D1453406

The Anglican chaplains who served in the Great War were changed by their experience of total war. They returned determined to revitalise the Anglican Church in Britain and to create a society which would be a living memorial to the men who had died. The chaplains who served in the army returned to a wide variety of church posts, bringing with them their experiences and expectations. They were to serve as parish priests, in cathedral chapters, teaching in schools and universities, as chaplains in prisons and hospitals and as full time workers for national institutions such as Toc H and the Industrial Christian Fellowship. A substantial number were destined to achieve positions of significant influence as bishops, deans, chaplains to the King and to be instrumental in matters concerning the influence of the church in industrial and political issues. These chaplains will be shown to have had an influence on Prayer Book revision, developments in theological thinking, moves towards church unity as well as having an important part to play in the resolving of industrial tension. Changes in society such as new divorce laws, the acceptance of contraception, and the responsible use of new media were aspects of the interwar years which former chaplains were to involve themselves in. They were also influential in shaping attitudes to rituals of remembrance in the 1920s and attitudes to pacifism in the 1930s. Given the changes that occurred in the Church of England, institutionally, liturgically and in its attitudes to a rapidly changing society, it is important that the role of former chaplains should be examined and their significance analysed.

This book argues that in the interwar years the impact of former chaplains was enhanced by their experiences in an unprecedented global conflict, which gave their actions and opinions more moral authority than would otherwise been the case. This question of the impact of former chaplains is considered in the context of debates about the effect that the war had on British society as a whole and on the Church of England in particular.

The interwar years have been described as "the long peace". As the former chaplains were coming to terms with the way in which the Great War had affected their lives and ministries the threat of the next war loomed. In the twenty years after their wartime chaplaincies, former chaplains had gone some way to fulfilling the hopes and aspirations articulated on their return from the front and could claim to have contributed greatly to both developments in the Anglican Church and in wider society.

Linda Parker combines teaching on a part-time basis with her writing and studying. Her main areas of interest are twentieth century military history, church history and the history of polar exploration. She is a member of the Western Front Association. She was born and educated in Wales, but now lives in Oxfordshire with her husband and their dog. She enjoys walking and travelling, ideally together, and her ambition is to visit Antarctica. This is her third book for Helion, following *The Whole Armour of God* and *Ice, Steel & Fire*.

SHELLSHOCKED PROPHETS

Wolverhampton Military Studies

www.helion.co.uk/wolverhamptonmilitarystudies

Submissions

The publishers would be pleased to receive submissions for this series. Please contact us via email (info@helion.co.uk), or in writing to Helion & Company Limited, 26 Willow Road, Solihull, West Midlands, B91 1UE.

Titles

Shellshocked Prophets

Former Anglican Army Chaplains in Interwar Britain

Wolverhampton Military Studies No. 6

Linda Parker

Helion & Company Limited

Helion & Company Limited
26 Willow Road
Solihull
West Midlands
B91 1UE
England
Tel. 0121 705 3393
Fax 0121 711 4075
Email: info@helion.co.uk
Website: www.helion.co.uk
Twitter: @helionbooks
Visit our blog http://blog.helion.co.uk/

Published by Helion & Company 2015

Designed and typeset by Bookcraft Ltd, Stroud, Gloucestershire
Cover designed by Paul Hewitt, Battlefield Design (www.battlefield-design.co.uk)
Printed by Lightning Source, Milton Keynes, Buckinghamshire

ISBN 978 1 909982 25 3

British Library Cataloguing-in-Publication Data.
A catalogue record for this book is available from the British Library.

For details of other military history titles published by Helion & Company
Limited contact the above address, or visit our website: http://www.helion.co.uk.

We always welcome receiving book proposals from prospective authors.

Contents

List of Illustrations

The Wolverhampton Military Studies Series
Series Editor's Preface

As series editor, it is my great pleasure to introduce the *Wolverhampton Military Studies Series* to you. Our intention is that in this series of books you will find military history that is new and innovative, and academically rigorous with a strong basis in fact and in analytical research, but also is the kind of military history that is for all readers, whatever their particular interests, or their level of interest in the subject. To paraphrase an old aphorism: a military history book is not less important just because it is popular, and it is not more scholarly just because it is dull. With every one of our publications we want to bring you the kind of military history that you will want to read simply because it is a good and well-written book, as well as bringing new light, new perspectives, and new factual evidence to its subject.

In devising the *Wolverhampton Military Studies Series*, we gave much thought to the series title: this is a *military* series. We take the view that history is everything except the things that have not happened yet, and even then a good book about the military aspects of the future would find its way into this series. We are not bound to any particular time period or cut-off date. Writing military history often divides quite sharply into eras, from the modern through the early modern to the mediaeval and ancient; and into regions or continents, with a division between western military history and the military history of other countries and cultures being particularly marked. Inevitably, we have had to start somewhere, and the first books of the series deal with British military topics and events of the twentieth century and later nineteenth century. But this series is open to any book that challenges received and accepted ideas about any aspect of military history, and does so in a way that encourages its readers to enjoy the discovery.

In the same way, this series is not limited to being about wars, or about grand strategy, or wider defence matters, or the sociology of armed forces as institutions, or civilian society and culture at war. None of these are specifically excluded, and in some cases they play an important part in the books that comprise our series. But there are already many books in existence, some of them of the highest scholarly standards, which cater to these particular approaches. The main theme of the *Wolverhampton Military Studies Series* is the military aspects of wars, the preparation for wars or their prevention, and their aftermath. This includes some books whose main theme is the technical details of how armed forces have worked, some books on wars and battles, and some books that re-examine the evidence about the existing stories, to show in a different light what everyone thought they already knew and understood.

As series editor, together with my fellow editorial board members, and our publisher Duncan Rogers of Helion, I have found that we have known immediately and almost by instinct the kind of books that fit within this series. They are very much the kind of well-written and challenging books that my students at the University of Wolverhampton would want to read. They are books which enhance knowledge, and offer new perspectives. Also, they are books for anyone with an interest in military history and events, from expert scholars to occasional readers. One of the great benefits of the study of military history is that it includes a large and often committed section of the wider population, who want to read the best military history that they can find; our aim for this series is to provide it.

Stephen Badsey
University of Wolverhampton

Acknowledgements

I should like to acknowledge the help and encouragement given by the following people:

My thanks to my supervisor at Birmingham University, Dr M. F. Snape, without whose support the PhD thesis on which this book is based would not have been completed, Mr D. Blake, curator and archivist, Royal Army Chaplains' Department Museum Amport, the Rev P. Howson for his support, and permission to quote from the unpublished diary of the Rev Ben O' Rorke, the staff of the University of Birmingham Special Collections, the staff of Lambeth Palace Library, and the staff of the Bodleian Library.

Nigel Parker, my husband was, as always, a source of help and inspiration. Duncan Rogers of Helion and Co. has given much encouragement in the process of turning the thesis into a book.

Introduction

Robert Keable,[1] an Anglican army chaplain writing in 1919, said of chaplains returning from the front: "It is inconceivable that they will not make an upheaval: if they do not, it will be the central disappointment of my life."[2] F. R. Barry,[3] writing in 1970, looking back over his life and ministry, argued that: "The social and religious revolution started on the Somme and the Salient."[4] These quotations are indicative of the mixed feelings and expectations of army chaplains on their return from the Great War and the awareness throughout their ministry that their experiences at war had shaped them irrevocably. There is a clear sense that a new era had began in which the chaplains, changed and in some ways strengthened by their experiences, were more self-consciously aware of the part they were to play in post-war church and society.

The role of the Anglican army chaplain during the Great War has in recent years received increasing attention from military and religious historians. Derogatory comments about Anglican chaplains, which gained credence in the interwar years as a result of accounts of the war by authors such as Siegfried Sassoon, Robert Graves and Guy Chapman, have to a great extent been refuted by Michael Snape and Edward Madigan. They have used a multiplicity of sources to paint a different picture, showing the way in which chaplains sought to adapt to their changing roles during the war and were able to provide spiritual and material help to the troops. During the war 3,030 Anglican chaplains served in the army,[5] so it can be seen that their return to their peacetime positions was likely to have an effect on the life of the Anglican Church.

---

1   Robert Keable had been teaching at St Andrew's Missionary College in the diocese of Zanzibar and served as a missionary in Basutoland until May 1917, when he was commissioned as a chaplain to the South African Labour Corps and was sent to France, serving mainly at Le Havre. M. F. Snape, "Church of England Army Chaplains in the First World War: Goodbye to' Goodbye to All That'", *Journal of Ecclesiastical History, Vol. 62, No. 2, April 2011*, p.328.
2   Robert Keable, *Standing By: Wartime Reflections in France and Flanders* (London, Nisbet & Co., 1919), p.42.
3   F. R. Barry, TCF 1915-1919, DSO 1916. Deputy Assistant Chaplain General, *Crockford's Clerical Directory*.
4   F. R. Barry, *Period of My Life* (London, Hodder & Stoughton, 1970), p.56.
5   M. Snape, *The Royal Army Chaplains Department, 1796-1953, Clergy Under Fire* (Woodbridge, Boydell Press, 2008), p.184.

The chaplains who served in the army returned to a wide variety of church posts, bringing with them their experiences and expectations. Evidence from *Crockford's Clerical Directory* shows them serving as parish priests, in cathedral chapters, teaching in schools and universities, as chaplains in prisons and hospitals and as full-time workers for national institutions such as Toc H and the Industrial Christian Fellowship. A substantial number were destined to achieve positions of significant influence as bishops, deans, chaplains to the King, and to be instrumental in matters concerning the influence of the church in industrial and political issues. Chaplains were to have had an influence on Prayer Book revision, developments in theological thinking, and moves towards church unity, as well as having an important part to play in the resolving of industrial tension. Changes in society such as new divorce laws, the acceptance of contraception, and the responsible use of new media were aspects of the interwar years in which former chaplains were to involve themselves. They were also influential in shaping attitudes to rituals of remembrance in the 1920s and attitudes to pacifism in the 1930s. Given the changes that occurred in the Church of England, institutionally, liturgically and in its attitudes to a rapidly changing society, it is important that the role of former chaplains should be examined and their significance analysed. Many of the chaplains considered in this book, especially those men who became national figures, were well-connected in the pre-war church and some reached senior rank in the wartime Army Chaplains' Department (AChD). This is significant, as an important part of any debate surrounding the role of former chaplains is the extent to which their post-war activities were influenced by their war experiences alone, or had their roots in their background, training and pre-war careers. Some might say that the impact of the returning chaplains, being largely of the younger generation of the pre-war clergy, could have been as a result of their youthful enthusiasm for reform, as seen in the actions of younger clergy who did not become chaplains, for example William Temple.[6] However, there is good evidence to show that in the interwar years the impact of former chaplains was not merely a generational issue. It was enhanced by their experiences in an unprecedented global conflict, which gave their actions and opinions more moral authority than would otherwise have been the case. This question of the impact of former chaplains must be considered in the context of debates about the effect that the war had on British society as a whole and on the Church of England in particular. F. R. Barry realised this when he commented: "The question of religion after the war was part of the very much bigger question about England itself after the war."[7]

6   William Temple, editor of the *Challenge* 1915-1918, secretary to the National Mission of Repentance and Hope, 1916, chairman of the Life and Liberty Movement 1917, Bishop of Manchester 1920, Archbishop of York 1929-1942, Archbishop of Canterbury 1942-1944 *Crockford's Clerical Directory* (London, Oxford University Press, 1940), p.1518.
7   Ibid., p.61.

Questions about the way in which returning chaplains functioned as positive elements in many areas of church and national life can be answered by examining them in the wider context of the results of war on the economic, social and psychological condition of the British people, and the way in which the church as a whole functioned in the interwar years. There was an enduring perception in the twentieth century that the pre-war Edwardian years represented a halcyon era in which: "there was an ordered way of life, a law, a temple, a city – a civilisation of sorts … a progressing and expanding civilisation."[8] Juliet Nicolson has written of the such ideas: "Some said that the twentieth century did not begin until 1914, that the extended Edwardian Idyll had lulled the English into a sense of that not only was everything all right with the world, but that it always would be."[9] She continued by pointing out, as other historians have done that: "In fact the structure of society had been changing, sometimes imperceptibly and sometimes … with great drama." Although it is questionable that the First World War represented a watershed after which everything changed, the perception that this was the case fed into the interwar years, which Richard Overy has described as "civilisation in crisis".[10]

The effect of the war on British society has been the subject of controversy. Adrian Gregory and Dan Todman have produced evidence of benefits and improvements to the lowest sections of British society. Todman has shown that, "For many Britons, the war was the healthiest time of their life. Wartime changes in social policy and behaviour meant better health care for many civilians and in particular, better diet and medical attention for their children."[11] Jay Winter has taken the infant mortality figures from the years 1914-1918 as evidence that material well-being had improved.[12] Adrian Gregory shows that: "In face of often fierce middle-class hostility members of the working class fought a modest war within the war, in the first instance to prevent intensification of exploitation and secondly to claw a modest amount of benefit from the situation."[13] He says that at the end of the war one in three workers was unionised.[14]

Both Gregory and Todman have refuted the idea that every family was affected by death on the battlefield and also that the flower of English manhood had disappeared. Both have sought to minimise the effect of war losses on the psyche of the nation, Todman by a statistical analysis of deaths, and Gregory by work on the concept of

8   Leonard Wolf, cited in R. Overy, *The Morbid Age: Britain Between the Wars*, (London, Allen Lane, 2009), p.2.
9   Juliet Nicolson, *The Great Silence: 1918-1920: Living in the Shadow of the Great War* (London, John Murray, 2009), p.2.
10   Overy, *The Morbid Age*, p.2.
11   Dan Todman, *The Great War, Myth and Memory* (London, Hambledon and London, 2005), p.45.
12   Figures cited in Adrian Gregory in *The Last Great War: British Society and the First World War* (Cambridge, Cambridge University Press, 2008), p.288.
13   Ibid., p.288.
14   Ibid.

mourning becoming institutionalised and nationalised. Richard Overy, in his book *The Morbid Age*, describes the collective anxieties of: "Cassandras and Jeremiahs who helped to construct the popular image of the interwar years as an age of anxiety, doubt and fear."[15] He argues that this nihilism was not the product of an intellectual fringe but gained widespread acceptance as "one of the defining features of contemporary culture".[16] The main strands examined are: "Fear of eugenic disaster, the diseases of capitalism, the dark side of the human mind, the inevitability of conflict, the power-lessness of reason and the fear of political extremism."[17] In contrast, Martin Pugh in *We Danced All Night*,[18] Roy Hattersley in *Borrowed Time*,[19] and to a certain extent, Juliet Gardiner in *The Thirties*,[20] stress the wide variations of experience in the interwar years, including new social trends, low prices, the growth of new light industry and new housing, as well as describing the plight of the economy, the effect of strikes and rising unemployment. However much they may differ in their perspectives and conclusions, the need to look at the role of the church and of the former chaplains is emphasised by the fact that these general, cultural histories of Britain in the interwar years have very little to say about the Church of England or its clergy.

Any consideration of the way in which former chaplains had an impact on religion and society in the interwar years must also take into account the debate concerning the secularisation of society in the twentieth century, as the success or failure of the Anglican Church, including former chaplains, should be seen in the light of changing ideas about religion in British society over a longer period. Hugh McLeod has questioned the views of Alan Gilbert, Robert Currie and John Kent, who considered that the Victorian era saw increasing secularisation. He points to the fact that in the period 1902–1914 the percentage of Anglican baptisms to live births was 66–70 percent. This figure had risen in late Victorian Britain reflecting the "process by which the Church of England put down roots in relatively newly-formed working class communities".[21] Callum Brown's work has denied that secularisation was necessarily the result of industrialisation and has called into question the concept of increasing secularisation occurring until the 1960s when it was exacerbated by the rise of feminism, cultural change and the growth of the permissive society.[22]

---

15   Overy, *Morbid Age*, p.2.
16   Ibid., p.364.
17   Ibid., p.364.
18   Martin Pugh, *We Danced all Night: A Social History of Britain Between the Wars* (London, Bodley Head, 2008).
19   Roy Hattersley, *Borrowed Time: The Story of Britain Between the Wars* (London, Little, Brown, 2007).
20   Juliet Gardiner, *The Thirties, An Intimate History of Britain* (London, Harper Collins, 2010).
21   Hugh McLeod, *Religion and Society in England 1850–1914* (London, Palgrave Macmillan, 1996), p.78.
22   Callum Brown, *Religion and Society in Twentieth Century Britain* (London, Pearson Longmans, 2005), Chapter Six.

Jeffery Cox[23] and Sarah Williams[24] have completed in-depth studies of areas of London which set out to prove that the church was active in society and in many ways encouraged a close relationship with the church and the local population. Michael Snape is of the opinion that Christianity "continued to exert a powerful and even defining influence on national and individual life".[25] This assessment of the strength of religion and the Church of England in these areas forms an interesting backdrop to the attempts of the returning chaplains to show the relevance of the church in the parishes to which they returned.

The role of chaplains in the war has been discussed by Alan Wilkinson, whose book *The Church of England in the First World War* presents a detailed account of the role of the Church during the conflict. He is inclined, however, to emphasise the difficulties and failures experienced by the chaplains such as the paradox of role confusion,[26] whereas Snape's work on the role of the chaplains during wartime is more positive, stressing the adaptation of chaplains to changing circumstances and emphasising the perception of the army commanders that the role played by the chaplains was of benefit to morale.[27] This theme has been continued in Edward Madigan's recent work.[28] The in-depth considerations that these historians provide into the thoughts, actions and motivations of the chaplains in wartime enables the effect of their wartime experiences to be debated. Wilkinson's book includes a discussion of the influence of former chaplains on rituals of remembrance, while Madigan's has a chapter giving an overview of the post-war activities of Anglican chaplains, with some case studies of the more famous characters.

Recent works which deal with the general history of the Church of England during this period include those by Keith Robbins[29] and Adrian Hastings.[30] Recent relevant biographies include John Kent's work on William Temple,[31] although for biographical accounts of some of the major Anglican figures one has to look to the 1960s and

23   J. Cox, *The English Churches in a Secular Society – Lambeth 1870–1930* (Oxford, OUP, 1982).

24   Sarah Williams, *Religious Belief and Popular Culture: A Study of the South London Borough of Southwark 1880-1930* (Oxford, University of Oxford, 1999).

25   Michael Snape, *God and the British Soldier: Christianity and Society in the Modern World* (London, Routledge, 2005), p.242.

26   A. Wilkinson, 'The Paradox of the Military Chaplain', *Theology,* (1984), p.249.

27   Snape, *The Royal Army Chaplains Department: Clergy under Fire* (Woodbridge, Boydell Press, 2007), p.260 and *God and the British Soldier,* Chapter 6.

28   E. Madigan, *Faith Under Fire, Anglican Army Chaplains and the Great War* (Basingstoke, Palgrave Macmillan, 2011).

29   K. Robbins, *England, Ireland, Scotland, Wales: The Christian Church 1900-2000* (Oxford, OUP, 2008).

30   A. Hastings, *A History of English Christianity 1920-2000* (London, SCM Press 1991).

31   John Kent, *William Temple: Church, State and Society in Britain, 1880-1950* (Cambridge, CUP, 1992).

1970s for such examples as Charles Smyth's biography of Cyril Foster Garbett,[32] F. R. Barry's work on Mervyn Haigh,[33] and F. W. Dillistone's biography of Charles Raven.[34] As a detailed guide to the general history of the Church of England in these years, Roger Lloyd's history of the Church of England up to 1965 is still relevant and informative.[35] John Maiden covers controversies surrounding liturgy and the revision of the Prayer Book in his study of the events of 1928.[36]

John Oliver,[37] E. R. Norman,[38] Keith Thompson,[39] and more recently Callum Brown[40] have investigated the role of the church in society. The Industrial Christian Fellowship was the subject of a detailed study by Gerald Studdert Kennedy.[41] To date there has been no recent work on the role of Toc H or biographical studies of Tubby Clayton or Geoffrey Studdert Kennedy. Historians dealing with remembrance after the war have included assessments of the role fulfilled by the Anglican Church and former chaplains include Mark Connelly,[42] who has looked at rituals of remembrance in South London parishes, and Bob Bushaway,[43] who linked rituals of remembrance with a political agenda of preserving the status quo. Patrick Porter has written about the insistence of former chaplains in Britain and Germany on the need to honour the dead by instigating reform, while David Lloyd has looked at the significance of battlefield tourism to the understanding of remembrance. Martin Ceadel has made an exhaustive study of the development of the pacifist movement in the twentieth century with an assessment of both Raven and Sheppard, but has not focussed on the significance of their careers as chaplains in wartime. Jill Wallis has chronicled the development of the Fellowship of Reconciliation. Several biographies of H. R. L. Sheppard

32   Charles Smyth, *Cyril Foster Garbett Archbishop of York* (London, Hodder and Stoughton, 1959).
33   F. R. Barry, *Mervyn Haigh* (London, SPCK, 1964).
34   F. W. Dillistone, *Charles Raven, Naturalist, Historian and Theologian* (London, Hodder and Stoughton. 1975).
35   Roger Lloyd, *The Church of England 1900-65* (London, SCM Press, 1968).
36   J. Maiden, *National Religion and the Prayer Book Controversy, 1927-1928* (Woodbridge, Boydell Press, 2009).
37   J. Oliver, *The Church and Social Order* (London, Mowbray, 1968).
38   E. H. Norman, *Church and Society in England* (Oxford, OUP, 1976).
39   Kenneth Thompson, *Bureaucracy and Church Reform: The Organizational Response of the Church of England to Social Change, 1800-1965* (Oxford, The Clarendon Press, 1970).
40   Callum Brown, *The Death of Christian Britain: Understanding Secularisation 1800-200* (London, 2000) and *Religion and Society in 20th Century Britain* (London, Routledge, 2006).
41   Gerald Studdert Kennedy, *Dog Collar Democracy, The Industrial Christian Fellowship 1919-1929* (London, Macmillan Press, 1982).
42   M. Connelly, *The Great War, Memory and Ritual: Commemoration in the City and East London, 1916-1939* (London, Royal Historical Society, 2001).
43   B. Bushaway, 'Name upon Name' in R. Porter (ed.) *Myths of the English* (London, Polity Press, 1993).

appeared later in the twentieth century,[44] and Dillistone wrote his biography of Raven in 1975,[45] but no recent assessment of Raven or Sheppard has been made.

Anglican theological trends have been looked at by Michael Ramsay, Roger Lloyd, Horton Davies and, most recently, by Alan Wilkinson in *Dissent or conform?*,[46] but otherwise, apart from specific topics such as Maiden's book on Prayer Book reform, there is a paucity of modern scholarship.

The main evidence from former chaplains themselves consists of the ideas and opinions of fifty former chaplains who have left testimony in the form of books, essays, articles, diaries and speeches written both during the war, and as a response to the post-war situations in which they found themselves, along with records of their actions. The essays in *The Church in the Furnace* were written in 1917 by serving army chaplains including many of the leading figures discussed in this book, for example, F. R. Barry, who was to become Bishop of Southwell, Geoffrey Studdert Kennedy, who was to be the chief missioner of the Industrial Christian Fellowship (ICF), and E. S. Woods, later bishop of Lichfield. Tom Pym, an activist for church reform and Geoffrey Gordon, later Bishop of Jarrow, wrote about their wartime thoughts and experiences in *Papers from Picardy*,[47] published in 1917. William Carey, a naval chaplain, wrote about the theological debates that had perplexed him in time of war in *Sacrifice and some of its Difficulties*.[48] Tubby Clayton's *Tales of Talbot House* was published in 1919.[49] Contemporary evidence of the wartime thoughts of more senior chaplains can be found in sources such as B. K. Cunningham's diary, which chronicles events at the clergy school at St Omer,[50] and the wartime papers of Harry Blackburne.[51] These and other books, such as Neville Talbot's *Religion Behind the Front and After the War*,[52] and Studdert Kennedy's *Rough Talks by a Padre*,[53] written while the chaplains' experiences were still fresh, cast a clear light on what they were thinking during the war and allow, in the light of later books and ministries, a judgement to be made on how far these experiences shaped their post-war lives and careers.

44   R. Ellis Roberts, *H. R. L. Sheppard, Life and Letters* (London, John Murray, 1942).
45   F. W. Dillistone, *Charles Raven, Naturalist, Historian and Theologian*.
46   Alan Wilkinson, *Dissent or Conform? – War, Peace and the English Churches 1900-1945*, (SCM, London, 1986).
47   Tom Pym and Geoffrey Gordon, *Papers from Picardy* (London, Constable, 1917).
48   W. Carey, *Sacrifice and Some of its Difficulties* (London, Mowbray, 1918).
49   P. B. Clayton, *Tales of Talbot House, Everyman's Club in Poperinghe and Ypres, 1915-1918* (London, Chatto and Windus, 1919).
50   Lambeth Palace Library (hereafter LPL), MS 2077 B .K. Cunningham, *Diary of B. K. Cunningham*,.
51   Royal Army Chaplains' Department Archives (hereafter RAChDA), Amport House, the papers of the Very Rev H. W. Blackburne.
52   Neville Talbot, *Religion Behind the Front and After the War* (London, Macmillan, 1918).
53   G. A. Studdert Kennedy, *Rough Talks by a Padre. Delivered to Officers and Men of the B.E.F.* (London, Hodder and Stoughton, 1918).

Many of the more prominent chaplains continued to publish books in response to events in the 1920s and 1930s. F. R. Barry wrote *The Relevance of Christianity* (1931) and one of the first books to address the new discipline, psychology, *Christianity and Psychology* (1923). Rogers contributed, among other works, *The Church and the People* (1930) and Studdert Kennedy published a stream of popular books in the early post-war years including *Lies!* (1919), *The Word and the Work* (1925) and *Democracy and the Dog Collar* (1921). Neville Talbot wrote an important book on unity, *Thoughts on Unity* (1920) and produced a range of publications during the 1920s and 1930s including *The Returning Tide of Faith* (1923) and *Before we Meet at the Lambeth Conference* (1930). Several prominent and senior chaplains, including Harry Blackburne,[54] wrote later about their experiences in the front line. The 1960s and 1970s saw several of the former chaplains writing autobiographies, including Barry with *Period of My Life* (1970) and William Drury with *Camp Follower* (1968). About the same time, biographies were written of Kenneth Kirk[55], Charles Raven,[56] Geoffrey Studdert Kennedy,[57] Tom Pym,[58] and Dick Sheppard.[59] Although these are secondary sources and come from an era when sources were often not extensively footnoted and were in some cases anecdotal, they often contain verbatim copies of the correspondence and papers of their subjects. The activities of other chaplains can be found in reports in the church press and parish magazines. Many of the leading figures among former chaplains were members of Convocation, the National Assembly or Church Congress, and their opinions and actions can be traced through the reports of speeches and minutes of these meetings during the interwar years. The papers of Archbishops Davidson, Lang and Temple provide interesting comments on, and information about, individual clergy and on institutions such as Toc H and ICF. Each theme considered draws on a variety of different evidence, although some sources are so significant they appear in each section.

The significance of the former chaplains' contribution to church and society can be looked at under several headings. First, the thoughts and actions of these men during the war and in the immediate post-war era. It is important to emphasise that the question of the post-war world was one which they thought about whilst experiencing war conditions and that these thoughts informed their plans and hopes for the future. There is no shortage of evidence that both men and clergy had their attitudes

54   H. Blackburne, *This Also Happened on the Western Front. The Padre's Story* (London, Hodder & Stoughton, 1932).

55   E. W. Kemp, *The Life and Work of Kenneth Escott Kirk* (London, Hodder & Stoughton, 1959).

56   Dillistone, *Charles Raven, Naturalist, Historian and Theologian*.

57   W. Purcell, *Woodbine Willie: An Anglican Incident, being some account of the life and times of Geoffrey Anketell Studdert Kennedy, Poet, Prophet, Seeker After Truth, 1883-1929* (London, Hodder & Stoughton, 1962).

58   Dora Pym, *Tom Pym. A Portrait.* (Cambridge, W. Heffer & Co., 1952).

59   C. Scott, *Dick Sheppard, A Biography* (London, Hodder & Stoughton, 1979).

changed in "the furnace" and that the change in their thinking would be reflected in the post-war years.

Another theme takes up the way in which chaplains realised some of their ideas concerning industrial relations and reform of social conditions. The church's response to social issues in the pre-war years is looked at, along with the chaplains' contribution to the changing post-war social and industrial landscape. Their contribution to key organs of the Church of England, such as Convocation and the Church Assembly can be traced in the church and national press, and their comments in the local press and parish magazines show how often industrial reconstruction and social justice occupied their thoughts. The reactions of the chaplains to the depression and unemployment in the 1930s is seen both in their autobiographical works and in their contemporary works in response to the situation. For example, the work of former chaplains in the Industrial Christian Fellowship will be considered, alongside the activities of prominent individuals who were involved in industrial issues such as Geoffrey Studdert Kennedy and John Groser.

The work of Toc H in the interwar years[60] can be traced by the coverage of the organisation in the national and church press, as well as the *Toc H Journal*. The contribution of Toc H to British society, founded by Tubby Clayton on the idealism and ethos of the wartime Talbot House, is probably one of the best-known contributions of a former chaplain to Britain after the war, but it is important to use the available evidence to show how the movement was not only an ex-service organisation but a way in which the next generation could learn to serve society and lessen class differences. The question is whether Toc H succeeded in becoming "The Living Memorial" that Tubby Clayton wished it to be.

Their experience of war had made some of the chaplains aware that the training received by Anglican clergy had not prepared them well for what had been expected of them. The way in which the returning chaplains both raised the problem of relevant training and helped to contribute to solving it is another theme. Evidence from the church press shows that this concern was widespread, along with concern about the numbers of men coming forward for ordination. The extraordinary venture of the Test School at Knutsford produced a large proportion of the next generation of priests for the Church of England, but was controversial. The efforts of other former chaplains such as B. K. Cunningham, head of Westcott House, and Christopher Chavasse, master of St Peter's College, Oxford, are investigated to add to the evidence of the concern of former chaplains about the training of the clergy. An offshoot of this was the role played by former chaplains in developments in academic theology, drawing largely on the works of such authors as Charles Raven, Kenneth Kirk, and E. G.

60   Toc H was an organisation set up by Tubby Clayton which was to keep the memory of the fellowship of Talbot House alive and continue the ethos of service to others created at Talbot house during the war. It was called Toc H after its letters in the wartime signalling alphabet – Toc being T, therefore Talbot House became Toc H.

Selwyn and Edwyn Hoskyns. Continuing the theme of academic debate and education the contributions of F. R. Barry and Tom Pym to the new discipline of psychology are also considered. The variety of contributions that former chaplains made to issues concerning the training of the clergy, theological debate and education is indicated.

The returning chaplains were also involved in the ecclesiastical controversies of the interwar years. The opinions of these men fed into the larger movement of Life and Liberty, the main reforming movement in the Church of England in the immediate post-war era, in which several former chaplains were prominent. The Padres' Fellowship, which sought to retain the fellowship which had existed in the trenches between padres of different denominations, was short-lived, but did indicate the large role former Anglican chaplains were to play in a major controversy of the interwar years; that of church unity. The way in which chaplains from both wings of the Anglican Church spoke out about unity is discussed. The contemporary works of the chaplains, alongside articles in the church and national press, show how influential former chaplains of various Anglican persuasions were in the cause of unity. Chaplains from the high, liberal and evangelical wings of the church all brought influence to bear on the debates concerning liturgical changes, leading to the attempts of the Church of England to reform the Prayer Book in the 1920s. John Maiden has examined in detail the debates surrounding the tortuous topic of Prayer Book revision and has accentuated the importance of the topic to debates surrounding church and state in the twentieth century. Former chaplains, especially those involved in producing the "Grey Book", made a significant contribution.

Later, the emphasis changes from ecclesiastical controversy to wider issues in interwar society. Written evidence from the chaplains, in their books, articles and letters and their speeches in debates in the Church Assembly and Convocation, shows the ways in which they responded to changes in society regarding divorce and remarriage, contraception and sexual morality: often differing sharply from the formal position of the Church of England on these matters. The attitudes of former chaplains to the uses of new technologies of radio and cinema is also considered. Dick Sheppard was a pioneer in the field of broadcast services and his work in this area was continued by his successor at St Martin-in-the-Fields, Pat McCormick, another former chaplain. Of course, this use of radio was not without controversy, which is well documented in letters to the press, debates in Convocation and Church Assembly. Probably more controversial was the growth of cinema after the war and in the interwar years. Particularly of concern was the Sunday opening of cinemas. Guy Rogers spent a considerable amount of time and effort in fighting a rearguard action in Birmingham against Sunday opening and the content of films to be shown on a Sunday. E. S. Woods had a different attitude. He realised that cinema was a fact of life and tried to find ways of using the technology in a positive way.

The ways in which the former chaplains played their part in shaping, and responding to, attitudes towards remembrance, and how this affected the later pacifism of some chaplains is extremely significant. Their attitudes are to be found in their published works and in private and public letters, but also important are their public opinions expressed at Remembrance services, and occasions such as dedications of memorials, sermons, and at Armistice Day ceremonies during the interwar years. Such sources showed that the chaplains were anxious to justify the sacrifices made in the war by attempting to build a better society. The discussion also assesses to what extent the Anglican chaplains' thoughts had changed to encompass a wider theology on sacrifice and redemption. As the international situation in the 1930s changed and developed, some Anglican Clergy became prominent in the pacifist movement. The opinions and action of Charles Raven and Dick Sheppard in particular gave a lead to the peace movement, and resulted in the setting up of the Peace Pledge Union.

Any consideration of the role of the returning Anglican army chaplains needs to be made in the light of their war experiences and the impact of their war service on their later opinions and actions. The extent to which their pre-war training and careers had an effect on their post-war lives is also relevant. However, the former chaplains did not exist in a vacuum, and in order to fully assess their impact on the interwar church, changes in both the Anglican Church and in wider society must be investigated, to gauge the way in which the former chaplains used the spiritual and pastoral skills acquired in the war to develop a leading role in many aspects of the Anglican Church's ministry in the interwar years. Former chaplains were able to respond positively to the challenges of post-war church and society, largely as a result of a flexible attitude to many controversial issues which had its origins in their service in the Great War.

1

Shellshocked Prophets

The term "'shellshocked prophets'" was used by the Rev. F. B. Macnutt,[1] in his essay in a wartime publication written by serving Anglican army chaplains, *The Church in the Furnace*:[2] a metaphor which has many echoes in the contemporary accounts of the war.[3] The collection of essays in which this appeared was written under wartime conditions and consisted of a wide-ranging series of ideas on how the chaplains could use their experiences to help renew the spiritual and practical life of the Church of England after the war.

The chaplains were presented as being moulded by the events of the war and empowered by new ideas and motivations. The essays in this volume gave the impression that the army chaplains emerged from the war with a whole new set of values and practical ideas which would help them set to right what they considered to be the failings of the established church in such matters as education, training of the clergy, the public worship of the church and its role in society. In 1916 it had already been recognised that the chaplains were in a good position to comment on the position of the church at home and at the front. George Bell, chaplain to the Archbishop of Canterbury, reporting on the replies of chaplains to questions posed by the Bishop of Kensington as part of the National Mission, talked about their "prophetic witness" and believed that: "The chaplains of the navy and army had special opportunities for observing the nature and character of the churches' influence on a large and important section of church members."[4]

---

1   Rev. F. B. Macnutt, Canon of Southwark Cathedral, served as Temporary Chaplain to the Forces (TCF) 1915-1918, becoming senior chaplain, *Crockford's Clerical Directory* (Oxford, OUP, 1940), p.870.
2   F. B. Macnutt, 'The Moral Equivalent of War', in F. B. Macnutt (ed.), *The Church in the Furnace* (London, Macmillan, 1917), p.15.
3   See for example, E. Milner-White, 'Worship and Services', *The Church in the Furnace*, p.176 and P. B. Clayton's article 'Two men's work', *The Times*, 29 October 1920, p.15.
4   *The National Mission of Repentance and Hope, A report on the chaplains' replies to the Lord Bishop of Kensington* (London, 1919), p.3.

The chaplains were indeed shellshocked, some in physical and mental ways,[5] but many more by the insights they had gained into the nature of religion, in wartime and in society. Many were prophets, in that they returned with a determination to revitalise the church, renew its mission and establish its place more firmly in society. Bishop Gwynne,[6] Deputy Chaplain-General in charge of the Anglican army chaplains in France, described "'The conviction that we must dare scrap that which is out of date and effete in our methods so as to be able to mobilise and unify the enormous Christian resources now lying dormant.'"[7] Kenneth Kirk,[8] former chaplain and future Bishop of Oxford, realised that some clergy had been changed in ways which would not permit them to return to parochial ministry. He wrote in his essay "When the Priests Come Home":

> Some of the chaplains who have seen action will never come home, that is as parochial clergy. The powers that they have discovered affect their view of the future so deeply that they will seek some sphere of work, the mission field or the colonies in which to minister with the freedom and opportunities they had in France.[9]

The use of the phrase "shellshocked prophets" was, in the context of Macnutt's essay, a pejorative one. He was referring to the opinions expressed by some 'sturdy apologists' about the validity of the new ideas expressed by what they saw as 'doubting Jeremiahs' who had returned from the war. Some churchmen felt that these radical opinions would subside when the "shellshocked prophets" recovered and returned to normal church life.[10] The expression, however, seems to be a useful one to encompass the wartime experiences of the chaplains and their impact on post-war church and society. Their prophetic role stemmed from the desire of many of them to revitalise the church, renew its mission and establish its place more firmly in society. Bishop Gwynne, writing in 1917, considered that the war had given the chaplains increased insight and knowledge which would inform their post-war lives: "This knowledge

---

5   For example, the story of Rev. H. Spooner in M. Moynihan (ed), *God on Our Side* (London, Secker & Warburg, 1983), p.42. Spooner spent sixteen years in hospital after experiencing a nervous breakdown post-war. Also the Rev. Cyril Hall, who committed suicide after being wounded in 1916 and suffering depression on returning to problems in his parish, *The Times*, 1 July 1919, p.9.

6   Bishop L. H. Gwynne, Bishop of Diocese of Khartoum (Sudan) 1908. TCF 1914-1919, Deputy Chaplain General in France 1915-1919. *Crockford's*, p.406.

7   L. H. Gwynne, in the introduction to *The Church in the Furnace*, p.xx.

8   The Rev. Kenneth Escott Kirk, TCF 1914-1919. *Crockford's*, p.1013

9   Kenneth Kirk, 'When the Priests Come Home', *The Church in the Furnace*, p.409. Some prominent examples include Bishop Gwynne, who returned to Sudan and in 1920 became the bishop of the new diocese of Egypt and the Sudan, and Neville Talbot, who took up a post as Bishop of Pretoria in April 1920.

10   Macnutt, 'The Moral Equivalent of War', *The Church in the Furnace*, p.15.

has given them dreams and visions of a great spiritual fighting machine, which if realised may overcome the spiritual foes of humanity and allow the Kingdom of God to operate on earth."[11] Guy Rogers commented:[12] "Chaplains have come home rejoicing in the freedom from institutional life, new contacts with men and new ideas fermenting in themselves."[13] The evidence points to the fact that many of them believed that they possessed a new vision of the church and its role and relevance in the world. Christopher Chavasse,[14] in taking up his appointment to a parish in Barrow-in-Furness after his return from the front, said in his parish magazine:

> The fact is we have begun a new age, everything is in the melting pot. ... We cannot take up the old state of things which existed in 1914 ... therefore the next year or two we must experiment, experiment, experiment.[15]

Tom Pym,[16] one of the chaplains most critical of the established church, summed up the attitude of the returning chaplains: "God will expect much of us now."[17] Three former chaplains, F. B. Macnutt, Neville Talbot and H. K. Southwell contributed to an appendix to the Archbishops' Second Committee of Enquiry, *The Worship of the Church* in 1918. This report was part of a series of enquiries set up in response to issues raised by the National Mission.[18] Macnutt, Talbot and Southwell felt they had the right to give their opinion: "As a body of men we shall be unable to go back to the old pre-war grooves."[19] An anonymous chaplain writing at the request of Bishop Gwynne in 1917 foresaw some difficulties: "We are convinced that, unless great distinctive methods are used, and also some definite changes made, England's church will not thus secure the robust and virile influences of England's manhood."[20]

In order to appreciate the impact that returning chaplains had on the post-war church it is, of course, necessary to consider the challenges faced by the Church of

11   Gwynne, Introduction to *The Church in the Furnace*, p.xx.
12   T. G. Rogers, TCF 1915-1916, MC 1916, *Crockford's*, p.1157.
13   T. G. Rogers, *A Rebel at Heart* (London, Longmans Green & Co,1956), p.129.
14   C. M. Chavasse, TCF 1914-1918, MC 1917, Croix de Guerre, 1918 *Crockford's*, p.1153.
15   *St George's Parish Magazine*, October 1919, cited in Selwyn Gummer, *The Chavasse Twins* (London, 1963), p.73.
16   Thomas Wentworth Pym TCF 1914-, DSO 1917, Deputy Assistant Chaplain General VIII Corps 1917, Assistant Chaplain General, Third Army 1918, D. Pym, *Tom Pym: A Portrait* (Cambridge, W. Heffer & Sons, 1952).
17   Pym, *Tom Pym: A Portrait*, p.57.
18   The Archbishops' Committees of Enquiry were published by SPCK. in 1918. The first was *The Teaching of the Church*, the second was *The Worship of the Church*, the third was *The Evangelistic Work of the Church*, the fourth was *The Administrative Reform of the Church* and the fifth was *Christianity and Industrial Problems*.
19   Appendix to The Archbishops' Second Committee of Enquiry, *The Worship of the Church* (London, 1918), p.33.
20   Anonymous, *Can England's Church Win England's Manhood? By an Army Chaplain* (London, 1917), p.8.

England at the turn of the twentieth century. Increasing industrialisation and urbanisation were seen as having engendered an increasingly secular outlook in society at large, particularly among the urban working classes, while a widely diffused confidence in human progress had led to a misplaced faith in human potential. Old orthodoxies were judged in the light of the new "God of science": some were discredited by the implications of Darwinian thought[21] and by developments in biblical criticism.[22] English modernism, under its main proponent, Hastings Rashdall, was challenging traditional theology,[23] and had initiated controversy which would continue into the interwar years. Problems faced by the Church of England included falling attendance, a decline in the number of candidates for ordination and the need to reorganise parishes in the light of demographic change. Nevertheless, the pre-war church had been adjusting to meet these challenges. Frances Knight, writing about church reform in the late Victorian period and the years leading up to 1920, has described how: "during this time religious identities and practices continued to be centrally important to large numbers of people", and that "Christians began ... to fight for the most effective use of whatever ground was available to them in a world where politics was moving to the centre, and religion to the periphery."[24]

In the first decade of the twentieth century the church was adapting to meet the demands being made by the changes mentioned above. There was much activity in cities. Jeffery Cox has described the situation in Lambeth. The church carried out poor relief, was involved in thrift societies, medical services, education, ran Sunday schools, clubs, the Church Lads' Brigade, the Girls' Friendly Society, women's clubs, and a plethora of sporting and recreational clubs provided popular recreation and entertainment.[25] According to Cox, the churches were not too disappointed with a lack of success in terms of congregation increase, as they were responding to the need of the church to become more associated with democracy and social reform. This situation prefigured the "holy grocery" dilemma that later faced priests in the trenches over the competing demands of the material and spiritual needs of the troops. Cox sees this as a reason for the later decline in the influence of the church as the role of the church in social concern was taken over by the welfare state.

21 R. Lloyd, *The Church of England in the Twentieth Century 1900-1965* (London, SCM Press, 1966), pp.141-142.

22 For example, A. Schweitzer, *The Quest of the Historical Jesus* (London, Adam and Charles Black, 1910).

23 Hastings Rashdall, an influential Anglican modernist theologian. Rashdall set out his ideas in *Anglican Liberalism* in 1908. *ODNB*.

24 Frances Knight, 'Internal Church Reform 1850-1920. An Age of Innovation in Ecclesiastical Reform' in Paula Yates and Joris van Eijnatten (eds.) *The Churches: The Dynamics of Religious Reform in Church, State and Society in Northern Europe, 1780-1920* (Leuven Univesrsity Press 2010), p.69.

25 Cox, *The English Churches in a Secular Society*, pp.64-87.

The church seems to have been becoming more aware of what Bishop Talbot called "diffusive Christianity".[26] He defined this as "The penumbra of the embodied Christian in the church".[27] He considered that the church "had an important influence on the lives of many people who seldom attended services."[28] Diffusive Christianity was a term made use of by the chaplains in the war whilst trying to understand both the appalling lack of religious knowledge and commitment on the part of the troops that they encountered, but also expressing the very real sense they had that men were not totally alienated from God.

Intellectually and theologically the church was also responding to the industrial and secular age with new theological initiatives. *Lux Mundi*, a collection of essays edited by Bishop Gore in 1889, introduced a more liberal trend in Anglo-Catholic theology. Horton Davies, summing up the pre-war decades, claimed that there was an optimistic religious immanentalism regarding social welfare and practising the social gospel. Other worldly transcendence was losing ground to liberal secularism which put emphasis on man's effort and he concluded that this was the means of alienating further the working class as mere worship seemed irrelevant.[29] Gore,[30] Temple and Inge[31] all had in common the desire to emphasise the importance of the Incarnation as part of sacramental practice. This emphasis on sacraments was to be one which struck many chords with chaplains at the front where the incarnate God became central to worship.

The matter of church reform was also one that came to prominence in the pre-war years.[32] The Church Reform League had been examining self-government for the church which also became an aim of the Life and Liberty Movement. *Essays in Aid of the Reform of the Church*, edited by Bishop Gore, appeared in 1898. Roger Lloyd summarised what Gore hoped for:

> The end of the sale of advowsons, the end of the particular form of establish-
> ment which so tied the church that she had no freedom to manage even the
> affairs committed to her by Christ herself, the power of the laity to stop improper

---

26   Edward Stuart Talbot, Bishop of Rochester 1895-1911, Bishop of Winchester 1911-1923. Talbot contributed an essay to *Lux Mundi* in 1889, *ODNB*.
27   Ibid., p.93.
28   Ibid., p.6.
29   Horton Davies, *Worship and Theology in England: The Ecumenical Century, 1900 to the Present* (Cambridge, W. B. Eerdmans, 1996), p.172.
30   Charles Gore, vice president of the newly formed Christian Social Union in 1889. He edited *Lux Mundi* in 1889. Gore was one of the founder members of the Community of the Resurrection, 1892. Bishop of Oxford 1911-1919, *ODNB*.
31   Ralph Inge, Dean of St Paul's Cathedral 1911, leading spokesman for the modernist wing of the Anglican Church and prolific author and journalist, *ODNB*.
32   Frances Knight, 'Internal Church Reform 1850-1920. An Age of Innovation in Ecclesiastical Reform' p.71.

appointments to benefices and to secure the removal of incompetent and lazy clergy, and the protection of the clergy from the tyranny of wealthy parishioners.[33]

Frances Knight points to the emergence and growth of new Anglican societies founded in late Victorian an pre-war era, such as the Church of England Men's Society and the Mother's Union.[34] Roger Lloyd claimed that the church was increasing in confidence by 1914, in contrast to increasing uncertainty in the political arena due to strikes, women's suffrage and Home Rule in Ireland.[35]

In order to come to some conclusions about the impact of the war on the chaplains who took part it is necessary to examine the background of the men who became temporary chaplains. Their experiences and opinions were developed before the intervention of war could possibly have coloured their evolving theology and thoughts on the church, even if it is accepted that the experience of war made them question many of these ideas. War in 1914 came as the Anglican Church was struggling with internal conflicts arising from the growth of the Anglo-Catholic movement, the problems posed by modern biblical criticism, and the rise of secularism. A study of the educational background of a substantial group of Anglican chaplains serving on the Western Front has been made by Edward Madigan.[36] He examined a sample of 723 chaplains mentioned in Bishop Gwynne's surviving 'Army Book'. He found that 411 of them were Oxbridge educated, with sixty-four from Trinity College Dublin. Madigan points out that they lived in 'an atmosphere of exclusive privilege'.[37] However, many of these men had had the opportunity of working for university settlements in the East End of London where they lived among the local population. Men who took this opportunity to widen their experiences and later became chaplains included P. B. 'Tubby' Clayton,[38] F. R. Barry[39] and Neville Talbot.[40] After

33   R. Lloyd, *The Church of England 1900-1965* (London, 1966), P.238.

34   Knight, 'Internal Church Reform 1850-1920, p.71.

35   Lloyd, *The Church of England*, p.238.

36   E. Madigan, *Faith Under Fire: Anglican Army Chaplains and the Great War* (Basingstoke, Palgrave Macmillan, 2011), pp.67-68.

37   Ibid., p.69.

38   P. B. Clayton. TCF 1915-1919, M.C. 1917. While at Oxford University, Clayton spent an evening every week helping at the Oxford and Bermondsey Mission at Bermondsey, B. Baron, *The Doctor, The Story of John Stansfeld of Oxford and Bermondsey* (London, 1952), p.207, *Crockford's*, p.251.

39   Barry recounted the efforts of Oxford undergraduates, including himself, at the Oxford House at Bethnal Green, where he first met H. R. L. 'Dick' Sheppard. Barry, *Period of My Life*, p.43.

40   Neville Talbot TCF 1914-1919, M C 1915, senior chaplain 6th Division 1915, Senior Anglican Chaplain of XIV Corps 1916 and Assistant Chaplain General to 5th Army 1916. Talbot was involved with the Oxford Medical Mission which was renamed the Oxford and Bermondsey Mission in 1910, M. Snape (ed.), *The Back Parts of War: The YMCA Memoirs and Letters of Barclay Baron, 1915-1919* (Woodbridge, Boydell & Brewer, 2009), *Crockford's*, p.1313.

ordination, opportunities in the worldwide Anglican Communion were varied. Some chaplains had served in large working-class parishes such as Portsea, which sent eight of its curates to serve as chaplains in the First World War.[41] Others served in the overseas mission fields or became chaplains to prisons or other public institutions. Familiar accounts of those who wrote of their wartime experiences underline this impression of varied pastoral experience before the war. F. R. Barry joined the Army Chaplains' Department (AChD) almost immediately after being ordained, following a brief spell as a fellow of Oriel College.[42] In contrast, Pat McCormick[43] served as a chaplain after ministering to mining communities in South Africa.[44] Neville Talbot was a former army officer and a bishop's son[45] while P. B. 'Tubby' Clayton had been a curate at Portsea.[46] It is clear, even from these few examples, that many of the Church of England's younger and more vocal chaplains had plenty of varied pre-war experience against which to gauge and understand their wartime experiences. It is evident from their accounts of their wartime experiences that many chaplains did see the war as a turning point in their careers and the cause both of disappointment and hope to the Anglican Church as a whole.

The Army Chaplains' Department had to be expanded rapidly to meet with the demand for its services throughout the war. At the outbreak of war the strength of the department was 117, from all denominations, but with the majority, eighty-nine, being Anglican. The department was to grow in strength until in August 1918 there were 3,416 chaplains, 1,941 of whom were Anglican.[47] Early recruitment was characterised by confusion, delay and rumours of a bias toward low churchmen by the Chaplain General, Taylor Smith. When chaplains set out with the B.E.F. in August 1914, there was no provision made for their attachment, rations, accommodation or transport. Harry Blackburne,[48] who had been a regular chaplain at Aldershot before the war, commented on the difficulty experienced by the first chaplains deployed to France: "those of us who went out with the original B.E.F. are not likely to forget how difficult it was for us to fit ourselves into machine so wonderfully woven together,

41   Smyth, *Cyril Foster Garbett*, p.137.
42   Barry, *Period of My Life*, p.40.
43   W. P. G. McCormick, TCF 1914-1919, D.S.O. 1917. *Crockford's*, p.855.
44   *The Times*, 17 October 1940, p.7.
45   F. H. Brabant, *Neville Stuart Talbot 1879-1943: A Memoir* (London, SCM Press, 1949), pp.12-16.
46   M. Harcourt, *Tubby Clayton: A Personal Saga* (London, Hodder & Stoughton, 1956), p.45. The parish of Portsea was a large, mainly working-class parish in Portsmouth, which had a tradition of pastoral work among men and boys. Former curates of Portsea who served as chaplains and played a prominent part in the Church in the interwar years include Bernard Keymer (see Chapter Two) and Freddie Hawks (see Chapter Five). Smyth, *Cyril Foster Garbbet, Archbishop of York*, p.133.
47   Snape, *God and the British Soldier*, p.89.
48   H.W. Blackburne, CF 1903-1924, M.C. 1914, D S O 1917, *Crockford's*, p.118.

and in which no clear decision had been made about the Chaplains' Department."[49] Peter Howson's work on the organisational structure of the chaplains' department in the Great War is entitled *Muddling Through*, and he considers this to be "a good description of what was happening in the Churches, and in the War Office Chaplains' Branch, as they responded to the rapidly developing military situation. … It is also an apt title for the experience of those first chaplains deployed in France."[50]

While the regular chaplains were participating in the retreat from Mons, and filling a variety of roles in the early mobile stages of the war, the temporary chaplains were experiencing difficulties at every turn. F. R. Barry described the situation:

> When the padres first went out with the B.E.F. the army had little idea of what to do with them. In battle they were left behind at base and were not allowed to go up to the fighting front. … A colonel would say 'nothing for you to do today, padre', meaning no corpses to bury.[51]

The Anglican chaplains were frustrated by orders forbidding them to visit the front line and this became a cause of criticism of their performance in the first part of the war. Robert Graves, Siegfried Sassoon, Guy Chapman and C. E. Montague were well-known literary figures that were later scathing of the chaplains' performance in the war. However, their criticism stands and can give us a good idea of the problems faced by chaplains with their public image. Graves's main criticism of the Anglican chaplains rested on the contrast between them and the Roman Catholic priests who were allowed to go the front line from the beginning of the war. He said of the Anglican chaplains: "Soldiers could hardly respect a chaplain who obeyed these orders, yet not one in fifty seemed sorry to obey them."[52] Guy Chapman also used this comparison: "The Church of Rome sent men into battle mentally and spiritually cleaned. The Church of England could only offer you a cigarette." Schweitzer believes that many British officers did not share Graves' views and claims that his doubts about the bible "got on his fellow officers nerves."[53] As a result of the efforts of chaplains like Neville Talbot,[54] Maurice Peel[55] and others who did go forward, and

---

49   Harry Blackburne, lecture to The Royal United Services Institute, February 1922, *RUSI Journal* Vol. LXV111 p.421, cited by Peter Howson, *Muddling Through, The Organisation of British Army Chaplaincy In World War One* (Solihull, Helion, 2013), p.58.

50   Howson, *Muddling Through*, p.58

51   Barry, *Period of My Life*, p.60.

52   R. Graves, *Goodbye to All That: An Autobiography* (London, Jonathan Cape, 1929), p.158.

53   R. Schweitzer, *The Cross and the Trenches: Religious Faith and Doubt Among British and American Great War soldiers* (Connecticut, 2003), p.85.

54   E. Madigan, 'The Life Lived Versus Balaam's Ass's Ears: Neville Stuart Talbot's Chaplaincy on the Western Front' *Royal Army Chaplains Department Journal vol. 47*. (2008).

55   Maurice Peel had insisted on going into front line battle with his men at Festubert in 1915. He was later killed bringing in wounded at Bullecourt in May 1917, J. Walker, *The Blood Tub, General Gough and the Battle of Bullecourt 1917* (Staplehurst, Spellmount, 1999).

the realisation by the generals that chaplains were good for morale, these orders were eventually rescinded. However, the damage had already been done to the reputation of the Anglican chaplains who are, even now, sometimes compared unfavourably by historians to the Roman Catholic chaplains.[56]

By the beginning of 1916 the situation had changed and chaplains were allowed to move freely. They were realising the importance of their work at the front line as well as their essential work at field ambulances and bases. E. C. Crosse[57] was convinced that the nearer the chaplain could get to the front line the better.[58] By this time the Army Chaplains' Department had overcome several ideological and practical problems relating to its deployment and was present at battalion level as well as being attached to base hospitals and field ambulances. Senior chaplains like Harry Blackburne had worked hard at the organisation of the Department. Chaplains met regularly at divisional level to discuss their work, pray and keep up morale.[59] This was sorely needed as tensions concerning the chaplain's role were ever present. Much of the chaplain's time was spent in what Neville Talbot called "holy grocery" that is, ministering to the material and social needs of the troops rather than their spiritual needs. Many chaplains, however, found that these were intertwined. Geoffrey Gordon felt this dilemma keenly:

> Those of us chaplains who feel ourselves pressed by our dilemma are occupying our time with things that the soldier would not describe as religious, but on every opportunity we are preaching insistently the inclusiveness of Christianity.[60]

This problem of priorities in the spiritual and material roles of the priest was often to inform the ideas and actions of returning chaplains.

During the war some of the chaplains were faced with the proximity of men who they would not have met in normal circumstances and whose values and ideas they would not have necessarily shared. However many chaplains had come from big industrial or slum parishes where the church was very active. Many had experience with men in the clubs that had been set up as part of the Church's attempt to appeal to the working-class men and boys in such parishes. The expectation that clergy would visit all the families in a parish regardless of attendance at church also ensured a wider pastoral experience. Cyril Foster Garbett, in his description of the work of the parish of Portsea, commented "Great importance is placed on

56   For example, S. Louden, *Chaplains in Conflict, The Role of Army Chaplains since 1914* (London, Avon Books, 1996), p.50.
57   E. C. Crosse, TCF 1915-1918, MC and DSO 1917, *Crockford's*, p.305.
58   Imperial War Museum (hereafter IWM), E. C. Crosse Papers, 80/22/1.
59   RAChD, TNA WO 95/2023, the papers of the Very Rev H. W. Blackburne, DSO MC. The war diary of the senior chaplain to the 18th Division, the Rev G. A. Weston, details regular meetings of the divisional chaplains.
60   G. Gordon and T. Pym, *Papers from Picardy* (London, Constable, 1917), p.112.

house to house visitation. ... It brings the clergy into touch with all sorts and conditions of men and not only those who are already connected with the church."[61] It
is possible that the chaplains were more in touch with working class life than the
officers, especially when one considers the variety of posts that the chaplains had
been pursuing pre-war. Many of the Church of England's younger and more vocal
chaplains had plenty of varied pre-war experience against which to measure their
wartime impressions.

The job of censoring letters often revealed to the chaplains the opinions of the
enlisted men on religion and a variety of other matters. Richard Holmes was of the
opinion that this "enabled them to see just how deep a current of belief flowed through
the army."[62] However, there was criticism of the chaplains from the ordinary soldiers
which has survived in memoirs such as *Old Soldiers Never Die* by Frank Richards.
Relationships with the chaplains were often soured by the remnants of pre-war class
tensions and anti-clericalism. Much of the criticism of chaplains arose from the
resentment of compulsory church parades, the perception that the chaplains were
identified with authority, and the conflict between the basic tenets of Christianity and
the experience of trench warfare. Corporal Houghton commented on the fact that
his padre had prayers about "not leading us into any kind of danger", and continued:

> I am sure the chaplain had not noticed the inconsistency of that phrase any more
> than the clergymen out here that profess a religion that teaches us that all men
> should be brothers and yet prays weekly for victory over our enemies.[63]

Although chaplains messed with the officers and probably had more in common with
them, they still had to work hard to win the respect of their officer colleagues. Guy
Rogers, chaplain to a Guards Brigade found this difficult at first but eventually his
determination and persistence paid off. By February 1915 he wrote: "Great discussions at lunch – they push me now to discuss all sorts of religious and philosophical
questions ... it is pleasant to feel one's position assured and it has given me the confidence to try and get further."[64] Although relationships with officers and men were
sometimes fraught, the chaplains worked hard to obtain a rapport. This job was made
easier by the increased freedom of action of the chaplains and the heroism of individual chaplains. Bishop Gwynne's Army Book contains many cuttings from papers
and comments by him on the circumstances in which a number of chaplains earned
military honours for bravery in bringing in the wounded. The difficulties experienced
by the chaplains made them more determined at the end of the war to build bridges

61   C. F. Garbett, *The Work of a Great Parish* (London, Longmans, Green & Co, 1915). p.112
62   R. Holmes, *Tommy, The British Soldier on the Western Front 1914-1918* (London, Harper
      Collins, 2004), p.522.
63   Malcolm Brown, *The Imperial War Museum Book of 1918: Year of Victory* (London, Pan,
      1998), p.13.
64   IWM, (7/107/1), T. G. Rogers papers.

with all members of society and to free the church from elitism and snobbery. Rogers also recommended that: "we must make ourselves accessible to all men. We must not burden ourselves with organisations; the impossibility of losing oneself in an organisation has been one of the chaplains' greatest safeguards at the front."[65]

The taking of services proved to be the most frustrating as well as the most rewarding part of the chaplain's job. Resentment of church parade and a growing sense of the importance of Holy Communion led them to concentrate more on voluntary service and communion services although Harry Blackburne and E. C. Crosse had a more robust attitude to church parade, seeing it as an essential part of the Army Chaplains Department's relationship with the army.[66] Both were effective in finding ways to make the parade service more accessible. Blackburne pioneered the breaking of the parade square formation to make a circle and also encouraged chaplains to experiment with more informal service styles and to dispense with the "parsonical" voice.[67] The numbers of candidates coming forward for confirmation were commented on in many chaplains' accounts of the war and Bishop Gwynne's diary shows that a considerable amount of his time was spent touring the Western Front to attend confirmation services.[68] This was possibly food for thought for chaplains as it reflected on the two-tiered system existing at home where it was automatic for middle and upper classes to be confirmed but not so for the working classes.[69] The memorial of Christ's sacrifice on the cross struck a chord with men about to give their lives in battle. Milner-White in his contribution to *The Church in the Furnace* recommended that after the war the Eucharist should be the chief service of the day. Julian Bickersteth was an advocate of as many communion services as possible, feeling that "We have fed the hungry with mattins and evensong for generations when all the time they were hungry for the bread of life."[70] Some chaplains had to revise some of their long-held beliefs about the administration of communion. It was realised that a fasting communion made no sense when services were quickly arranged and had to fit with army routine. Blackburne realised not long after his arrival in France, "We have communion services at all hours of the day and night, one has to change one's ideas out here."[71] Informal services in dugouts became commonplace. Eric Milner-White[72] in his contribution to *The Church in the Furnace* summed it up: "liturgy vanished with peace and rubrics

65   IWM, (7/107/1), T. G. Rogers papers.
66   IWM, (80/22/1), E. C. Crosse papers.
67   RAChD, the papers of the Very Rev H.W. Blackburne, MC DSO.
68   Church Missionary Society Archives (hereafter CMSA), XACC/18/F/1,the diaries of Bishop L. H Gwynne.
69   Lloyd, *The Church of England*, p.163.
70   J. Bickersteth, (ed) *The Bickersteth Diaries*, (London, Leo Cooper, 1995), p.82
71   H. Blackburne, *This Also Happened on the Western Front*, p.16.
72   E. Milner-White, TCF 1914-1918, DSO, *Crockford's*, p.925.

paled in a redder world."[73] He also described the Book of Common Prayer as "semi-usable and semi-used."[74]

The burial service came under a lot of criticism from chaplains. C. I. S. Hood related an experience common to many chaplains when taking a burial service: "No light or book, so by heart I used what prayer seemed useful."[75] The net effect of the experience of the chaplains using the Book of Common Prayer in the trenches was that the services of the Church of England had to be changed, that they were too archaic and complicated for many of the congregation at home and at the front. Milner-White concluded that "It appears that the Prayer Book as it stands is a volume which serves only those who are highly instructed in the faith."[76]

The expected revival of religion in the officers and men of the British Army did not materialise, and chaplains had developed a pessimistic view of the depth of religious feeling at the front. F. R. Barry asserted in his article in *The Church in the Furnace*: "It is untrue … that war is a reviver of religion."[77] Philip Crick wrote in 1917: "It would seem that the mobilisation of a large section of the young men of England has made it clear that the church has not succeeded in impressing upon the majority of them a sense of allegiance to her teaching and practises."[78] Neville Talbot believed that the gauging of religious feelings in the men was a complicated business. He was increasingly aware of the "inarticulate religion" of the ordinary soldiers: "deep in their hearts is a great trust and faith in God. It is an inarticulate faith but expressed in deeds."[79] *The Army and Religion*[80] report was initiated by D. S. Cairns,[81] while he was at the base camp at Rouen. Michael Snape has pointed out that as the report was financed by the YMCA and Cairns was working for the YMCA and influential in raising funds for the association In Scotland, that he was given a free hand to indulge in his pessimistic view of the state of religion in the army.[82] The committee that produced the report was set up under the chairmanship of Bishop Edward Talbot. Snape has called the Cairns Report 'deeply flawed' as it excluded evidence from Welsh and Irish sources and minimal input from Roman Catholic sources.[83] Many of the replies to the questions posed by the committee can be summed up in the remark attributed to Neville

73   E. Milner-White, 'Worship and Services', p.175.

74   Ibid., p.177.

75   IWM, (90/7/1), C. I. S. Hood Paper.

76   Milner-White, 'Worship and Services', p.184

77   Barry, 'Faith in the Light of War' *The Church in the Furnace*, p.36.

78   Philip Crick, 'The Soldier's Religion' in *The Church in the Furnace*', p.371.

79   N. Talbot, *Thoughts on Religion at the Front* (London, 1917), p.8.

80   D. S. Cairns (ed.) *The Army and Religion* (London, YMCA, 1919).

81   D. S. Cairns, United Free Church of Scotland minister and theologian.

82   M. Snape (ed.) *The Back Parts of War*, p.88. Snape cites YMCA Archives, University of Birmingham, YMCA, K27 YMCA War Work No. 14. France, a letter from E. C. Carter to O. McCowen to illustrate the financial considerations involved.

83   Ibid., p.87.

Talbot: "The soldier has got Religion, I am not so sure that he has got Christianity."[84] There was respect for Jesus in that men often revered him as a fellow sufferer and the opinion seemed to be that "All the best instincts feel that man will get a fair judgement in another world."[85] The troops were reported as considering Christianity to be a negative set of ideas and as something irrelevant in their lives. In Chapter Four of the report, "Misunderstandings", a "chaplain of experience" said that "institutional religion is widely identified with respectability and a negative code, but a generous or unselfish act was called "really Christian"."[86]

Having established a general opinion on the unsatisfactory nature of religion in the army the report went on to speculate on the reasons. The social and economic conditions of life in post-Industrial revolution Britain was blamed for a spirit of materialism among the men at the front.[87] The educational systems of both church and state were blamed for the general ignorance of men about religion and doctrine. A senior chaplain found that it was not only in working men that this ignorance was found, "The crude religious ideas expressed in officers' messes are generally lamentable."[88] Neville Talbot also blamed the absence of a religious revival on both the nature of total war and the lack of spiritual equipment to deal with it; he considered: "We have been overtaken by the cataclysm of war in a condition of great poverty towards God."[89]

The chaplains had many issues militating against the work of preaching the gospel and expanding religious awareness at the front. Unrealistic expectations from church leaders and civilians at home who were expecting a religious revival led to disillusionment and heart-searching on the part of the chaplains. Even when the realities of war hit home, the religious condition of the troops in the army proved unsatisfactory. The Cairns Report confirmed what chaplains and committed laymen like Donald Hankey already knew,[90] that religion in the trenches, where it existed, was inarticulate, deistic and not specifically Christian.[91]

At home the church had been responding to war by formulating plans for a National Mission of Repentance and Hope. This was in response to the failure of the expected national religious revival to materialise and an attempt to identify the church with the struggle of the nation at war. Wilkinson described it as "an attempt to discharge

---

84   D. S. Cairns *The Army and Religion*, p.9.
85   Ibid., pp.23-24.
86   Ibid., p.70.
87   Ibid., Ch. Five, 'Materialism and the Social Environment'.
88   Ibid., p.109
89   Talbot, *Thoughts on Religion at the Front*, p.17.
90   Donald Hankey, pre-war ordinand and volunteer at the Oxford and Bermondsey Mission. While serving in the Royal Warwickshire Regiment he wrote a series of article for *The Spectator* under the nom de plume of *A Student in Arms*. Following his death in action in October 1916 these essays were collected in *A Student in Arms* (London, Andrew Melrose, 1916).
91   D. Hankey, *A Student in Arms* p.110.

its vocation to act as the Christian conscience of the country."[92] Although even its critics worked hard to prepare for the mission it was generally judged to be a failure. F. Iremonger, a leading Anglican cleric, summed it up "There were no signs of a renewed desire on the part of the people of England to identify themselves and their ideal with the fellowship and worship of the national church."[93] The results of the mission in terms of the church trying to understand where it had gone wrong, in the reports of the Archbishops' Committees of Enquiry, are fruitful sources of the thinking of the immediate post-war church about what had gone wrong and how to proceed in the future.

As part of the soul-searching involved in the National Mission, the Bishop of Kensington[94] sent out a questionnaire to gather the ideas of serving army and navy chaplains. In a letter to chaplains the bishop posed four questions, asking them about their difficulties in their work, to what extent they felt the church responsible for these difficulties, and asking for their suggestions for remedying these faults and preparing for the return of the troops to civilian life. He said:

> We felt there was no body of men better qualified to give us an account of the religious state of the nation than those who are now in a special position to observe and judge what great masses of men think and feel on the vital subject of religion.[95]

Many were evidently anxious to get things off their chest as the Bishop of Kensington continued in the introduction: "The letters are a record of the intense eagerness to serve the cause of God and his church, which we are thankful to know has character-ised the work of the chaplains."[96]

The questionnaires were sent to 1,300 army chaplains and 300 navy chaplains. Their replies, which were commented on by George Bell[97] as part of the report, gave a clear picture of the preoccupations of the chaplains.[98] Bell particularly wanted to draw the committee's attention to two themes arising from the answers: firstly, the misconceptions about the gospel and the church's responsibility for this and, secondly, the misunderstandings which had alienated people from the church. As in the Cairns

---

92   Wilkinson, *The Church of England and the First World War* (London, SCM Press, 1978), p.70.

93   Cited by Wilkinson, Ibid., p.79.

94   John Primatt Maud (1860 – 1932) was the second Bishop of Kensington from 1911-1932, *ODNB*.

95   *The National Mission of Repentance and Hope*, A report on the chaplains' replies to the Lord Bishop of Kensington (London, 1919), p.5.

96   Ibid., p 5.

97   George Bell was at that time domestic chaplain to the Archbishop of Canterbury.

98   *The National Mission of Repentance and Hope*, 'A report on the chaplains' replies to the Lord Bishop of Kensington' (London, 1919), p.6.

Report, the chaplains commented on the widespread ignorance they had found. Another similarity to the Cairns Report was the comments of the chaplains on the good qualities of the men they had come across: "Of the splendid national qualities of devotion to duty, loyalty, cheerfulness and courage, chaplains do not weary of speaking."[99] A complaint of the chaplains was the very few number of recommendations of soldiers from parish priests that they had received which seemed symptomatic of "the failure of the clergy to know the men."[100] The conclusion of the chaplains was that the church was responsible for the difficulties in their work at the front. They blamed the church's failure to teach and the failure to keep hold of young men and boys, along with divisions within the church, the organisation of the church and the nature of the church services, and warned that special efforts must be made in preparation of "a real welcome by the church and the offer of service to all who return."[101]

The emphasis on both the Cairns report and the Bishop of Kensington's report on the failure of education showed the importance the chaplains put on this reason for the difficulties of working and evangelising with troops at the front, but the situation cannot have come as such a large shock. Their consternation must be looked at in the light of changes in the nature of society and in the education system. The secularisation of society had been increasing side by side with the effort of the churches to ameliorate social conditions as we have seen above. Masterman, in his *The condition of England*[102] published in 1909, had commented on this contradiction:

> The churches are extraordinarily active, endeavouring in this way and that to influence the lives of the people. Their humanitarian and social efforts are widely appreciated. Their definite dogmatic teaching seems to count for little at all. They labour on steadily among a huge indifference.[103]

The 1870 Education Act had resulted in the start of the process by which the state took more control over elementary education, lessening the voluntary sector's influence and diluting or eliminating the influences of denominational religious education. Literacy, however, rose significantly. In 1891 the Registrar General reported a national literacy rate for males at 94 percent.[104] Although the Sunday schools remained influential in the years leading up to the war, especially in big parishes such as Portsea, clergy and teachers were lamenting the almost inevitable loss of boys after the age of fourteen or fifteen. Given these developments, it is possible that chaplains in their comments on the poor state of education were over-compensating for a feeling that it was not

99   Ibid., p.10.
100 Ibid., p.12.
101 Ibid., p.22.
102 C.F.G. Masterman , *The Condition of England* (London: Methuen, 1909).
103 Cited in Lloyd, *The Church of England*, p.61.
104 J. Lawson and H. Silver, *A Social History of Education in England*,(London, Methuen, 1973), p.324.

so much ignorance as indifference that was the problem with the troops' attitude to religion.

The necessity for chaplains of all denominations to work closely together in the war had prompted the Anglican chaplains to think more deeply about the issues that united them and divided them from the nonconformist denominations. The Rev Linton Smith in his contribution to *The Church in the Furnace*, "Fellowship in the Church", commented on the good relationships established in the front line: "A real awakening of the religious spirit, the desire for fellowship has been very widely felt."[105] William Wand in his memoirs said "It has been interesting to see how the chaplains of various denominations got on together. It may be that this shared experience had a salutary effect on the lowering of barriers which was to become the most obvious element in the ecclesiastical history of the twentieth century."[106] Peter Howson considers that it needs to be recognised that "the experience of chaplaincy during the war period provided a shift in the way in which those from different church backgrounds could regard each other."[107] Harry Blackburne pointed to the fact that, under war conditions, positive aspects of cooperation between different denominations and different church parties were emphasised and negative ones ignored: "One has to change one's ideas out here".[108] Returning chaplains could not see why the absence of denominational strife could not continue after the war. Guy Rogers was of the opinion that "it seemed intolerable to return to the type of life where churches could not get together at the table of the Lord."[109] Phillip Crick, writing in 1917, believed that men who had found faith in wartime would "simply have no use for any church that formulates religion in terms of division", and that the church would lose these men. He urged that: "If there cannot be unity, there must be at least uniformity of aim."[110] *The Times*, reporting on Archbishop Davidson's visit to the front in January 1919, commented:

> The chaplains have realised that ... in the face of the forces of evil, the whole church must close up her ranks and have a united front towards the real enemy.[111]

It was not only Anglican chaplains that felt this urge to better peacetime relationships. From the chaplains' conference held in March 1919 at the chaplains' school at St Omer, a letter was sent to *The Times* signed by representatives of chaplains from the Anglican, Scottish Presbyterian, Wesleyan and Baptist churches and the YMCA which set out their hope for the future of church unity. They suggested conferences and conventions to share ideas "as a regular and normal part of the life of the churches", and

---

105 M. Linton Smith, 'Fellowship in the Church' in *The Church and the Furnace*, p.119.
106 W. Wand, *The Changeful Page*, (London, Hodder & Stoughton, 1965) p.69.
107 Howson, *Muddling Through*, p.198.
108 Blackburne, *This Also Happened on the Western Front*, p.16.
109 Rogers, *A Rebel at Heart*, p.310.
110 Crick, 'The Soldier's Religion', *The Church in the Furnace*, p.365.
111 *The Times*, 28 January 1919, p.5.

that intercommunion be allowed "at least on such occasions as joint conferences and retreats where the spirit of fellowship already existing is deepest and fullest."[112] The YMCA had been instrumental in organising united services in its huts, conducted by Anglican and Nonconformist clergy.[113] A measure of cooperation between the chaplains' department and the YMCA can be seen in the fact that after the war Neville Talbot was offered, but declined, the position of the religious work secretary to the YMCA.[114]

The experiences and difficulties that chaplains endured under the conditions of war caused many chaplains to give careful thought to their own beliefs and theology. As the Dean of Worcester, W. Moore Ede, put it in his introduction to Geoffrey Studdert Kennedy's *The Hardest Part*: "These pages express the thoughts which come to the writer amid the hardship of the trenches and the brutalities of war. It is literally a theology hammered out on the battlefield."[115] Studdert Kennedy wrote *The Hardest Part* as a response to the question frequently asked of him: "What is God like?" He was drawn to emphasise increasingly the immanence of God and his ability to suffer with us: "It is funny how it is Christ on the cross that comforts, not God on the throne."[116] Like many other chaplains and soldiers he identified the suffering Christ with the soldier's predicament but emphasised the eventual triumph of the crucified suffering God: "The true God is naked, bloody, wounded and crowned with thorns, tortured but triumphant in his love."[117] Frank West in his biography of F. R. Barry said of Barry and Studdert Kennedy: "Both felt instinctively that the transcendent impassible God would not commend the gospel to an increasingly sceptical public. A God wholly removed from the sufferings of his children just would not do."[118] Mervyn Haigh questioned the ability of the diffusive Christianity prevalent in the trenches to mesh with a post-war church. He questioned whether the church was wide enough in its theology and its attitude to provide a home for the men who had discovered an "inarticulate" religion during the war:

> There are others, who reverently recognising the source of all diffusive Christianity is the work of the Christ through the church his body, yet begin to question whether the church is wide enough in its theology or in its outreach, to gather men such as this within its fold or embrace the God given opportunities now open before it in a post-war society.[119]

---

112 *The Times*, 1 April 1919, p.9.
113 Snape, *The Back Parts of War:* p.86.
114 Ibid., p.86.
115 G. A. Studdert Kennedy, *The Hardest Part*, (London, Hodder & Stoughton, 1918), p.ix.
116 Ibid., p.8.
117 Ibid., p.71.
118 F. West, *F. R. B. Portrait of Bishop Russell Barry*, (London, Grove Books, 1980).
119 F. R. Barry, *Mervyn Haigh* (SPCK, 1964), p.55.

His thinking widened his ideas on salvation. Studdert Kennedy also pursued this theme of the church's ideas not being flexible enough, theologically, to keep up with the wartime developments in thinking by the chaplains: "Everywhere the followers of Christ are found outside the church. The Church of Christ has ceased in these days to be a pillar of cloud and fire ... and has become a weak and inefficient ambulance brigade."[120]

The chaplains, then, confronted in the war events which were to make them question the nature of their own faith, face the reality of a vast ignorance about Christianity, consider the failure of religious education and appreciate the poor image the Church of England had among ordinary men. However, they had also discovered the large extent of inarticulate religion and diffusive Christianity existing in the army and were determined to build upon that in tackling the issues that awaited them in returning to their peacetime ministries. In what ways could the lessons, both negative and positive, of being witnesses to God in four years of war be put to best use in Britain in the future? Amongst the reactions of the chaplains was a clear sense of optimism and opportunity. Milner-White emphasised the changes that the war had brought about: "An immense, spontaneous, amicable anarchy has sprung into being and this has been the church in the furnace."[121] He went on: "We are a new race, we priests of the furnace, humbled by much strain and much failure, revolutionaries not at all in spirit, but actually in fact."[122] This revolutionary spirit among some army chaplains had been brewing since mid-war. In 1915 in a book dedicated to the men who had died, F. R. Barry was thinking about the end of the war and his response to it: "A merely different world is not enough, we must see that it is a better one ... what part will the church play in the building of the new world?"[123]

The church at home came in for a great deal of criticism from the chaplains at the front. Macnutt compared the "Heights to which men ... rise to in the pursuit of duty, the self giving, the sacrifice," with "the cold calculating uninspired profession of Christianity which forms so large a part of the practical religion of the church."[124] He added that the churches' failure must be recognised: "to recognise it is the only possible attitude for faith." In his contribution to *The Church in the Furnace*, 'The Moral Equivalent of War', he recommended self-government for the church, escape from parochialism, a readiness to face social evils and an end to sectionalism. Tom Pym was one of the most outspoken critics of the established church. This critical attitude was coupled with a strong sense of how the returning chaplains were to play a part in its future. He had been an extremely successful and popular chaplain who had been promoted to Deputy Assistant Chaplain General of XIII Corps. In spite of his

---

120 Studdert Kennedy, *Hardest Part, p.158.*
121 Milner-White, 'Worship and Services', *The Church in the Furnace*, p.176.
122 Ibid., p.176.
123 F. R. Barry, *Religion and the War* (London, Methuen, 1915), p.1.
124 Macnutt, 'The Moral Equivalent of War', *The Church in the Furnace*, p.5.

privileged and establishment position before the war as curate and chaplain of Trinity College Cambridge, he had spent his vacations living and working in Camberwell in the East End of London. He contributed an essay on religious education and training of the clergy to *The Church in the Furnace*[125] and was thinking seriously about church reform in the later stages of the war. He was asked to be present at the first meeting of the Life and Liberty Campaign, a pressure group which had been set up to campaign for changes in the way the Church of England was run. His views on the church after the war were considered by some to be extreme. He thought of a scheme called "Plus and Minus", known as PAM, whereby groups of clergy would pool their resources and make a pledge to accept no church endowments or patronage until either the church was disestablished or it had had the chance to put its own house in order. Another outspoken critic of the status quo, Neville Talbot, felt that Pym had gone too far and that he was in danger of losing support and becoming a martyr to his own cause. He took to calling him "ig" and warned: "You don't want to become a modern Ignatuis Loyola do you Tom?"[126]

Pym's ideas were discussed at a chaplains' conference in March 1918 and the scheme was rejected. However, he continued to agitate and had not changed his ideas when writing to his wife in May 1918:

> We talk of scandals and abuses disqualifying the church in preaching righteous-
> ness and the Kingdom of God. Surely they even more disqualify the individual
> parson who depends on that system for his worldly advancement.

He urged chaplains and clergy at home to: "Resign and refuse livings and curacies. Don't take the church's preferment or the church's money."[127] In November, a few days after the Armistice, Pym went to stay the night with Bishop Gwynne, who according to Dora Pym, his wife, talked to him at length about his attitudes.[128] Ben O'Rorke,[129] a regular army chaplain who had been captured in the retreat from Mons and only released from a prisoner of war camp in 1915, kept a diary in 1918 and recounted in his entry for 23 November the genesis of the revolutionary ideas of some of the chaplains which took place at a conference for Assistant Chaplain Generals:

> Chiefly notable for a caucus which took place in [J. V. Macmillan's] room
> after dinner. They came back to the dining room and read out a new scheme
> for a community arising out of the reconstruction propaganda. Members of the
> community to pool their incomes and pledge themselves not to accept benefice

---

125 T. Pym, 'Religious Education and Training of the Clergy', *The Church in the Furnace.*
126 Pym, *Tom Pym: A Portrait*,p.50.
127 Ibid., p.51.
128 Ibid., p.56.
129 Ben O'Rorke, pre-war regular army CF. He was mobilised with the 4th Field Ambulance at Bordon on 10 August and was captured in the retreat from Mons.

while the church continued on present lines. They would work amongst the poor and live simple lives among the working classes.[130]

Archbishop Davidson[131] in his visit to the front in January 1919 held conferences at all the army headquarters and addressed chaplains and other officers. Bell said in his biography of Davidson: "The subjects were this time far more concerned with the future, than with immediate needs. ... They included church unity, demobilisation, church and labour, the permanent diaconate."[132] The Archbishop obviously picked up the unrest among army chaplains. Bell continued: "There was a plan for equalising stipends in the benefices and curacies to which the chaplains would return." Another scheme was for "rovers in each diocese – a kind of flying squadron of special missioners under authority."[133] According to Bell, Davidson sympathised but did not find the chaplains very constructive in their views. He apparently thought the unrest and rebellion were due to an unwillingness to face the old parochial grind: "possessing so much freedom, how should they be servants again?"[134] Barry remembered:

> We too were getting frustrated and developed our own view of "we" and "they" the chaplains at the front and the home church. We tended to blame everything on "the system" and particularly "the bishops" – always the whipping boys of dissatisfaction.[135]

B. K. Cunningham had some sympathy with the discontent: "without claiming to find any great remedy for past failure, this very restlessness and discontent is surely begotten of God and is consequently full of hope."[136]

The chaplains had had to consider throughout the war the way in which the role that they had been performing had changed them and how prepared they had been for war. This led many to consider the role of ordination training and its suitability in providing able clergy in peace and war. Before the war the number of ordination candidates had been decreasing and by 1900 the situation had become critical. By 1908 the deficit in clergy was 5,204. The problem was compounded by the growth of the population and its concentration in industrial centres. To hold parishes in plurality or to create new parishes meant a special act of parliament for each individual case.[137] Candidates for ordination were predominantly upper or middle class. It was very

130 *The Diaries of The Rev B. O'Rorke.*
131 R.A. Davidson, Archbishop of Canterbury 1903-1928, *ODNB.*
132 Bell, *Randall Davidson*, p.942.
133 Ibid., p.943.
134 Ibid.
135 Barry, *Period of my Life*, p.62.
136 B. K. Cunningham, contribution to Anon, *Can England's Church win England's Manhood?*, p.43.
137 Lloyd, *The Church of England*, p.75.

expensive to be ordained, involving years of education. Roger Lloyd estimated a sum of £500 after secondary education. Also, unless a private income was available, taking up a poorly paid benefice was impossible. Bertie Bull,[138] a colleague of Charles Gore at the Community of the Resurrection, said: "We have invented a class priesthood with a money qualification."[139] After 1900 some bishops were beginning to waive the requirement to have a degree and colleges such as St Aidan's, Birkenhead, were training increasing numbers of non-graduate clergy. The bishops were also starting to insist on some type of theological training, although they did not enforce this until 1917. Neville Talbot in his contribution to *The Church in the Furnace*, 'The Training of the Clergy', commented on how the chaplains had to overcome a pre-war aversion to the clergy and proved themselves worthy of respect and pointed to the gaps in training shown up by the stresses of war. He continued that theological training, when it existed, was too short and rushed.

P. B. "Tubby" Clayton, who had set up the Every Man's Club at Poperinghe in the war, had been in a good position to judge the state of religion among the troops and officers as they poured through the doors of Talbot House. He too was concerned with the training of ordinands but in a different context. Many of the men he had come into contact with had expressed a desire to be ordained if they survived the war. Clayton had kept a record of their names and thought up a scheme for a test school, that is, a pre-ordination educational centre to assess the suitability of the candidate and bring his education up to the standard required. The two French temporary test schools set up in 1919 were joined together and the great venture of the test school started, which was to provide priests who would have an influence on the Church of England for the next forty years. The setting up of Knutsford test school established the principle that in future none should be debarred from ordination training because of their lack of educational opportunities or financial background.

With the school at Knutsford well established, Clayton turned his attention to his other post-war ambition, which was to start a club in London along the lines of Talbot House. What was to become the international movement of Toc H started at a meeting on 19 November, 1919, and the first HQ or "Mark" as the houses were to become known, was set up in a flat in Red Lion Square, soon spilling over to two other London locations. The aims and actions of the new organisation were soon being advertised on the London underground. The basis of the ideology of Toc H was apparent at this stage: the perpetuation of the active service atmosphere of fellowship, the extension of this tradition to the younger generation, and the continuation of the Talbot House tradition of service, thought and conduct.

---

138 Bertie Paul Bull, Community of the Resurrection 1894, Chaplain to South African Forces, *Crockford's*, p.180.

139 Ibid., p.150.

The discussions at the Pan Anglican Congress in 1908[140] had shown clearly that Christian Socialist movements, for example the Guild of St Matthew[141] and the Christian Social Union,[142] had had an influence out of proportion to their small numbers. The question which was addressed in their session on social issues was: "Does Christianity point to a socialist society and if so, ought the church to be allied to the Labour Party?" The answer to these questions was a "resounding yes."[143] The fifth report of the Archbishops' Committee of Enquiry, *Christianity and Industrial Problems*, gave a clear lead on the ways in which industrial problems and social inequalities could be dealt with: "We would urge our fellow Christians to ask themselves once more whether an economic system which produces striking inequalities of wealth is compatible with the spirit of Christianity?" The report continued, discussing the living wage, unemployment, sickness, industrial injury and child labour and expected the parish priests "to take the lead in the application of the Christian faith to social and industrial problems."[144]

The report formed the basis of the Industrial Christian Fellowship, which in the interwar years evangelised in industrial areas. Through its missions and crusades, educational work and political influence, it created an impression of the concern of the church for the condition of the working class. The ICF was led by P. T. R. Kirk, an ex-chaplain, and its chief missioner was the Rev Studdert Kennedy, who travelled around the country evangelising and leading crusades. It was supported to a large extent by ex-chaplains. M. B. Reckitt explained that they were ideally positioned to support it. They had "endured the hardships, shared the same searching questions and gained thereby an insight into the needs of body soul and spirit."[145]

Of the 111 in-service bishops in *Crockford's Clerical Directory* in England and Wales in 1940, thirty-two of them were ex-chaplains, that is, 29 percent, which seems to show a healthy career path for many former chaplains. Among them were chaplains who became bishops of large or important dioceses: Salisbury-Woodward at Bristol,[146]

140 The Pan Anglican Congress was held in London in the summer of 1908 and was attended by 17,000 delegates from every church in the Anglican Communion. The Archbishop of Canterbury called it "a week without parallel on our history", W. E. Gibraltar, 'The Pan Anglican Congress' in the *Irish Church Quarterly* Vol. 1. No. 4 (October, 1908, pp.274).

141 The Guild of St Matthew was formed by Stewart Headlam, prominent Christian Socialist, in 1887. It was a society for high church clergy and laity sympathetic to socialism. *ODNB*.

142 The Christian Social Union was formed in 1889 and studied social conditions and social injustice. It was merged with the Navvy Mission to form the Industrial Christian Fellowship in 1919.

143 Lloyd, *The Church of England*, p.193.

144 The Archbishops' Fifth Committee of Enquiry, *Christianity and industrial Problems* (1918).

145 M. B. Reckitt, *Maurice to Temple. A Century of the Social Movement in the Church of England* (Scott Holland lectures, 1946).

146 Clifford Salisbury-Woodward, TCF 1916-1917, MC 1916, *Crockford's*, p.158.

E. S. Woods at Lichfield,[147] Mervyn Haigh at Coventry,[148] F. R. Barry at Southwell, Christopher Chavasse at Rochester, Kenneth Kirk at Oxford and Geoffrey Lunt[149] at Ripon. There are also numerous entries of former chaplains who had either been overseas bishops and retired or returned home to a parish in England (for example, Neville Talbot, who had been Bishop of Pretoria).

We have seen how former chaplains were convinced even before the end of the war that they had something specific to give to the post-war life of the church. The years before the Second World War would see changes in the church's relationship with state and people. Former chaplains were to be involved in many of them, from the rise of the pacifist movement to the first use of the broadcast media by the church. The agendas for the first Church Congresses to be held since the war, in 1919 and 1920, show that former chaplains were represented prominently in major forums for the church's discussions. The variety of topics they covered prefigured the extent to which they would be involved in church affairs the interwar years. In 1919 Tom Pym spoke on: "Social centres and welfare work"; B. K. Cunningham on: "The faith that could move mountains"; and E. K. Talbot[150]on: "The church of tomorrow".[151] In 1920 Geoffrey Studdert Kennedy spoke on: "Christ and the Labour movement"; F. R. Barry on: "Incarnation"; and Timothy Rees[152] and F. B. Macnutt led a discussion on the implications of the Lambeth resolution on unity.

The Rev Kenneth Kirk in his article "When the Priests Come Home", said of the returning chaplains: "In so far as they are able to codify their experience, and keep it intact under the disintegrating influence of peace it will modify their methods in parochial work in many directions."[153] The following chapters will show in more detail to what extent their hopes and ambitions were achieved.

147 E .S.Woods, TCF 1914-1919, *Crockford's*, p.822.
148 Mervyn Haigh, TCF 1916-1919, mentioned in Despatches 1918, *Crockford's*, p.289.
149 Geoffrey Lunt, TCF 1917-1919, *Crockford's*, p.1137.
150 Edward Keble Talbot, TCF 1914-1920, *Crockford's*, p.1313.
151 *The Times*, 9 October 1919, p.9.
152 Timothy Rees, TCF 1916-1919, J. Lambert Rees, *Timothy Rees of Mirfield and Llandaff* (London, Mowbray, 1945).
153 K. Kirk, 'When the Priests Come Home', *The Church in the Furnace*, p.419.

2

Chaplains, Industry and Society

In his contribution to *The Church in the Furnace*, E. S. Woods, later Bishop of Lichfield, believed with many other chaplains that the church had a post-war opportunity to make a difference in society. He thought that "The problem of securing justice and mercy in the world of industry",[1] was one which the church could legitimately address and advised the church to "Go on a crusade for the social justice and brotherhood of man."[2] Gerald Studdert Kennedy describes the experience of the war as being "both an accusation and a challenge"[3] to the returning chaplains, and that they returned with "A sense of corporate identity and a number of readily agreed objectives." *The Church in the Furnace* became, according to him, "a kind of tract for frontline reformists."[4]

Any assessment of the role of returning chaplains must take several criteria into account in making judgements about their significance in industrial and social affairs during the interwar years. Firstly, the extent to which their thoughts and actions were influenced by their pre-war experiences, secondly to examine the evidence that their conduct was based on their wartime experiences. Thirdly, it is necessary to put the evidence of their impact in the context of other initiatives by the church in these years. To what extent did the chaplains stand out as leading the field in their concern for social and industrial justice? Finally the extent to which the Church of England was continuing to be relevant to working men and business interests must be assessed in order to judge the returning chaplains' effect on them.

It is possible that the returning chaplains, despite being aware of the evidence to show that the churches' "opportunity" in the trenches had not resulted in a religious revival, were conscious of a change of attitude towards the clergy, developed in the comradeship of chaplains and men in the trenches. This realisation could form

---

1   E. S. Woods, 'The Great Adventure', *The Church in the Furnace*, p.440.
2   Ibid., p.447.
3   Gerald Studdert Kennedy, *Dog Collar Democracy:, The Industrial Christian Fellowship 1919–1929* (London, Macmillan 1982), p .51.
4   Ibid., p.51

the basis of new work that the churches could do in society and industry. Bernard Keymer,[5] in his contribution to *The Church in the Furnace*, attempted to make sense of "the revelations of war" and the way in which the increased understanding created during the war between different social groups could be continued. He seemed to have a realistic appreciation of the changes war had made in the perceptions of the combatants. He claimed that "War is dealing shrewd blows every day to prejudice, criticism and suspicion", but that there was still work to be done: "The wage earners are filled with a vague but profound sentiment that the industrial system ... denies to them the liberties, opportunities and responsibilities of free men."[6]. He considered that the heart of the question was in "The general status of labour, its insecurity and lack of freedom."[7] The church must take the lead in a new attitude:

> It is up to the church to spiritualise the ideas of the industrial world. If the Church is to exert any influence it will be learning to see men as they really are, by trusting them and understanding the difficulties of rich and poor alike. Unless we are willing to learn, the church will be seen as having a patronising attitude.[8]

The Rev A. Lambardine, a former chaplain, preaching at Bishopsgate in March 1919 commented on his perception that there was a sense of expectancy as to how the church would respond to the post-war world. "The Labour world, conscious of its growing power is watching and waiting to see what the church is going to do" and continued "Millions of men have learned from what they have seen and heard of the padres that a clergyman is out for more than taking services and sitting on committees."[9] The Rev Christopher Chavasse who became Vicar of St George's church, Barrow in Furness after demobilisation, said in one of his first letters to parishioners: "In industry there is the problem of the union between capital and labour which we must have and to which we are groping."[10] Chavasse considered that in the days of troubled industrial relations immediately after the war that "There was one of two things imminent – one was a revolution; the other, a great revival."[11] He seemed convinced that it was a revival which would sweep the country.

The Rev Linton Smith,[12] later to be Bishop of Rochester, in his essay in *The Church in the Furnace*, believed that the chaplains had been successful in breaking down some

5   RAChD archives, Bernard Keymer, TCF 1916-1918, chaplain to the RAF 1918.
6   Bernard Keymer, 'Fellowship in Industrial Life', *The Church in the Furnace*, p.130.
7   Ibid., p.130.
8   Ibid., pp.141-142.
9   *Church Times*, 21 March 1919, p.282.
10 Barrow in Furness Record Office, BPR11/PM/2 C. Chavasse, *St George's Parish Magazine, January 1920.*
11 Ibid., May 1921.
12 M. Linton Smith TCF 1915-1917, DSO 1917, *Crockford's*, p.1248.

of the class barriers in fellowship with men of all sorts during the war, and had come to admire the personality traits of officers and men: "The chaplain has learned to revise his standard of judgement … he has learned as never before to know men, and knowing them, to love and respect them."[13] He continued "It must be made clear that the interest of the church lies in men because they are men, not because they have a position of wealth and position." He talked of the "absolutely unique" opportunity given to them in the war: "Through their close association with men of all classes, of obtaining an insight into their lives and thoughts which is quite impossible … under the conditions of parochial life."[14] He was not alone in regarding the post-war era as one in which a new relationship with the population could be built up. The Archbishop of Canterbury, speaking at the memorial service for chaplains who had died, said:

> Up and down the land a fellowship of mutual knowledge and mutual trust is now aflame with a larger outlook, a manlier sympathy and a new found loyalty to our Lord. See to it brothers that henceforth it should never wane and that the national church should be more and more the church of the people.[15]

P. B 'Tubby' Clayton was anxious that fellowship engendered in the war should not dissipate in the class tensions of peace:

> The pit boys of today cherish an almost racial antagonism against the classes whose sons led the pit boys of yesterday against uncut wire. If the Talbot House movement can go forward with its programme of reconciliation—much good may come of it.

He continued, "The church must teach industry and commerce to say prayers together."[16]

Kenneth Kirk, in his essay, "When the Priests Come Home", in *The Church in the Furnace* compared the relationship of church and government to the work of the chaplain in the trenches:

> There are brigadiers in France who refer almost every question affecting the well-being of the men to the chaplains for comment and advice. When the character of the priesthood is so developed that county council and committees do the

---

13   M. Linton Smith, "Fellowship in the Church", in *The Church in the Furnace*, pp.108-109.
14   Ibid., p.116.
15   *Church Times*, 4 July 1919, p.7.
16   *The Times*, 29 October 1920, p.15

same by the clergy at home, the Church of England can be certain that the ministry has absorbed the lessons of the war.[17]

For some chaplains, then, their experiences in the war made them optimistic about the way in which their increased social awareness would impinge on their efforts toward creating a more equal society in the post-war era. They were also, ironically, more aware also of the negative opinions of many men to the church as an institution, and the problems that faced the church in its projected efforts to aid social equality and industrial harmony. Guy Rogers dismissed the idea that the war would result in a revolution in labour relations as a "pathetic delusion".

The opinions of some chaplains in their replies to the questions asked in the Bishop of Kensington's report showed that they believed that there existed a high degree of anti-clericalism and also that the identification of the church with the upper classes still persisted. The Bishop of Kensington in his introduction to the report said. "To the thousands of men and women who labour, we have come to be regarded as, and identified with, what is classy and socially exclusive." He realised that "The church simply does not count as a live factor for social betterment."[18] Bishop Bell's report on the answers of the clergy to the questions posed contains comments by the chaplains on the "social exclusiveness" of the church and the "social barrier" between clergy and people. One reply mentions "The failure of the church to witness in social things."[19]

Macnutt, in his essay in *The Church in the Furnace*, summed up what should be the attitude of the chaplain and the church in the post-war era. He quoted the Bishop of Oxford, Charles Gore, who had said in sermon at a pre-war Church Congress that the clergy should have a "permanently troubled conscience." Macnutt stressed that "We must face the social evils with a new spirit, no longer regarding them with the mild uneasiness which evaporates with talk." He advised that the "permanently troubled conscience" should "never rest until the spirit of Christ has won."[20]

The Church in the Furnace was reviewed by the *Church Times* in January 1918, and it was recommended as being of use to the reconstruction of the church after war. The review recommended that its study might "With profit be taken as a basis in Rural Decanal chapters and other church meetings."[21]

Gerald Studdert Kennedy, commenting on the ex-chaplains who joined the Industrial Christian Fellowship, was aware of the effect their war service had on them:

A small but articulate proportion of the temporary chaplains returned from the war guilty at the failure of the church as a national institution, traumatically

---

17   Kirk, 'When the Priests Come Home', *The Church in the Furnace*, p.426
18   *The National Mission of Repentance and Hope, A report on the chaplains' replies to the Lord Bishop of Kensington* (London 1919), p.17.
19   Ibid., p.33.
20   Macnutt, 'The Moral Equivalent of War', *The Church in the Furnace*, p.30.
21   *Church Times*, 25 January 1918, p.64.

initiated into the dilemma of a socially effective faith and with some collective sense of issues requiring attention.[22]

An inaugural meeting of the Chaplains Fellowship in October 1918 had as one of its objectives "To do all in our power to arouse the conscience of the church with regard to social reform."[23] The Bishop of Peterborough, F. T. Woods, brother of E. S. Woods, speaking in the Convocation at Canterbury in February 1918, considered that:

> It was incumbent upon the church at the present time to do all in its power to second the efforts now being made in many quarters to inaugurate a truer fellowship ... between all who are engaged in the industries of the nation and particularly in view of the critical period which will follow the conclusion of peace.[24]

As part of the Anglican Church's response to the war and as a follow-up to the National Mission, the Archbishops set up Committees of Enquiry to look at the tasks of the post-war Church. The fifth report was called *Christianity and Industrial Problems*. The introduction recommended the need for a new beginning in industrial affairs and also a recognition that the church was in need of repentance of its past role, that of "An undue subservience of the church to the possessing, employing and governing classes of the past." There was the realisation that any action would "require a conflict with political economy." The main themes of the report were: the living wage, adequate leisure, full employment, the status of labour, the adequate provision of education and health and housing. The basic incompatibility of the churches' message and capital was stated:

> We would urge our fellow churchmen to ask themselves once more whether an economic system which produces the striking ... excessive inequalities of wealth which characterise our present society is one which is compatible with the spirit of Christianity.

The clergy's role in the front line of social and industrial matters was emphasised: "They might rightly be expected to take the lead in the application of the Christian faith to social and Industrial practice."[25] Historians have praised the Fifth Archbishops' Report as an important part of the development of the post-war church in its effort to further the social gospel. John Oliver called it "an outstanding expression of Christian thought about post-war society"[26] Gerald Studdert Kennedy claims that the report

---

22   Studdert Kennedy, *Dog-Collar Democracy*, p.51.
23   *Church Times*, 11 October 1918.
24   *Church Times*, 8 February 1918.
25   The Archbishops' Fifth Committee of Enquiry, *Christianity and industrial Problems* (London 1918).
26   Oliver, *The Church and Social Order*, p.49.

became "The charter document of the Industrial Christian Fellowship."[27] However, the ideas and actions, both of the post-war church as an institution and the returning chaplains, must be seen in the context of the attitude and work of the church in the nineteenth century and in the years leading up to the war. E. H. Norman is of the opinion that the post-war church concentrated too much on its failures, and public repentance for them, and was over-critical of its record on social action. He quoted the report of the Third Archbishops' Committee of Enquiry, *The Worship of the Church:*.

> It is undeniable that the church's own record in the past stands in its way today. Old abuses, child labour, sweated labour, the intolerable conditions of housing and the monstrous evils of the slums … long continued to exist with scarcely a protest from the church at large."[28]

He commented: "The authors' ignorance of the positive passion found in the nineteenth century church for social improvement is remarkable."[29]

How far had the church been involved in social reform in the nineteenth century? The term "Christian Socialist" was used by the Maurice group in the 1840s and for the first time brought two hitherto mutually incompatible terms together. The wave of Christian socialism in the 1880s was reflected in the speeches of the Church Congresses. The publication of *Lux Mundi* in 1889 was important for its influence on ideas about society as well as its theological significance. Two of its essays were purely social, and later in the year its editor co-founded the Christian Social Union to further the social gospel. Its aims were to research the ways in which a better social order could be achieved. It campaigned through its publication *The Commonwealth*, pamphlets and public meetings on such issues as housing. At its height in 1910 it had 6,000 members. Wilkinson said of it:

> It attracted the largest number of members of any organisation for social reform in the history of the Church of England, and created a tradition of social thought which continued long after its demise in 1919.[30]

John Oliver claims that it secured the passage of the factory act in 1901 and that the Christian Social Union had raised the profile of social and industrial issues amongst church people. This can be seen in the proceedings of Church Congress in the years leading up to the war. In Manchester in 1908 it discussed "The conditions of factory life" and "The main problems of Industry and commerce." It is significant that *The*

27   Studdert Kennedy, *Dog-Collar Democracy,* p.51.
28   Norman, *Church and Society in England,* p.230.
29   Ibid., p.230.
30   Alan Wilkinson, *Christian Socialism: from Scott Holland to Tony Blair* (London, Presbyterian Pub Corp, 1999), p.29.

Times newspaper saw this emphasis as right and proper. An editorial at the time of the conference said "It is entirely right, in Manchester it is probably inevitable, that there should be papers read on socialism."[31] In 1913 the congress debated "rural betterment" and "the ethics of property". In *The Times* report on these debates it was stated: "Here were four uncompromising collectivists preaching the ethics of the socialist gospel in undiluted form and by and large not with tolerance but with active sympathy."[32] The importance in which social and industrial issues were regarded by the church can particularly be seen in the Pan Anglican Conference in 1908.

In the preface to section A in the report of the congress, the authors T. C. Fry and J. Carter explained the main areas considered. Point five dealt with "the problem of unemployment" which "urgently requires the immediate attention o the community of the whole." Point six considered that "That religion and ethics can never be rightly severed from the motives of economic life." Point nine asserted that "fearlessly to assist in the evolution of a just and efficient organisation of society, by the exercise of her prophetic office, without committing herself to any partisan politics is a permanent duty of the church."[33]

Several former chaplains, such as E. S. Woods, Harry Blackburne, Charles Raven[34] and Tom Pym became involved in the Life and Liberty movement which started agitating for church reform from 1917 onwards. Its leaders were involved in social reform in other spheres of interest such as the I C F and C.O.P.E.C., and it was inevitable that some of its publications took a strong line on social and industrial issues. Its pamphlet *The Social message of the Church* said that: "The principles of a Christian social gospel should be cooperation, fellowship and mutual service. The implications of our existing social system are competition, profits and self-interest."[35]

The proponents of the involvement of the church in the politics and practicalities of the social gospel after the war therefore had a sound basis in pre-war Christian Socialism. However, in the writings of the former chaplains the impression remains of their perception of the post-war era as being significantly different; with the church facing many and varied opportunities and challenges. How different was the interwar period to the challenges that faced Britain before the war? Social conditions on the home front during the war had improved for the poorest members of society. Richard Overy is of the opinion that: "Standing back and taking an overview, there can be no doubt that the working classes made relative gains in the war."[36] The bargaining power of the unions had also increased in times of acute labour shortage. He claims

31 *The Times*, 3 October 1908, p.4.
32 *The Times*, 4 October 1913, p.9.
33 *The General Report of the Pan Anglican Congress 1908*, Vol 2, pp.iii and iv.
34 Charles Raven, T C F 1917-1918 *Crockford's*, p.1109.
35 C. O. P .E. C. booklet *The Social Message of the Church*, cited by Thompson, *Bureaucracy and Church Reform*, p.149.
36 Overy, *The Morbid Age*, p.282.

that the end of the war one in three workers was unionised.[37] Unions particularly in South Wales, Sheffield, Merseyside and 'Red' Clydeside became more politicised. The growing confidence of the unions can be seen in the fact that between 1919 and 1921, 150 million working days were lost through stoppages.[38]

The post-war boom had resulted in many of the returning troops gaining employment in the post-war industrial economy. However, the boom was short-lived, as the traditional industries, shipbuilding, mining and railways had been over-stimulated in the war and now faced shrinking world markets. In the 1918 election the Labour Party had increased its vote from half a million to two and a half million, winning 63 seats and becoming the official opposition party. Juliet Nicholson summed up their stance: "Labour's goals included the immediate nationalisation and democratic control of vital public services, including mining, shipping, armaments and the electric industry."[39] The mine owners were opposed to nationalisation and wages and working conditions in mines varied throughout the country.[40] Miners' strikes broke out in February 1919 and by the end of the month, London was reduced to three day's supply of coal.[41] The government's response to the slump was to bring forward decontrol of the coal industry, resulting in more strikes in April 1921, only ending in "Black Friday", when the prospect of a general strike was averted by the collapse of the Triple Alliance of the transport, rail and mine workers.

The abandonment of building programmes during the war had worsened the housing shortage. Even though the Town Planning Act of 1919 required local councils to begin clearing slums and start building programmes, progress was slow and high rents caused by housing shortages meant homes were often out of reach of the unemployed. The immediate post-war boom was followed in 1920-21 by a recession. The Archbishop of Canterbury in his New Year's message for 1921 said: "More than two years have passed since our guns were silent. What of the hopes that were ours at Christmas 1918? Who without a sinking of heart can look thoughtfully ... on the rise of and character of unemployment in England?"[42]

Conversely, those in work had a higher standard of living as food prices fell in the 1920s, accompanied by an increase in real wages between 1914-1924.[43] There was a shift from old industries to newer ones, such as electrical, automobile, rayon, hosiery, chemicals and scientific industries. Other activities to benefit were commerce,

37   Ibid., p.288.
38   J. Wallis. *Valiant for Peace: History of the Fellowship of Reconciliation, 1914-89* (London, Fellowship of Reconciliation, 1991), p.45.
39   J. Nicolson, *The Great Silence: 1918-1920, Living in the Shadow of the Great War* (London, John Murray, 2009), p.75
40   C. Mowat, *Britain Between the Wars 1918-1940* (London, Methuen & Co, 1955) p.119.
41   Ibid., p.79.
42   *Church Times*, 7 January 1921, p.26.
43   Mowat. *Britain Between the Wars*, p.205.

building, utilities, entertainment and sport, and the manufacture of food, drink and tobacco.[44]

These developments did not help those who had always worked in the more traditional primary industries. Numbers employed in the coal-mining industries fell from 1,259,000 in1924 to 1,069,000 in 1930. In the Iron and steel industry over the same period the numbers declined from 313,000 to 287,000. As well as this lowering of employment the percentage of their workers who were unemployed rose. In 1927 unemployment as a whole stood at 11.3 percent, but unemployment in the coal, metal, engineering, woollens and shipbuilding industries stood at 15.8 percent.[45]

The general world recession after 1929 did not help employment. A change from reliance on exporting traditional products such as coal to providing consumer goods for the home market meant that the employment situation was different in different parts of the country, with those employed in new manufacturing industries experiencing a good standard of living at the same time as the Jarrow hunger marchers protested about unemployment, lockouts and falling wages. A slow economic revival in 1932-1937, helped by the government investing in housing schemes, was followed by a boom resulting from rearmament. It can be seen, then, that the church both locally and nationally had to react to a wide variety of circumstances over a period of twenty years.

The Church, Former Chaplains and the 1920s

The issues discussed in the Church Congress and Church Assembly reflected the engagement of the church with the post-war problems. The former chaplains had an important part to play in these discussions. In the 1920 Church Congress Studdert Kennedy was speaking on "Labour and church membership". He started by saying that "The relationships between the church and organised labour are very bad." He went on to develop his theme using "a racy dialogue between two imaginary characters – one representing organised religion and the other the organised labour movement." The *Church Times* correspondent described his speech as "A clear and concise examination of the actual position of the church and labour opinion."[46]

The Conference on Christian Politics, Economics and Citizenship (C.O.P.E.C.), met in April 1924. It was attended by 1,200 delegations from all Christian denominations excepting the Roman Catholics. Prominent among its participants were Charles Raven and Tom Pym, both former chaplains, as was J. V. Macmillan who was tasked by Archbishop Davidson with publicising the conference to the whole

---

44   Ibid., p.273
45   Ibid., p.274.
46   *Church Times*, 29 October 1920, p.214.

Anglican Church. E. K. Talbot, Geoffrey Studdert Kennedy, Oliver Quick,[47] F. R. Barry and R. G. Parsons[48] were members of the conference.[49] Charles Raven, as one of the two secretaries, was a prime mover in its organisation. Four years before the conference, studying and campaigning began. Iremonger, William Temple's biographer, described its object: "To seek the will and purpose of God for men and women in every relationship in their lives, political, social, industrial and the rest."[50] The organisers described their vision for the conference in their commission reports in 1924: "It is the first time in history that qualified and representative Christians have come together for considered and prolonged study of such questions in a common search for the will of God in society."[51] Twelve commissions were set up and 200,000 questionnaires filled in by seventy-five centres. All of 1923 was devoted to studying the replies and producing the commission's reports. 1,500 delegates were present at the town hall in Birmingham.

In its first session, Charles Raven gave the report of the group working on "The Nature of God and His Purpose for the World". The report discussed the reversal of the world's standards of value if true Christianity was to be achieved. True Christianity, he said, "Gives honour not to great position or wealth but to the man who walks humbly with his God."[52] The report of the group looking at "Christianity and Industry" was critical of the industrial affairs in Britain. Their resolution read:

> The immediate aim of Christians with regard to industry and commerce should be the substitution of the motive of service rather than the motive of gain. ... All talk of democracy has a note of irony while men are valued mainly for what they have, a little for what they do, but least of all for what they are.[53]

The Times report suggested that the comments of the "Christianity and Industry" group were "more or less an unqualified indictment of the existing industrial system". The report on "The Social Function of the Church" said that: "On class distinctions, the conference declared that Christians could recognise none in the church, and in the world must use their influence against any distinction which might offer an obstacle to true social communion."[54]

---

47   Oliver Quick, TCF 1917-1918, *Crockford's*, p.1100. He assisted B. K. Cunningham at the chaplains' retreat centre at St Omer.
48   R.G. Parsons, TCF 1916-1917, *Crockford's*, p.1259.
49   C.O.P.E.C. *The purpose, Scope and Nature of the Conference* (London, 1923), p.3.
50   F. Iremonger, *William Temple, Archbishop of Canterbury: His Life and Letters* (Oxford, OUP, 1948), p.334.
51   The C.O.P.E.C. Commission Reports (London, 1924), p.5.
52   C.O.P.E.C. Commission Report: *The Nature of God and his Purpose for the World* (London, 1924), p.18.
53   The C.O.P.E.C. Commission Reports (London, 1924) p.289.
54   *The Times*, 12 April 1924, p.8.

Some delegates realised that this was all revolutionary opinion and that it could have far-reaching implications. Mr Herbert Pickles, a working weaver, after hearing the report on "Christianity and Industry", warned the conference that: "In the resolutions that it was about to adopt it was playing with social dynamite." Mr H. H. Elvin, after listening to the debate on "The Social Function of the Church", prophesied:

> If the churches carried out the recommendations of the commission to work for a Christian solution of social, political and economic questions, as he thought they ought to, it would result first in the emptying of many of the churches of their present occupants and then refilling them with a totally different set of men and women.[55]

At the end of the conference, the delegates came up with resolutions on a variety of topics, including education, the home, the relation of the sexes, leisure, the treatment of crime, industry and property, industrial relations, Christianity and war, and politics and citizenship.[56] The resolution on unemployment stated:

> The conference considers that the continual recurrence of unemployment on a large scale ... constitutes a challenge of primary urgency and calls upon the government either to hold or to invite and assist the Christian churches to hold, a searching enquiry into the causes of unemployment."[57]

Archbishop Söderblom[58] praised the organisers of the conference: "It was a living thing, with a father, the bishop of Manchester, a mother, Lucy Gardener and a soul, Charles Raven."[59] Despite having spent nearly four years on the project, Raven did not keep closely involved in the follow-up initiatives. The continuation committee of C.O.P.E.C. was supported by the creation of "The Companions of C.O.P.E.C.", resulting in regional conferences held in 1924, which established regional committees, which created the Tyneside Christian Social Council and the Birmingham Home Improvement Society.[60]

What had been achieved by C.O.P.E.C.? F. W. Dillistone, Raven's biographer, described the long-term effect of the conference: "The C.O.P.E.C. report could well

55 Ibid.
56 The C.O.P.E.C. Commission Reports (London, 1924), pp.277-292.
57 *The Times*, 12 April 1924, p.9.
58 Nathan Söderblom, from 1914 Archbishop of Uppsala and Primate of the Church of Sweden. http://justus.anglican.org/resources/bio/199.html.
59 B. Sunkler, *Archbishop Söderblom*, cited in Dillistone, *Charles Raven*, p.334.
60 G. I. T. Machin, *Churches and Social Issues in Twentieth-Century Britain* (London, Hodder & Stoughton, 1998), p.34.

be regarded as a blueprint for the Welfare State."[61] Raven, in a letter to *The Challenge* in November 1922, described the venture as:

> Unique in religious history, and should strike the imagination as no individual should do. Our quest is a cooperative effort in which every Christian communion in the country to pledge itself to take part.[62]

The *Church Times* in December 1926 reported that: "C.O.P.E.C. is, we understand, in the last days of its life. It was never intended to be more than a temporary association, with a mission to carry out the proposals of the Birmingham conference." The report continued, crediting C.O.P.E.C. with serving "an admirable purpose in quickening the Christian social conscience."[63] The overall achievement of C.O.P.E.C. has been debated, it being questionable whether in the long term the effects of C.O.P.E.C. were ideological or practical. Machin, writing on churches and social policy in the interwar years said: "The effects of C.O.P.E.C. and its reports, certainly when set in the general context of collectivist discussion and planning which marked the interwar years, were far from insubstantial."[64] Dillistone credited Raven with the opinion, expressed towards the end of his life, that: "Whereas the foundations of a Christian society had been well and truly laid [at C.O.P.E.C.] no group of thinkers had carried on the task of raising the building above ground."[65] E. R. Norman criticised the conference as containing only what had been said for several decades but also considered that its main achievement had been "The extent to which social radicalism had penetrated the leadership of the church."[66] He also considered that Raven had in mind significantly more radical consequences to the conference than those envisaged by William Temple.[67] However, when Raven was asked by the Fellowship of Reconciliation (FOR), of which organisation he was chairman, to write a series of articles setting out the FOR's aims on its social and economic responsibilities, he was unable to find time to complete this task and passed it back to the FOR social responsibility group to do.[68] The shift in his interest from Christian social policy to pacifism will be discussed in Chapter 6.

The encyclical letter of the Lambeth conference in 1920 considered social and industrial questions worth devoting some space to. In its comments on "Industry and Commerce" it said, "We seem to be involved in an internecine conflict between capital and labour ... the message of Christianity in this matter is to make men see that they

61   Dillistone, *Charles Raven*, p.120.
62   *Challenge*, 17 November 1922, p.123.
63   *Church Times*, 12 November 1926, p.569.
64   Machin, *Churches and Social Issues*, p. 34.
65   Dillistone, *Charles Raven*, p.122.
66   Norman, *Church and Society in England*, p.280.
67   Ibid., p.287.
68   Wallis, *Valiant for Peace*, p.87.

can and must 'in love serve one another.'"[69] It continued: "An outstanding and pressing duty of the church is to convince its members of the necessity for nothing less than a fundamental change in the spirit and working of an economic life."[70] When the Labour party became the main opposition party after the 1923 election, 500 Church of England clergymen signed a memorial to Ramsey Macdonald congratulating him and assuring him of their support. It read:

> As a result of this, we look forward to the more serious consideration and more adequate treatment of the pressing problems and difficulties of our time—our particular calling, with its pastoral experience, gives us direct knowledge of the sufferings and deprivations ... to which numbers of our fellow citizens are subjected to. ... To find a remedy for which is the chief purpose and aim of the labour movement.[71]

It is interesting to note that G. A. Studdert Kennedy and P. T. R. Kirk did not sign the memorial, probably because of their position in the non-political and non-denominational ICF. Among the selection of the 500 signatures published by the *Church Times*, however, could be found former chaplains Harry Blackburne, F. R. Barry, B. K. Cunningham, O. Quick, C. S. Woodward and E. K. Talbot. Gerald Studdert Kennedy has pointed out that this action was not one without risk of censure. It was not "a gesture an Anglican clergyman could afford to make without thought.[72]" According to A. M. Scott, one of his congregation, C. Salisbury Woodward, lost at least one leading member of his congregation as a result of his signing the memorial.[73]

One of the most important of the efforts of Christians to engage with the industrial world and one in which former chaplains played a prominent part was the Industrial Christian Fellowship (ICF). Gerald Studdert Kennedy, author of a study of the ICF, *Dog Collar Democracy,* considered it to be: "An organisational response, easily the most effective and vigorous, to the catastrophic revelations of secularisation and aliena-tion that emerged during the war."[74] The Rev Lambardine, a former chaplain, in a sermon considering the role of the church in social and industrial questions of March 1919, reckoned that the ICF: "Was going to be the one which would save the situ-ation for the church."[75] It developed out of a merger of the Navvy Mission and the

69 *The Lambeth Conferences (1867-1948): the Reports of the 1920, 1930, and 1948 Conferences, with Selected Resolutions from the Conferences of 1867, 1878, 1888, 1897 and 1908,* (SPCK, 1948), p.30.
70 Ibid., p.51.
71 *Church Times,* 16 March 1923, p.297.
72 Studdert Kennedy, *Dog Collar Democracy,* p.124.
73 A. M. Scott, *Diaries,* 12 June 1925 (University of Glasgow). Cited in ibid., p.124.
74 Gerald Studdert Kennedy, 'Woodbine Willie: Religion and Politics after the Great War', *History Today,* (December 1986), p.42.
75 *Church Times,* 21 March 1919, p.282.

Christian Social Union. Its leader, the Rev P. T. R. Kirk,[76] who had been a chaplain in the war, felt that the term "mission" was out of date in the post-war world and smacked of condescension to the working class, and that the term fellowship was more appropriate. The headed notepaper of the ICF proclaimed "We stand for Christ and his principles – independent of party."[77] The fellowship had a headquarters staff and clerical area directors. It sent agents or missioners to factories and canteens, to address trades unions, to stress the application of "Christian principles as the solution to their problems"[78] 'These agents or lay missioners were men who had been employed in factories, mines and workshops, but the fellowship's other evangelical staff were the clerical directors and messengers who visited Rotary Clubs, Chambers of Commerce, and groups of businessmen. The fellowship was concerned with the practical application of the gospel: "We have to show them that God is love and that the Christian religion has a value for this life as well as for the life to come."[79] They took part in many conferences between the church and the industrial world. Kirk found he needed a clerical messenger and, after hearing Studdert Kennedy speak, said of him: "I had no doubt his was the voice, and his the message for which we had been waiting."[80]

Kirk set out the aims of the fellowship in his chapter on the ICF in Modern Evangelistic Movements: "The only hope lies in the evangelisation of the great labour movement. If the masses will not come to the church, the church will go to the masses." Although the ICF was not afraid to be political, the constant theme was the necessity of following Christian principles in commercial life. In Chapter Two of the ICF crusade manual Kirk described: "How society could only be changed by everyone leading a life guaranteed by Christian principles." The Bishop of Croydon, in an article on the ICF in the *Manchester Guardian* in February 1920, set out some of the ways in which the movement was progressing:

> We are holding conferences in all parts of the country, which are free and open to all to come. The sternest criticism is welcomed, either of the church and labour, provided the name of Christ is respected. In this way we are giving trades unionists ... the opportunity to explain their desires and requests, and equally, the clergy and laity can show by their presence that they are dissatisfied with the spiritual and industrial conditions of England and that they no longer intend to remain silent in the face of injustice and wrong. ... Everywhere the results

---

76   P. T. R. Kirk, TCF 1915-1918, *Crockford's*, p.771.
77   LPL: the papers of Archbishop Lang Vol. 117, ff. 246, Letter from P. T. R. Kirk to Archbishop Lang, on ICF headed notepaper.
78   P. T. R. Kirk, 'The Industrial Christian Fellowship' in D. P. Thompson (ed.), *Modern Evangelistic Movements* (New York, 1924), p.77.
79   Ibid., p.77.
80   P. T. R. Kirk, 'Studdert Kennedy, ICF Crusader', in J. K. Mozley (ed.), *G. A. Studdert Kennedy, By His Friends* (London, Hodder & Stoughton, 1929), p.166.

have been full of encouragement in destroying misunderstanding and expelling prejudice"[81]

The ICF became a broad church politically, with influences from both the organisations that had merged at its foundation. Writing in *The Times* in 1926 Studdert Kennedy made his thoughts clear on this issue: "The fellowship refuses to associate itself with any particular policy or party as being Christian to the exclusion of others."[82]

The active lay supporters of the ICF were influential figures on the fringes of high politics and represented elements of all political opinion, among them Lionel Hitchens, director of Cammell Laird, Donald Maclean MP, Ben Spoor MP, H. Slesser, lawyer, and trade unionists H. H. Elvin and E. L. Poulton.[83] As well as Kirk and Studdert Kennedy other chaplains who were to become leaders of the post-war church were also members of the Industrial Christian Fellowship, including Tom Pym, F. R. Barry, David Railton,[84] Charles Raven, Guy Rogers and C. S. Woodward.[85] Neville Talbot remained a supporter even after becoming Bishop of Pretoria. Many of the chaplains saw hope of new relationships between men of different backgrounds. Former chaplains did not always agree with this point of view. Tom Pym was sceptical, and was described by Gerald Studdert Kennedy as: "Looking ahead to the intensification of class hostilities in a society that would not reproduce the sense of common purpose and common danger informing the army."[86]

The council of the ICF met regularly to discuss the issues of the moment and to decide action. In January 1921 under the chairmanship of the Bishop of Lichfield, J. A. Kempthorne, it met to discuss unemployment, which seemed to be a result of the disintegration of the post-war boom. Their resolution – "the duty of every citizen and of the church and nation to give attention to the matter"[87] – was affirmed, and in July of that year the ICF was instrumental in helping set up an outdoor preaching pitch in the market at Leicester for local churches to preach and encourage debate. The ICF's regular column in *The Challenge* reported successful open-air preaching campaigns in Hull in March 1921. The preaching location was also one used frequently by communists. The report quoted "a Bolshevist" as saying of the ICF preaching "It is the most honest thing that has come to Hull."[88]

In 1920, the ICF organised a number of special services on the Sunday before Labour Day, which became known in succeeding years as "Industrial Sunday." This

---

81   *Manchester Guardian*, 13 February, 1920, p.118.
82   *The Times*, 19 November 1926, p.10.
83   Studdert Kennedy, *Dog Collar Democracy*, pp.22-23.
84   David Railton, TCF 1911-1919, MC 1916, *ODNB*.
85   LPL, MS 4042, The minute book of the ICF Council for 1920-1926 shows former chaplains well represented on the ICF Council.
86   Studdert Kennedy, *Dog Collar Democracy*, p.51.
87   *Church Times*, 14 January 1921, p.34.
88   *Challenge*, 25 March 1921, p.343.

was a success, which helped Kirk establish the ICF as a bridge between labour and industry, as the occasions were generally accompanied by the issues of letters signed by both leaders of the labour movement and industrial management.[89] The insistence that the solution to the social and industrial ills of the country could be only solved by adherence to Christian principles was the common theme of ICF preachers.

The links that some prominent ICF figures had with the Brotherhood Movement proved a useful conduit to the Trades Union Movement.[90] This movement had grown from a local artisan improvement society founded in West Bromwich in 1875 into a national labour movement, which stressed individual responsibility to social needs. Due to these links the ICF developed a role at Trades Union Congress. The report of congress in 1921 recorded: "Special sermons were preached in eight of the churches of the city, the arrangements being made by the Industrial Christian Fellowship."[91] At the Trades Union Congress in 1922 Geoffrey Studdert Kennedy preached to a large congregation on "The law of combat giving way to the law of mutual service."[92]

At the beginning of 1926, it had become apparent that industrial trouble was brewing as the results of the Samuel Commission on the future of the coal industry[93] were awaited. In an uncharacteristically downbeat sermon delivered at York Minster in January, C. S. Woodward admitted that in his opinion both the affairs of the church and the country seemed to be uncertain: "We are on shifting sand and we are bound to confess that we cannot see clearly … The church, like the community as a whole is marching in the dark."[94] In addressing the Church Assembly in February 1926 the Archbishop of Canterbury referred to the possibility of serious industrial trouble in the early summer.[95]

The principles of the ICF were involved, not directly but through Kirk in the miners' dispute and the General Strike of 1926. Together with Henry Carter, a prominent Wesleyan, he set up a group pledged to bring together the opposing parties. Stuart Mews, in his essay on the strike, recounted how a meeting with Thompson, a coal owner and Conservative MP, resulted in a set of conciliatory proposals, which were to form the basis of the Archbishop of Canterbury's intervention.[96] The BBC did not broadcast the Archbishop's statement so Kirk and Carter chartered a car and deliv-

---

89   Studdert Kennedy, *Dog Collar Democracy* p.144.
90   Studdert Kennedy, *Dog Collar Democracy*, pp.145-147.
91   Trade Union Congress Report 1921, p .418, cited by G. Studdert Kennedy, *Dog Collar Democracy*, p.147.
92   Ibid., p.149.
93   The Commission, reporting in March 1926, recommended sweeping changes to the coal industry, including a reduction of miners' wages and a withdrawal of the Government subsidy. D. H. Robertson, 'A Narrative of the General Strike of 1926', *The Economic Journal* Vol. 36, no. 143 (September 1926), p.376.
94   *Church Times*, 8 January 1926, p.55.
95   *Church Times*, 12 February 1926, p.179.
96   S. Mews, 'The Churches', in M. Morris (ed.), *The General Strike* (London, Historical Association, 1976), p.328.

ered a copy of the appeal and a statement about the BBC ban to as many manses and churches as possible, and it was published in *The Times*[97] and the *British Worker*. After the strike was settled, a 'Standing Conference' of churchmen, including Kirk, the Bishop of Lichfield, the Bishop of Birmingham, and Charles Gore met at the headquarters of the ICF. They attempted to bring together the miners' unions and mine owners to stop the miners' strike which was ongoing. Their efforts were not successful and were criticised in some quarters. Hensley Henson, then Bishop of Durham, wondered "why it is that sincere and devout men ... are ever proposed to dogmatise 'in the name of the Lord', about practical problems of which neither morality nor religion can provide the solution."[98] Gerald Studdert Kennedy described how the recriminations which followed the ICF's attempts to intervene both before and after the strike resulted in "a widespread scepticism" over the ICF's claim that it was a "Non partisan interdenominational and impartial social concern and that it was a public instrument of reconciliation".[99]

In a letter to *The Times* in August 1926 Kirk and Carter explained their actions. "The first and essential function of the church when face to face with intense industrial conflict is that of peacemaker" and continued: "We are convinced it is our bounden duty to ascertain the true position of the contending parties."[100] William Temple's biographer, Iremonger, considered that:

> A result at least had been achieved by the churches group ... its intervention changed completely the miners' attitude towards the churches. By organised labour organised religion had hitherto been held to embody the reactionary sprit of a privileged caste.[101]

Gerald Studdert Kennedy, in his study of the Industrial Christian Fellowship, has placed much emphasis on the level of support for the organisation from Anglican clergy and lay people. Working from Studdert Kennedy's engagement diary he drew up a list of 130 incumbents who had been visited by him, some more than once. By comparing a random sample with this group he revealed some useful information on the sort of incumbent likely to be a supporter of the ICF. For example, they were more likely to have had a faster career promotion to a large parish, and their parishes were usually well endowed and generally had more curates. Bringing military service as chaplains into the equation, Gerald Studdert Kennedy found that ICF clergy ordained before 1900 were 20 percent more likely to have gone to war than those in the random sample but that over 50 percent of the ICF clergy of those ordained

97 *The Times*, 15 May 1926, p.4.
98 *The Times*, 13 August, 1926, P.11.
99 Studdert Kennedy, *Dog Collar Democracy*, p.135.
100 *The Times*, 5 August, 1926, p.11.
101 Iremonger, *William Temple*, p.343.

1900-1910 had volunteered. These statistics give us some evidence that ex-chaplains figured largely among those clergy who supported the ICF in the post-war years.[102] This impression is reinforced by evidence from Studdert Kennedy's engagement diary that many of the most frequently visited incumbents were former chaplains. From this statistical evidence we can conclude that the aims of the ICF were close to the heart of many returning chaplains.

The Role of Individual Former Chaplains

Geoffrey Anketell Studdert Kennedy

The most famous missioner for the ICF was Geoffrey Studdert Kennedy. He was the son of a vicar in Leeds. Ordained in 1908, he was placed in charge of the slum part of a parish in Rugby and showed promise in his preaching. William Purcell, drawing on conversations with staff who worked with Studdert Kennedy in Rugby, came to the following conclusion: "Geoffrey gravitated towards the slum area of the parish as a compass swings to North because it has a built-in disposition to do so. It was part of the man."[103] As a curate in Leeds he developed his gift for open-air public speaking, encouraged by Samuel Bickersteth, the vicar. Like several clergy who went on to be popular with the troops in the war, he cut his teeth with men's and boy's clubs. His first parish of St Paul's Worcester was a poor parish, giving him plenty of experience of the poverty that existed in industrial towns. The *Church Times*, reviewing *The Hardest Part* in November 1918, described his patch: "The block house, a modern suburb of distressingly mean streets and iron works."[104]

P. T. R. Kirk in his chapter about Studdert Kennedy in *Geoffrey Studdert Kennedy By his Friends*, emphasised the way in which his wartime experience had influenced his colleague: "The sympathy which he felt for the suffering in battle was transmuted into an even more tender compassion for the hard-pressed in industrial struggles."[105] Purcell, in his biography of Studdert Kennedy also emphasised the changes wrought in him by the war:

> If he had become a national figure, he had also become a different man. The chaplain of the Rive Gauche canteen was dead. In place of that ingenuous participant in a just war there stood now an infinitely more mature person equally convinced that no war could be just.[106]

102 Studdert Kennedy, *Dog Collar Democracy*, pp.128-129.
103 William Purcell, *Woodbine Willie: An Anglican incident, being some account of the life and times of Geoffrey Anketell Studdert Kennedy, poet, prophet, seeker after truth, 1883-1929*, (London, Hodder & Stoughton, 1962), p.60.
104 *Church Times*, 5 Nov 1918, p.356.
105 Kirk, '*Studdert Kennedy, I C F Crusader*', p.167.
106 Purcell, *Woodbine Willy*, p.159.

Kirk talked about the way in which Studdert Kennedy had no patience with partisanship in either a political or ecclesiastical sense: "He poured contempt upon those who talked as if it were an easy matter to settle our modern problems under a capitalist or socialist order."[107] Studdert Kennedy, in a letter to *The Times* claimed:

> Not a single one of the ICF activities has fallen under the control of socialists. If any of them did, I would sever my connection with the society immediately. I am not a socialist and spend a considerable amount of time, exposing popular Socialist claptrap, which is a curse to sane thinking, as popular Tory clap trap is on the other side. Bother them both.[108]

Studdert Kennedy spent much of his time and energy rushing around the country preaching on behalf of the ICF. In February 1921 he was preaching at the annual service of the ICF in the northern province held at York Minster and impressed the correspondent of the *Church Times* who reported: "Mr Kennedy gave what one member of the congregation called "The finest exposition of economics he had ever listened to." He went on to quote Studdert Kennedy: "The service of humanity, the dignity of the priesthood of love are the ideals which alone call forth the efforts needed, that alone can heal the interminable wrangling of capital and labour". The sermon was then described as: "A very distinct advance in the development of a modern prophet."[109]

At the ICF annual meeting in 1926, the *Church Times* correspondent described his speech: "His is ever the stuff to give to any spineless Christians who lurked in that great audience of idealists." Studdert Kennedy told the meeting:

> I hate warming my hands at a fire, the coal for which has been grubbed out of the ground by men who are unable to live in proper dignity. I hate living in a world in which there is a nice end of town where presumably all the nice people live and an end of dirty ramshackle pigsties where apparently all the nasty people live.[110]

Studdert Kennedy was not a rebel speaking out against the establishment continuously, according to Gerald Studdert Kennedy: "His refreshing eccentricities thinly disguised an obedient churchman."[111] It was important that in working for the ICF he did not irritate the establishment too much, but he was not afraid to criticise. Moreover, he was not always preaching on the social gospel. In August 1926 he gave a series of devotional addresses at the Anglo-Catholic Summer School and made a vivid impression on the *Church Times'* special correspondent:

---

107 Kirk, 'Studdert Kennedy: I C F Crusader', p.172.
108 *The Times*, 19 November 1926, p.10.
109 *Church Times*, 11 February 1921, p.238.
110 *Church Times*, 4 June 1926, p.616.
111 Studdert Kennedy, *Dog Collar Democracy* p.57.

No words can convey, to anybody who has not heard him the impression of the amazing personality of this priest ... A man working himself to death for God and the poor.[112]

A review of *Lies* in the *Church Times* in December 1919 commented on the effect of his war service on his subsequent career:

We doubt that any priest of our communion ... has such a gift of startling speech. But then no priests in history have ever gone through such experiences as those of our chaplains in the Great War and of those chaplains few, we suppose, were poets. Plunge a man with the soul of a priest and the heart of a poet into the horror of war in Flanders and something amazing must have been the result.[113]

Geoffrey Studdert Kennedy died in March 1929. The many tributes to him, services organised and memorials instigated, show his popularity and importance to many sections of society. He died in Liverpool and after a requiem mass at St Catherine's, Abercromby Square, 2000 people filed past the coffin. The vicar had received requests from working men to hold the memorial at a time convenient to them. The body was then taken to Worcester where once again: "Thousands of people, mainly working class, paid their reverent homage. Crowds packed the streets to see the passing of the cortege to the cathedral. A large contingent of unemployed men, wearing war medals brought wreaths with them."[114] In a service at St Martin's-in-the-Field, held simultaneously with the funeral, Dr Maud said of Studdert Kennedy: "He combined in his personality so many striking elements that they knew they had in him something entirely original. He had in him that human touch with men of every class which made him the friend of those who had no friends."[115]

In March 1929 Kirk talked on "Woodbine Willie as I Knew Him" and commented on his work for the Industrial Christian fellowship: "His love for his work was indescribable. It was his mission in life to help men out of their doubts and he would have gone to the end of world to reclaim a criminal or win a soul for Christ."[116] A close friend and colleague of Studdert Kennedy, the Rev J. K. Mozley, preached at a later requiem for him in April 1929 and summed up what many people felt. "From time to time, men have been raised up by God, inspired by the Holy Spirit with a message to deliver ... such a man was Studdert Kennedy. There was no doubting his call or his message."[117]

112 *Church Times*, August 6 1926, p.157.
113 *Church Times*, 6 December 1919.
114 *Church Times*, March 15 1929, p.331.
115 Ibid.
116 Ibid.
117 *Church Times*, 26 April 1929, p.492.

Tom Pym

On his return from France, Tom Pym did not compromise the principles laid out in his P. A. M. campaign, and took a job as Head of the Cambridge House Settlement. He was no stranger to the poorer areas of London as he had spent his vacations from his job as chaplain of Trinity College Cambridge in a workman's flat he had rented in Battersea. Here he had made friends with his neighbours and worked with young offenders in Wormwood Scrubs Prison. One of the his neighbours said of him: "He knew he could never be like us; he could always go up to the West End or stay with friends or relations, *but he did not go*; that drew him to us; even if he was not like us, *he was with us.*"[118]

At the Cambridge House Settlement he set about raising the profile of South London in the consciousness of Cambridge University. He needed workers for clubs, committees and all the activities already in existence. During his time at Camberwell Pym made many visits to Cambridge to find workers for the many clubs, care committees and the new ventures he had in mind. In his efforts to arouse the interest of Cambridge scholars, he preached in Trinity College in a memorial service for students who had died in the war and made it an occasion to preach on social service: "An appeal is being made in the university this week for a greater sense of comradeship between class and class within our nation. The appeal is being made to you to study the problems of our times ... and to find how you yourselves can help to bring in a new order founded on righteousness."[119] He continued: "Shall we who have been spared the last claim of human comradeship ... shrink from any lesson gained?" According to Dora Pym, his wife, he "Immediately embarked on new ventures where he thought a university settlement should pioneer."[120] Examples of these new ventures were a mixed club for a poor area: "Where gangs of wild boys and girls roamed the streets every night". There was also a Cambridge House library and bookshop designed for young adults who he felt would be unlikely to join in more formal structures such as a public library or an evening class.

Cambridge House also became a centre for training in social and educational work. The *Church Times*, reported in January 1921 that it was "Recognised as a hostel for the training of continuation school leaders and by the London School of Economics for practical training in social work." The reporter thought that Cambridge House was in a position, considering its wide range of activities, to "gather up the threads and make them into a serviceable whole".[121] From July 1921 Cambridge house published *The Cambridge House Bulletin*, which was a "serious attempt to provide facts for thinking people",[122] and to encourage a sense of proportion in arguments about

---

118 Pym, *Tom Pym, A Portrait*, p.42.
119 Ibid., p.60.
120 Ibid., p.61.
121 *Church Times*, 28 January 1921.
122 Pym, *Tom Pym*, p.65

industrial disputes. Dora Pym reported that: "A vast variety of technical fact and history was condensed in these short papers; readers began to realise their ignorance of the intricacy of the economic structure and the complexity of fact behind industrial news."[123] This was supplemented by the Camberwell Model Parliament to encourage practice in debate and knowledge of current affairs. In 1922 Tom Pym was appointed Rural Dean of Camberwell, and in the general election of that year published a pamphlet in the name of the clergy of the Rural Deanery, aimed at "all people of goodwill who whether or not they hold the Christian faith, are prepared, in recording their vote, to put the common welfare before their own personal interests"[124].

Christopher Chavasse

Chavasse was demobilised from the Army Chaplain's Department on Easter Monday 1919. His background was that of an Anglican in the evangelical tradition, as he was the son of Bishop F. J. Chavasse of Liverpool. After a degree at Oxford where he and his twin brother Noel excelled at sport, he was trained for ordination by his father, together with other ordinands. His first curacy had been in the industrial town of St Helens. The twins' biographer describes how Christopher continued his sporting activities, playing rugby for the town and earning for himself a considerable reputation as a character in the process.[125] On demobilisation he was offered the living of St George's in Barrow in Furness. Selwyn Gummer painted a picture of the problems he would face: "Seldom can a ministry have started under less propitious condition and with higher hope. There was mass unemployment, dire distress on all sides, disillusion on the part of returned conscripts and a local industrial situation which had been so geared to war as to offer no promise for the years of peace."[126]

In his letter to parishioners in November 1920, Chavasse talked about the "grim spectre of unemployment" which, he said, would "stalk among our towns this winter." He was writing at the time of the miners' strike and appealed "for us to refrain from all recrimination and bitterness".[127] This point of view was echoed by a *Church Times* writer in 1921, in an article about the purpose of an ICF crusade: "From the church point of view, Barrow is a most difficult town. Church building has not been able to keep up with growth of population."[128]

In an article in his parish magazine, Chavasse set out his objectives:

> The fact is we have begun a new age. Everything is in the melting pot. My ministry among you coincides with the conclusion of the war. Even before the

---

123 Ibid., p.65.
124 *Church Times*, 28 January 1921, p.93.
125 Gummer, *The Chavasse Twins*, pp.42-43.
126 Ibid., p.71.
127 Barrow –in-Furness Record Office, BPR11/PM/2, C. Chavasse, *St George's Parish Magazine* November 1920.
128 *Church Times*, 30 September 1921, p.329.

war changes were being mooted in the church. The war delayed them, but on the other hand, hastened and focused their intensity. We cannot take up the old state of things which existed in 1914. If we do so we stand still while the rest of the world continues in advance; and the people simply ignore the church as a useless out of date old dear.[129]

Twelve months after arriving and summing up the situation at St George's, Chavasse revealed his war memorial scheme to his parishioners, part of which was to clear the debt off St George's hall and refurbish it as a men's institute: "What better memorial to those who answered the call of duty than to give the parish its long-needed home where the comradeship of the trenches can be practised by our church people at home?" he asked. It was Chavasse, who according to the *Church Times*, was a prime mover in inviting the ICF to mount a crusade in Barrow in September 1921. All the clergy of the area agreed, and "well knowing the working class character of their parishes, had a genuine desire to hold out the right hand of fellowship to labour."

In announcing the coming crusade in the parish magazine of June 1921 Chavasse referred to the full church on the occasion of the St George's Labour Day service, which showed, he said, that:

The time is ripe for such an adventure, and that Labour is Christian at heart, though prejudiced against organised religion. To look at that full church on May the first, and to note all the prominent leaders of labour present, must have filed us all with thankfulness and with longing.

He asserted that the object of the crusade would be to try and bridge the gap between the church and labour and their needs in Jesus Christ.[130]

In the July edition, Chavasse continued to publicise the crusade.

What is a crusade? It is a war of the cross.
What does the cross stand for? It is the symbol of self-sacrifice?
What is the curse of the world? Selfishness.
What does the cross seek to do, then?

1.   To wage war on selfishness
2.   To put self-sacrifice in the place of selfishness
3.   To establish the cross in your world, your nation, your home and your heart.

If the world, Europe, England, Barrow followed Christ, would things get better?
You know they would.

---

129   Gummer, *The Chavasse Twin,s* p.73
130   Barrow-in-Furness record office BP11/PM/2, C. Chavasse, *St George's Parish Magazine*, June 1921.

He finished his piece with the exhortation: "Throw in your lot with Christ and with the crusade. Join his army and defend his cause."[131]

Chavasse explained to his readers in the August magazine some of the arrangements for the week, advertising services, meetings, visits to the factories and docks and open-air meetings nightly. He emphasised the non-political nature of the crusade, but also said that "no presentation of the gospel is complete today which does not take into account the conditions and environment of Christian men and women." The official letter, which went out all over Barrow and was printed in the August magazine, talked about "the importance at this time of such an effort to create in all men a spirit of fellowship in Industrial relationships."[132]

The Crusade seems to have been a success, with large crowds gathering at the open-air meetings, as well as attending the main Sunday meeting. On the Friday night, Studdert Kennedy addressed a "huge public meeting and made a great impression." At the end, "The crusaders expressed themselves as greatly encouraged by their reception."[133]

Writing in the parish magazine for November, Chavasse commented on the crusade; "No effort could more manifestly been blessed by God". He was particularly impressed by the quality of the lay missioners: "Trade Union men, who were enthusiastic Christians, and came to labour with a message as from one of themselves, and to which they were bound to listen." He continued with the news that the churches of Barrow were combining together to acquire a permanent missioner for the town.[134]

John Groser

After a tough independent upbringing on an Australian outback mission station, John Groser was trained at Mirfield, and after ordination, spent a year in a dockside parish, All Saints, Newcastle on Tyne, before becoming a temporary chaplain to the forces in 1915. In Newcastle, he ministered to parishioners in the local doss house and prison and in a futile attempt to get local businesses interested in their plight, first became aware of the general lack of interest in improving the lives of the poor:

> I thought in my ignorance that all that was needed was to make the fact known and the natural decency of people would rise up to deal with the situation. But I was mistaken. … I was receiving my first practical lesson in politics … I only know that I trod on the toes of some of the business people of Newcastle; that I was lifting the lid off a hell that stank and was not pleasant to behold; that I was

131 Ibid., July 1921.
132 Barrow-in-Furness record office BP11/PM/2, C. Chavasse, *St George's Parish Magazine,*
     August 1921.
133 *Church Times,* 9th September 1921, p.328.
134 Barrow-in Furness Record Office, *St George's Parish Magazine,* November 1921.

being called political because it was public policy to keep that underworld as far as possible out of sight and sound.[135]

His war service has been described by Lieutenant-Colonel A. Hanbury Sparrow, who described how Groser would spend the evenings visiting rather than sitting in the mess. He also described a situation in which he pressed Groser to take over the lead of a section in the heat of battle and Groser refused. Groser's biographer, Kenneth Brill, thought that Groser's radical nature was already showing signs of its development in the war and that Hanbury Sparrow's account of his work as a chaplain showed:

A man whose angularity and uncompromising sense of righteousness were already plain. Before the end of the war he was already convinced that it had been unnecessarily prolonged – he was beginning to see, what many came to accept as fact later, that the war itself was a crime against humanity.[136]

Moreover, he was making it known openly that he was doubtful of the Allied cause.[137]

After a year unsuccessfully trying to persuade ex-servicemen to return to church, as a representative of the Church of England Men's society, Groser came under the influence of Conrad Noel[138] – the red priest – whose ideas reinforced Groser's opinion that the church should be involved in politics. In his book *Politics and Persons* Groser described the effect the war had on his ideas: "I found myself up against a new set of problems in personal relationships which seemed more closely to demand political judgements."[139] In October 1922 Groser moved to St Michael's, Poplar. A parishioner in a later parish described Groser's parishioners in Poplar as "Dockers, unemployed, ex-servicemen and others who lived in uncertain poverty."[140] Groser and his colleagues started successful street corner meetings, using the crucifix, the cross of St George and the red flag as their symbols. He became the spokesmen for groups of workers in their battle with the Poor Law authority, the police and employers, negotiating in strikes and lockouts. His revolutionary interpretation of the gospels became very popular. His abilities as a speaker led him to appearances on trade union and Labour party platforms, supporting the miners in the lead up to the General Strike. His attitude to the relationship of government with the unions was clear: "The breaking of the power of the Trades Union movement in Britain enabled the government to continue

---

135 Kenneth Brill, *John Groser, East End Priest* (London, Mowbray, 1971) p.9.
136 Ibid., p.12.
137 Wilkinson, *The Church of England in the First World War*, p.143.
138 Conrad Noel, Vicar of Thaxted, Christian Socialist and founder of the Catholic Crusade, *ODNB*.
139 John Groser, *Politics and Persons*, (London, SCM Press, 1949) p.8.
140 Brill, *John Groser*, p.32.

to promote quite ruthlessly and without opposition, a policy which led to the slump of the 1930s, the growth of fascism and World War Two."[141]

His political activities of course encountered opposition, with attacks on him in the local and national press, and actual threats of violence to him and his family. This political thread of his ministry came to a head when he was injured in a baton raid by the police while trying to calm down a potentially violent confrontation in front of the town hall in Poplar in May 1926.[142] He described the incident, which had started when he went in front of the crowd alone to speak to the police:

> I asked them if they could tell me what was wrong but received no answer. I said that the crowd was waiting for orders, and suggested that if they wanted the crowd to disperse they should give them time to do so------ Then suddenly I was floored by a rain of batons which left me half senseless on the ground.[143]

Escalating disagreements with his vicar, C. G. Langdon, had already led to his receiving notice to leave the parish, with his fellow curate, Jack Bucknell, despite the protests of the parishioners who visited the Bishop of London to object. The arrival of a new vicar postponed Groser's departure from Poplar for two years, but by March 1927 he had decided to leave. He wrote to the bishop "I have no idea where I am to go or what I am to do." His political views and activism had made him an unsuitable candidate as vicar for most parishes. He was eventually placed as curate in charge of Christ Church, Watney St, and fourteen months later, Dick Sheppard, then Dean of Canterbury, confirmed him in the living. He was to stay at Christ Church until it was bombed out in 1941. He was again in conflict with the Bishop of Stepney in February 1929 over his decision to use the parish hall to offer hospitality to hunger marchers.

In 1932 Groser was nominated by the labour party as a co-opted member of the committee dealing with applications for poor relief. He campaigned against the practice of "test work" – compulsory retraining of the unemployed in the local workhouse at Belmont: "He used to tell stories of holes dug and filled in again and of dockers trained to make mats and baskets in consequence of which other mat and basket workers fell out of work".[144] He was also part of the ongoing battle over rents in the district in the interwar years. The standard of the rented accommodation was very low, and landlords would not spend money on renovation. As a result the tenants refused to pay their rents and were threatened with eviction. The suffragan Bishop of Stepney recalled how "Groser took me and other, more influential, people to see these dwellings for ourselves and we found many of them in a disgusting condition. He also arranged a meeting at my house between representatives of both sides and

---

141 Groser, *Politics and Persons* p.51.
142 Jack Boggis, 'John Groser, Man of God', *The Christian Socialist*, No. 32, May 1966, p.11.
143 Brill, *John Groser* p.47.
144 Ibid., p.98.

the borough council ... some of the landlords agreed to take action, but there were others who held out."[145] His involvement with the rent strikes culminated in June 1929 when tenants barricaded themselves in a tenement block in Alexandria buildings, Commercial St, and Groser was one of a group of men, including both the Bishop and the Mayor of Stepney, who went to the landlord to argue the tenants' case and negotiate an agreement.

A letter written to all Christian denominations in the area in 1932 shows his continued concern with conditions endured by local people: "We are arranging a conference in Stepney Deanery to discuss the social problems arising out of unemployment and the means test and to consider ways and means of making known the Christian attitude on these problems."[146] In December 1938 the Stepney Defence League sent him a letter "thanking you for the invaluable assistance you have given."[147]

The 1930s

Timothy Rees

South Wales was one of the areas most affected by the slump in traditional industries. In 1931 Timothy Rees was enthroned as Bishop of Llandaff. He was one of eighteen Mirfield fathers to be a chaplain. He had served in Gallipoli, Egypt and on the Somme, being mentioned in dispatches and being awarded the Military Cross. After the war he was in charge of the Leeds hostel attached to Mirfield and also took part in some of the earliest ICF crusades. Llandaff was a diocese that had been at the centre of the industrialisation of South Wales and was then in the grip of the depression, which was having an extreme effect on the South Wales valleys. Unemployment figures in the diocese of Llandaff in 1936 ranged from 23–65 percent in the mining areas of Merthyr, Rhondda and Bridgend.[148] Added to this were the problems experienced with the crisis of disestablishment and disendowment.[149] In his enthronement address he said:

> My heart goes out in sympathy to the broken lives and broken hearts that are the result of this depression. Would God that I could do something to help.

145 Ibid., p.100.
146 Lambeth Palace Library, MS 3428, f.126, the Papers of John Groser.
147 Ibid., f.11.
148 *Church Times*, 26 October 1936, p.595.
149 The Welsh Church Act, passed in 1914, was implemented in 1920. Disestablishment created the Church in Wales, which ended the Anglican Church's special legal status in Wales. Welsh Bishops were no longer allowed to sit in the House of Lords. Disendowment meant that the endowments of the Anglican Church were distributed among local authorities and the University of Wales. Tithes were no longer payable to the Anglican Church.

Would God that I could make some contribution to the solution of this crushing problem.[150]

The worsening situation in the South Wales valleys was brought to Archbishop Lang's attention by a letter from another former chaplain based in Wales. The Rev E. Iltyd Jones wrote in December 1930:

Never was South Wales – in a mining sense – so depressed as today. In my own parish of 6,000 people the only colliery which provided employment has closed. ... The result is that poverty and suffering are very acute. ... I would dearly love placing the situation before some of our churches, by preaching our Lord's compassion to them – because probably thousands think that the unemployed are thriving on the dole.[151]

In March 1932 Timothy Rees was preaching in Cardiff in Holy Week, and was aware of the problems created by the moving of population to the suburbs of Cardiff. This he realised was "creating new responsibilities for the church." In the meantime, according the report of the *Church Times* on his Holy Week sermons, "He is getting to know the city itself and takes every opportunity of meeting the leaders of the civic and business life."[152] In April 1932, Rees launched "The Bishop of Llandaff's Appeal" and asked *Church Times* readers to contribute. He said that:

The economic depression with which the whole world is struggling is felt nowhere more acutely than South Wales. In this diocese of Llandaff ... is concentrated half the population of Wales. There are whole areas in it where the percentage of unemployment is higher than in any part of the United Kingdom.

He went on to remind the readers that without new funds, "Priests and women workers would have to be withdrawn from parishes where they are desperately needed.[153]

His contribution consisted of overseeing the social needs of the diocese. He regularly held open house at Llys Esgob (bishop's house) for groups of the unemployed. As chairman of the Llandaff Industrial Committee he discussed ways of alleviating the situation with local politicians and Industrial leaders. In November 1935 he led a deputation to Whitehall to ask for government help in the rejuvenation of South Wales. His biographer described how he made available a "band of young missioners",[154] – a

---

150 *Church Times* 26 October 1936, p.595.
151 E. Iltyd Jones to Lang, 16 December 1930, LP 103 FOS. 180-82 cited by Machin, *The Church and Social Order* p.41.
152 *Church Times* 18 March 1932.
153 *Church Times* 22 April 1932, p.509.
154 J. Lambert Rees, *Timothy Rees of Mirfield and Llandaff*, (London, Mowbray, 1945), p.103.

small unit of unmarried clergy who were dispatched to the neediest parishes in order to help with relief work.

Although aware of the problems facing Wales and other depressed areas of Britain, Rees was adamant that defeatism would not help the situation. In a sermon to the Church Congress, held in Bournemouth In 1935, he commented on this defeatism: "There seems to be within the souls of men the haunting dread that the forces which mould our modern world are not only beyond man's control but also beyond God's control. It would appear to some that Christ is exulted not to the right hand of power but to the right hand of weakness". He continued: "Brethren, there has never been a time when it was more necessary than it is today to stress the fact of the complete and absolute victory of Christ ... it is the vision of the victorious Christ that alone expels the spirit of defeatism."[155] Although a prominent member of the Welsh establishment he was definitely on the side of the working man. Lord Rhys Williams said:

> Bishop Rees was among the first to see the great moral wrong committed by the British people as a whole against the people of the depressed areas in the 1930s. ... The part played by him in remoulding the political thought of his time and risking the censure of the country well may have been more significant than we know.[156]

Guy Rogers

Guy Rogers became vicar in the parish of West Ham after the war. When describing the reforming ideas of the returning chaplains he said:

> No one, I think, was more thoroughly aroused and more sensitive to these new hopes or more anxious to turn the Church of England upside down than I was. I can see from the letters I wrote from the Front how eager I was to put into practice what I really believed the Spirit of God was teaching me about freedom in the approach to the Bible, human relationships ... and the reconstruction and rehabilitation of parish life.[157]

Rogers made efforts to get and keep in touch with Labour. Although he admitted that, "Like others who have worked in great industrial areas ... I could never attract many to my Labour friends within the ranks of organised religion,"[158] he accepted invitations to speak at Labour organised meetings and "preach from their platforms the

155 *Church Times* 18 October 1935, p.439.
156 Lambert Rees, *Timothy Rees of Mirfield and Llandaff*, p.118.
157 Rogers, *A Rebel at Heart*, p.130.
158 Ibid., p.138.

social gospel as I saw it."[159] An example of this is his presence at a meeting organised in the rail strike by Jack Jones. He was humble enough to admit that in his early days at West Ham he got, as he put it, "the psychology of the working man wrong"[160] and often made gaffes. He moved to Birmingham in 1925 to take charge of the famous St Martin in the Bull Ring. He recalled:

> During the sad days of the General Strike I addressed the crowd every night in the Bull Ring. It was tricky business trying to keep out of politics and keep within the gospel. But it was not impossible to talk about their homes and families and how we all might help each other in times of stress.[161]

He then set in motion preparations which culminated in the ICF crusade to Birmingham in 1930.The crusade was organised under the auspices of the ICF and was nondenominational. The preparation for the crusade was carried out by all participants together, and local crusade leaders were trained to take their part with the ICF agents and other visitors. The ICF crusade syllabus was the "agreed doctrinal basis" and it was stated: "United prayer and worship shall be regarded as an essential part of the preparation, but this does not necessarily involve intercommunion or exchange of pulpits."[162] As Rogers pointed out, this did not rule out the possibility that these would take place. The fact that the churches were working together was appreciated by the city officials and when, on the first day of the crusade, the processions of the crusade entered the Town Hall: "The Lord Mayor was waiting to receive them, and express the city's welcome to organised religion."[163]

Rogers described how a new relationship with the Labour Party emerged as the crusade progressed. He admitted that "The record of the church in the long struggle of trades unionism for recognition and power is not a very sympathetic one", but those more cordial relations were established. The editor of a Labour paper wrote an open letter to those engaged on the crusade and threw the columns open for an official reply. The reply "Produced a good impression and the appeal to let bygones be bygones was not without effect." This was followed by a crusade official speaking to the Trades and Labour council to explain the crusade, and "A new feeling of sympathy was created and the position of members of our committee who happened to be engaged in labour politics was immensely strengthened."[164]

159 Ibid., p.138.
160 Ibid., p.139.
161 Ibid., p.221.
162 T. Guy Rogers, *The Church and the People: Problems of Reunion, Sex and Marriage, Women's Ministry, Etc.* (London, Sampson Low, Marston and Co., 1931), p.56
163 Ibid., p.59.
164 Ibid., p.61.

The crusade was led by E. S. Woods, who had recently been made Bishop of Croydon, and Dr Herbert Gray.[165] The evangelists worked for ten days in the factories, at open-air pitches and in the parks. The resolution on "The Scandal of the Slums" was not, Rogers thought, "a mere pious resolution". The resolution was asserted on behalf of all present at the large public meeting:

> We record our solemn protest against the unchristian conditions under which so many of our fellow citizens live in the slums of Birmingham. We recognise frankly our share of the blame. We pledge ourselves in the name of Christ to do what lies in our power, *and to face the cost involved*, to secure the removal of this blot upon the fame of the city to which we are proud to belong.[166]

The crusade in Birmingham led to the setting up of the Christian Social Council, which was chaired by Rogers for seventeen years. In his autobiography he gives an account of the varied activities and campaigns it took part in, including a long struggle against the Sunday opening of cinemas. A more positive side to its work was the creation of the first community centre for the unemployed, in the years of depression and unemployment in the early 1930s. This led to the city picking up the idea: "The city gradually followed suit in a real attempt to combat the physical and mental wastage of the life of its citizens."[167]

Developments in the 1930s

During the 1930s the Anglican Church as a whole continued to show its commitment to the social gospel. Men such as Cyril Foster Garbett, later Archbishop of York, and Basil Jellicoe were prominent in the cause of better housing. Under Jellicoe, the St Pancras House Improvement society in the interwar years did much to transform the Somers Town area. Charles Jenkinson, vicar of St John's Leeds, was the mastermind of the "Leeds housing policy". The bishops of the Church of England were supportive of these and other ventures. Lloyd, in his discussion on the role of the church in housing said "Anyone who reads the debates of bishops in *The Chronicles of the Convocation of Canterbury* during the period 1919 to 1939 would be cured of the popular delusion that bishops as a class took no interest in social welfare."[168] Cyril Foster Garbett took the lead in these debates. In 1930 in a debate on housing in Convocation, many of the

---

165 A. H. Grey, Scottish Presbyterian minister and former army chaplain, who had worked closely with Harry Blackburne during the war. M. Snape, *The Royal Army Chaplains Department 1769-1953: Clergy Under Fire* (Woodbridge, Boydell Press, 2008), p.231.
166 Rogers, *The Church and the People*, p.56
167 Rogers, *A Rebel at Heart*, p.219.
168 Lloyd, *The Church of England*, p.323.

Bishops pooled their knowledge to build up "a knowledgeable survey of the housing problem in most of England"[169]

Writing in the *Southwark Diocesan Gazette* in November 1932, R. G. Parsons, former chaplain, now Bishop of Southwark, gave his opinion on what church people could do about unemployment: "I hope that every incumbent and every church in the diocese will deliberately set aside time to consider unemployment". He recommended that, firstly, every one tried to understand the problem, and secondly, for every parish to ask itself if it could do anything practical. He gave some examples. The parish must keep in contact with employers in the area to find out the names of the recently unemployed. Some parishes had provided voluntary work for the unemployed in the neighbourhood. "Although they were paid nothing they were glad of the employment and the companionship and interest the employment brought." He also recommended opening and heating parish rooms as reading rooms for the unemployed: "I lay it on the consciences of all the parishes to consider carefully what they ought to do."[170] Again in the *Southwark Diocesan Gazette* on 24 May 1933 he made a strong plea for centres for the unemployed where "opportunities of definite occupation are offered", as opposed to merely recreational facilities. He continued, "It is the duty of the Christian church to convince the public opinion of the nation to consider … new projects for dealing with fundamental maladjustments in our own economic and industrial system of which unemployment is such a symptom."[171] In April 1924, he tackled the problem of housing. Referring to the London City Council's decision to improve the area around Waterloo Bridge, he suggested a widening of the scheme:

> What a splendid opportunity for erecting a new housing area for the poorer citizens of the capital closer to the centre of the city! Are we really incapable of making use of it? If we are indeed a free country, where there is a will there is a way.[172]

He also had an opinion on what church people could do about unemployment:

> I hope that every incumbent and every church in the diocese will deliberately set aside time to consider unemployment … I lay it on the consciences of all the parishes to consider carefully what they ought to do.[173]

On 11 November, 1932 the *Church Times* published an article on "The Church and Unemployment". It reported that: "The cathedrals are being moved by the prevailing

169 Ibid., p.324.
170 Quoted in the *Church Times*, 4 November 1932.
171 Quoted in the *Church Times*, 24 May 1933.
172 *The Times*, 14 February 1930, p.16.
173 Ibid.

distress. Canon Woodward has put the case for the workless from the pulpit of Westminster Abbey, in connection with the establishment in Westminster of a new centre where the unemployed can rest and work." The article also reported a scheme proposed by P. T . R . Kirk. "For those men, Mr Kirk said, who suffer from a nameless existence in which they are losing skill and will power ... places of recreation are not enough." Kirk suggested a barter system. "If they are banded together in centres working as Christian communities, the man who can carpenter will exchange his work with that of a man who can make a pair of boots."[174]

The Industrial Christian Fellowship was making its views felt on the reduction of benefits to the unemployed. In March 1934 the Archbishop of York wrote to the Chancellor of the Exchequer to suggest that: "If he finds himself in a position to reduce taxation, the restoration of the cuts in benefit for the unemployed shall have precedence over any other concessions, including the reduction of income tax."[175] Preaching in St Paul's Cathedral in March 1934, John Groser denounced the means test as an "inquisition". "Can you imagine, what it means to be unemployed for so long ... to be subjected to the inquisition of the means test? To have all your resources inquired into ... you know that no neighbour can help you, because anything he may spare will be deducted from the small sum the state allows you to keep body and soul together." He continued, "These people need bread, but they need more than bread. They need to feel that they matter, that the nation cares about them, recognises their right to work."[176]

The report of the Industrial Committee of the Church Assembly was published in January 1935. It had considered social credit, banking and the economic system. Guy Rogers and P. T. R. Kirk were among its signatories. The report received a mixed reception in the Church Assembly in February. It was criticised because it put forward three different solutions to unemployment and also because some members did not see the need for the church to be concerned with such problems. R. G. Parsons defended the report. "The report did not aim to secure the assent of the assembly about any one proposal for such elimination (of employment)" and continued, "but no one could pretend to ignore the appalling significance of the wilful destruction of the fruits of the earth and the prevention and restriction of production."[177]

James Geoffrey Gordon, by 1932 the suffragan Bishop of Barrow, had served as an Assistant Chaplain General on the Western Front. As Bishop of Jarrow he identified with the plight of the unemployed. In 1934 he was part of a committee which set up a residential centre for the unemployed at Hardwick Hall and in 1935 joined the North Eastern Development board for housing. In July 1936 he wrote to *The Times* during

---

174 *Church Times*, 11 November 1932, supplement. I-iv.
175 *Church Times* 16 March, 1934, p.333.
176 Ibid.
177 *The Times*, 8 February 1935, p.16.

the negotiations for a syndicate to set up a steel works in Jarrow, which was being opposed by the iron and steel federation:

> We who live in Durham County do not think of the unemployed as merely a problem, but as persons, men and women, boys and girls, in urgent need. I would plead with the industrial magnates, not in the dust of their controversy to lose sight of the individual peoples of Jarrow, whose hopes have been so consistently raised during the past two years and as constantly disappointed.[178]

On October 5 1936 the Jarrow marchers set off to London to present a petition to Parliament. At the civic service Gordon blessed the march, but caused controversy by a letter to *The Times* denying that he gave his approval to the crusade: "To pray for God's blessing on the marchers was and is surely a duty, but it by no means involved support for a march, the wisdom and usefulness of which many of us are more than doubtful."[179] Eileen Wilkinson, MP for Jarrow was disappointed: "His blessing at our starting point has meant a lot to the men, and it hurt when he explained that that was only because the mayor asked him to come."[180]

There seemed more emphasis on the political voice of the church. In March, C. S. Woodward, speaking for the first time as chairman of the ICF, said:

> Today politics touched every section and every part of human life and if it was held that the Christian Church had to keep her hand away from everything that might conceivably be called political, it meant that the Christian Church must seek to take a part in influencing ordinary life.

However he stopped short of being politically partisan. "He urged that they should understand in every party there were some sincere and genuine Christian men."[181] In May of that year Timothy Rees was more downbeat in his assessment of the national situation. He talked about "the turn of events in the world of politics, commerce and industry ... preparations for war, a vast army of the unemployed," but continued in a more positive vein. "In the ICF they had a body of men who believed it was not enough to preach Christian principle, but that these principle must be applied to everyday life." He appealed to the parties in industrial disputes to go to arbitration rather than having strikes and lock outs. He ended with a stirring assertion that God was in all of these problems:

---

178 *The Times*, 13 July 1936, p.16.
179 *The Times* 17 October 1936, p.8.
180 Tom Pickard, *Jarrow March*, (London. Allison & Busby, 1981), untitled press cutting used as illustration, p.117.
181 *Church Times*, 6 March 1935, p.250.

They cannot keep God out of commerce and industry because he was there already. In every workshop and mine, every meeting of a board of directors, every conference of trade unions. He stood there, either despised and rejected or acclaimed as leader and king.[182]

John Groser had no qualms about the political nature of Christian activities on behalf of the poor. After his adventures in the General Strike, and following various disputes with the Church authorities over his activism, in 1929 he settled in a parish in Watney Street, Stepney, and continued his social and political agenda. In February of 1938 he was asked to speak to the clergy of the Archdiocese of York. He explained to them why the working class was suspicious of the Church:

> The working classes as a whole are becoming aware of the class struggle as an important fact. They are learning to think of the state as organised primarily in defence of the rights of the ruling classes … practically everyone thinks that the state can count on the support of the organised religion when the real interests of the ruling classes are threatened.[183]

He recalled in later life his opinion of the religious establishment:

> In England, every large-scale religious organisation, whether established or not, has in modern times, become so tied up in the social order with which their privileges, power and economic independence are so inextricably bound up that their leaders have tended to equate the decision of the governing body of that social order with the will of God.[184]

He described how in the late 1930s: "In a situation in which untold millions were available … for armaments, in which luxury abounded in one section of society and another section was subject to conditions which were an insult to Christ in the person of His poor, the church seemed officially to acquiesce in a scale of values and proprieties which are the reversal of the of those of Christ."[185]

Throughout the later 1930s the Church continued to comment on social and industrial problems. Former army chaplains were prominent in their contributions. In October 1935, seven thousand churchmen met in the Albert Hall to "Voice their abhorrence of slums, unemployment, materialism and social evils".[186] Temple was in the chair and of the twelve bishops on the platform, six were ex –chaplains: Haigh of

182 *Church Times*, May 1935, p.665.
183 *Church Times* 11 February 1938.
184 Groser, *Persons and Politics*, p.85.
185 Ibid., p.85.
186 *Church Times* 1 November 1935, p.553.

Coventry, Havard of St Asaph,[187] Woods of Croydon, Moberly of Stepney,[188] Simpson of Kensington[189] and Rose of Dover. C. S. Woodward, Bishop of Bristol, spoke on housing. He said that a decent house was "an indispensable condition of a full and complete life ... because it is where boys and girls grow up and where their characters are made." He went on to spell out the minimum requirements for a decent house and that there were still tens of thousands of families who had not reached that minimum.

He recommended the setting up of "A social service committee in each PCC to acquaint itself and enlighten the congregation about housing conditions."[190] He also recommended that the rents charged by local councils should be monitored. As an outcome of this meeting a memorial was sent to Stanley Baldwin, Prime Minister. It called his attention to:

> The pledge taken by up to six thousand members of the Church of England to urge upon you our desire that the government will adopt such courageous policy in dealing with social evils as we believe that public opinion at the last election expected and favoured.

It continued:

> We are much concerned ... with the claims of the miners for a wage which will assure them comparative comfort. ... We, baptised members of the Church of England, affirm that we are most deeply disturbed in conscience by the unreason and injustice of prevailing social conditions.

The signatories to this memorial included E. S. Woods, C. S. Woodward, Dick Sheppard and P. T. R. Kirk.[191]

As a result of an appeal made by *The Times* in July 1936 by C. S. Woodward, Dick Sheppard and F. R .Barry, the Jarrow Unemployed Social Centre received enough funds to continue for another twelve months. C. S. Woodward "won the hearts of many of our working men" when he addressed an outdoor meeting on problems in Wales in November 1936. Speaking in Bath, later in the month, he reminded his audience that: "In South Wales there were thousands out of work and endless homes unworthy of the name of a home. Christian people should have a "permanently troubled conscience".[192]

187 W. T. Havard, TCF 19115-1919, mentioned in despatches 1916. DSO 1917, *Crockford's*, p.1177.
188 R.H. Moberly, TCF 1917-1919, *Crockford's*, p.1280.
189 A. C. Rose, TCRN 1914-1919, *Crockford's*, p.375.
190 *Church Times*, 1 November 1935, p.534.
191 Ibid.
192 *Church Times*, 27 March 1936.

The Industrial Christian Fellowship had an opinion on the education act of 1936. This raised the school leaving age to fifteen but provided for a significant loophole. The executive committee of the ICF passed a resolution which said: "The provision of exemption on the grounds of beneficial employment go far towards defeating the primary purpose of the bill; and we would urge the government of the desirability of deleting such provisions and of providing for the payment of such material allowances ... as will enable children to remain at school to the age of 15".[193] In November 1936 the Church Assembly devoted a morning to debate on the distressed areas. P. T. R. Kirk moved a long resolution explaining the Assembly's deep concern at: "The continuation of severe and prolonged unemployment in the depressed areas". Unemployment, he explained, had only been brought down by workers moving out of the areas. The resolution stated that the assembly "is concerned that the palliative measures adopted have shown themselves wholly insufficient". The resolution went on to demand the revision of the Special Areas Act by giving the commissioners more power, and also urged the government "To investigate all possible way of securing a more balanced economy".[194]

On St Andrew's Day 1936, Bishop Walter Carey,[195] a former naval chaplain, preached at a city church. The sermon was reported by the *Church Times* under the headline: "A bishop beards Mammon in the city. Vested interests and means test arraigned". He first dealt with what it meant to be Christian. "It means to say to the Lord, I am yours: no longer my own." His prayer that morning had been: "Lord Jesus here's another day, and I belong to you, hooray!" He then turned to the state of England: "I look around England, all is not well: there are 36 millions who live in fear about the future, many are liable to lose their jobs at four hours' notice ...when they are old all they can expect is an old age pension". The report went on: "The bishop feels it is desperately unfair, while people like himself can be reasonably sure of an income". He then moved on to the distressed areas where he thought: "The real difficulty is vested interests ... But I say if we were to waste 50 millions it would not be wasted really, on giving them heart and hope and a job in the distressed areas, It would be worthwhile even if it were uneconomic. Don't let us go putting wages and dividends and profits before human beings". He then moved on to the means test:

> The politicians don't mean any harm, they just don't understand what it means for the poor. It makes them spongers on their relatives. It is causing more broken hearts and misery and backbiting in working-class houses than the politicians can conceive.

193 Ibid.
194 *Church Times* 27 November 1936, p.932. The Special Areas Act, 1934, identified South Wales, Tyneside, West Cumberland and Scotland as areas with special employment requirements, and invested in projects like the new steelworks in Ebbw Vale, South Wales.
195 Walter Carey, TCRN, 1914-1919. Bishop of Blomfield, South Africa, 1921-1934, *Crockford's*, p.209.

He ended by making clear his political independence. "I do not care tuppence ... whether I vote for Conservative or Liberal or Socialist. I want to get things done and I am ready to vote for the man who will get things done."[196] In August 1936 Carey wrote an article in the *Church Times* on "The modern Dilemma – the Church, Communism and Fascism". He considered that if what the church meant by being Christian meant being "apathetic to the establishment of righteousness, well being and love on earth", then it was "Sheer unchristianity", and that "the communists and fascists will be more right than us". He urged that:

> When we leave church we have worshiped one who says "go and make my Kingdom come". We pick up the paper and read of heartbroken men who are losing their manhood through not being wanted. We read of boys and girls being taken into factories and businesses and then turned off to join the unemployed, to make room for more cheap youth. In the Kingdom of God on earth these things would not be.

He asked the question, "Can we Christianise the social and economic basis of all life?" He wondered if: "We are right doing it in small bits – perhaps the communists are right in doing it by a crisis. But unless a Christian Church can do the job properly through a democracy, the communists will certainly do it someday in their way".[197]

An article on the Birmingham C.O.P.E.C. housing association in the *Church Times* in December 1936 shows that this follow-on from the conference was still functioning usefully in the late 1930s. The association had decided that renovating housing was good, but that what was really needed was new housing. In the previous few years they had built both houses and maisonettes on land formerly occupied by slum tenements: "All the houses have a bath, hot and cold water and indoor sanitary arrangements. Each house also has a small garden. A children's playground has been provided." The report continued on the work of
C.O.P.E.C. "There is still urgent need for the work of the C. O. P. E. C. Society. In the past ten years it has carried out various experiments that have inspired other housing reformers."[198]

In February 1938 the ICF announced a crusade for the Rhondda valley for May. The Bishop of Llandaff would commission forty crusaders. G. Snowden, missioner for Cardiff, stressed the importance of the crusade: "To allow a community to suffer and degenerate as the people in the Rhondda valley have done was to violate all Christian teaching about the sanctity of human personality."[199] Canon A. l. G. Shields, an

196 *Church Times* 4 December 1936, p.675.
197 *Church Times*, 11 December 1936, p.706.
198 *Church Times*, 11 December 1936, p.706.
199 *Church Times*, 11 February 1938, p.142.

ex-chaplain, led the crusade and Bishop Kempthorne was the chaplain. The Bishop of Llandaff, Timothy Rees, wrote in the crusade handbook:

> All the Rhondda valley should welcome the crusade, because the crusade brings a message of hope. The forces of defeatism and despair are striving to posses the soul of the Rhondda. Unemployment, poverty and the migration of the cream of the population by the thousand every year, have all left their mark on the district: yet it is with a profound thankfulness that we note that the people of these valleys have not lost their morale: they are reaching to respond to the message of hope."[200]

A week later there was a report from a *Church Times* correspondent on the crusade. He reported that: "The Rhondda Valley is a very "special" area where the tyranny of mass unemployment has called for special measures to deal with the resultant conditions". He commented on the 30 percent unemployment figures, despite large-scale migration of younger workers. He then went on to explain some bad feeling in the area towards the church. He quoted an aged workman at one of the meetings, "I am fed up with religion ... the Churches are manned and financed by the bosses who grind the face of the workers." The report continued: "The critics represent no inconsiderable number of members of unemployed men's clubs." However the report went on to describe the crusaders, in the words of Canon Shields, as "hard-boiled nuts" capable of holding their own against hecklers, and concludes that the results as "surprising – both in the pitches and in the indoor meetings". It concluded that the even though the crusade was a "splendid gesture of help at a critical hour", it did no more than "enhearten the clergy to wrestle with the huge task". The reporter claimed that "Resources of men and money are not adequate to the work and despite some tentative palliatives, the Church in Wales has quite failed to respond to the urgency of a crying need."[201]

Conclusion

Much of the work of the Anglican Church on social and industrial issues had been progressing from pre-war days and had its roots in the Christian socialism of the second part of the nineteenth century. The war had emphasised the necessity for action and had resulted in one of the Archbishops' Committees of Enquiry being devoted to these problems.

The backgrounds of army chaplains of course varied, from clergy who had shown considerable concern for the social gospel before the war, such as P. B. "Tubby" Clayton, Tom Pym and Geoffrey Studdert Kennedy, to men straight from ordination and

200 *Church Times*, 20 May 1938, p.591.
201 Ibid.

university posts such as F. R. Barry. The evidence shows that many Anglican army chaplains returning from war had clear and urgent ideas about the need for social reform and the changing of the industrial systems. They had experience in the amelioration of class differences that could occur under difficult circumstances and the benefit of disciplined and determined cooperation by all in a desperate task. They considered the post-war situation a desperate task and were often despairing of the entrenched views and values of both management and work force, preventing a fairer and more equal social and industrial system. The activities of the former chaplains show that they possessed "the permanently troubled conscience", and they set about, in various ways, the easing of this conscience. The economic problems of the interwar era did not make the progression of the collectivist ideas held by many clergy easy. As Machin explained: "Christians who wanted social reform through collectivism had little hope of gaining what they wished in the interwar years. The Governments of the time were probably less sympathetic to their point of view than they would have been if the economy had been healthier".[202]

The work of the Industrial Christian Fellowship is an important part of the evidence for former chaplains' involvement in social and industrial matters. Although formed from two pre-war societies, the Christian Social Union and the Navvy Mission and was an interdenominational movement, it was led by an ex-chaplain and received support from many others, including those who had reached prominent positions in the Church hierarchy, such as C. S . Woodward and E. S. Woods. Its practical effect in the organisation of meetings, crusades and campaigns was a vital part of assuring the working population that the Church was on their side and fighting for them, despite apparent evidence to the contrary. To complement this, ICF had contacts with the managers and owners of industry and was able to work on persuading them to take a Christian view of industrial relations. Gerald Studdert Kennedy, in his study of the ICF, considers the major impact of the movement took place in the 1920s: "If it made a politically significant contribution to public consciousness it was in the first decade of its existence",[203] but it continued to bring before the churches and society the particularly serious problems of industrial life in the 1930s. It did not conform always to mainstream Anglican opinion. Bishop A. C. Headlam complained in Convocation in 1933 about "the enormous amount of harm which the ICF is capable of doing",[204]

---

202 Machin, *The Church and Social Order*, p.35.
203 Studdert Kennedy. *Dog Collar Democracy*, p.9.
204 Convocation of Canterbury 19 January 1933, ix, 3, pp129, 139, cited by Machin, p.43.

and Michael Furse,[205] Bishop of St Albans defended the fellowship by denying that "It was in the pay of the Bolsheviks".[206]

It is debateable whether the influence of C.O.P.E.C. had a large effect in a practical sense, but it certainly set out the arguments for radical change and has been praised, as we have seen, for containing in it much that was to be achieved by the welfare state. It certainly set standards to which other initiatives and movements could aspire. However, the work of individual and sometimes high-profile former chaplains continued in the 1920s and 1930s. P. T. R. Kirk, in a personal role rather than as a representative of the ICF, was involved, as we have seen, in the attempts of churchmen to intervene in the General Strike. John Groser was an overtly political supporter of the working man in London. Studdert Kennedy in his preaching and writing did much to explain the Christian social gospel to a popular audience. Timothy Rees was a champion of workers in the South Wales valleys. Tom Pym worked practically and in raising political awareness in Camberwell. The Church press and the national press of the interwar years had many accounts of former chaplains who became bishops, particularly Woodward, Parsons and Woods, speaking out on social reform issues such as housing, education and unemployment.

The Anglican Church as whole made an effort to respond to the living and working conditions in interwar society and the effects of the changing industrial and economic landscape. However, not all clergy approved of liberal and left-wing action and the church was often split over such issues as the General Strike. Callum Brown described the effect of the war and changing circumstances on some: "The impact of the war, the Russian Revolution of 1917 and the rise of Labour militancy in its wake all frightened the churches ... Many clergy became deeply opposed to labour and the trades unions and the gap within Christian politics widened".[207] Brown thinks that after the General Strike, "Many working class communities ... regarded the mainstream churches as agents of capital ."[208] Often the official line of the Anglican Church was timid and inclined to compromise. Talking about our "present distress" at Convocation in January 1933, Cyril Garbett said: "Where economists, statesmen and banks have all failed it was not likely that the church would have the knowledge to solve the most difficult problems".[209] As we have seen, this was not an attitude held by

205 Michael Furse, Bishop of Pretoria 1909-1920, translated to St Albans in 1920. Although not a TCF, he spent several months on the Western Front in 1915. On his return to Britain, he lobbied the Government on the necessity for conscription and on the shortage of munitions. He also took part in discussions leading to the appointment of Bishop L. H. Gwynne as Deputy Chaplain General. *Crockford's* p.1176, M. Furse, *Stand Therefore: A Bishop's Testimony of Faith in the Church of Our Fathers* (London, SPCK, 1953), pp.73-80.

206 Convocation of Canterbury 19 January 1933, ix, 3, pp129, 139, cited by Machin p.43.

207 C. Brown, *Religion and Society in Twentieth-Century Britain* (Harlow, Pearson Longmans, 2006), p.145.

208 Ibid., p.157.

209 Canterbury Convocation 19 January 1933. ix.3, p123, cited by Machin.

all. The significance of the stand made by the clergy,including many former chaplains, in offsetting this opinion by their concern and action must have been considerable.

Callum Brown considers that the old-fashioned evangelistic crusade had outgrown its usefulness by 1930, although he does except the Rhondda crusade from his criticism because of its "Discussion groups on the social implications of the gospel".[210] Despite the picture he draws of an increasing gulf between working-class communities and the churches, he admits that: "There is little evidence that the Depression caused a significant membership crisis for Christianity".[211]

Looking at the bigger picture of the economic, social and industrial changes and challenges in the interwar years, it can be seen that former chaplains played a significant part on the stage of industrial and social reform. Perhaps some of their motivation was from their pre-war experiences, but when considering their writing and speaking at the end of the war and post-war, it can be seen that the war had had an effect on their ideas of what the post-war era should look like. E. S. Woods in his book *Everyday Religion* in many ways summed up the attitude of the returning chaplains. "The life in which God moves is the life of societies and nations, indeed a better correspondence with that life in industrial and international relations is the only hope for the future of the world."[212]

210 Brown, *Religion and Society* p.159.
211 Ibid., p.160
212 E. S. Woods, *Everyday Religion* (London, Hodder & Stoughton, 1921) cited in a review in *The Challenge*, 12 January 1921, p.12

3

P. B. "Tubby" Clayton and Toc H

Philip Clayton has become an iconic figure, both as an army chaplain and as the founder and leader of Toc H. He was universally referred to as "Tubby" and both his wartime ministry at Talbot House and his post-war ministry as founder of Toc H became symbolic of the ways in which something positive could emerge from war. In assessing his role as a clear example of the way in which former Anglican army chaplains contributed to church and society, several questions must be asked. To what extent was the Toc H organisation an extension of the fellowship and Christian witness of Talbot House and a symbol of remembrance of the losses of the war? To what extent was its aim to provide a new generation of Christian leaders and to perpetuate the wartime ethos of service in peacetime? To what extent was it dependent on the personal strength and dynamism of Tubby himself?

Philip "Tubby" Clayton had nothing obvious in his background that predisposed him to working for social reform and equality and for setting up Toc H. His educational background was conventionally upper middle class, reading Theology at Oxford and progressing to ordination in 1908, after a period as a research student with the Dean of Westminster in Deans Yard, London. Tubby's family had its roots in the north of England, his grandfather being a clergyman. However, Tubby was the son of tough and courageous ex-colonials who had farmed in Australia before returning to England when Tubby was a small boy. Money in his childhood was scarce and he won scholarships enabling him to attend St Paul's School and Exeter College, Oxford. At school and at Oxford he gained a reputation for high intelligence combined with a very sociable personality: "The general testimony of his school friends seems to be that Philip was already what he has been ever since, the most socially minded of human beings with a positive genius for universal friendliness."[1] His later disregard for rank and status was prefigured by his habit of walking and discussing issues as "pal with pal" with the High Master of St Paul's, George Walker.

---

1   T. Lever, *Clayton of Toc H* (London, John Murray, 1972), p.13.

At Oxford his sociability continued, drawing to him a wide variety of friends who would drop into his rooms at Exeter at all hours of the day and night. Tubby came under the influence of Henry Scott Holland and Christian Socialism, contributing some articles to the *Commonwealth*, edited by Scott Holland. He also met Dr John Stansfeld and became involved in the work of the Oxford Mission at Bermondsey. Charles Booth described Bermondsey in 1899 as "The greatest area of unbroken poverty in England."[2] Alec Paterson said of the area, "The part that lies closest to the river is far poorer than the rest. On these streets poverty has set a seal, and its many problems have sunk their tangled roots deep into the life of the people."[3] Dr Stansfeld encouraged students from Oxford to spend weekends and vacations at the mission, where they started clubs and classes. Tubby described how "The Franciscan figure of Dr Stansfeld had passed through the 'varsity and bidden us to the boys' clubs at 'Dockhead', 'Gordon' and 'Decima.'"[4] Tubby spent Thursday evenings in these places where, as Barclay Baron put it: "His own missionary spirit, trailing a cloak of delicious whimsy, was perfectly in tune."[5] Tubby often said that Bermondsey was the true cradle of Toc H.[6] It was Barclay Baron's opinion that the "Toc H spirit" was in fact the same spirit that had inspired the workers at Bermondsey: "Had they not been used to the phrase 'The OBM spirit' for years? Were the two spirits, at their best, not identical?"[7] Lord Nathan,[8] in his preface to a mature work of Tubby's, said of Tubby in these years: "Tubby, like so many of his generation was caught in the upsurge of the social conscience that marked the first decade of the century. It caught him, it held him, he never forgot."[9]

As a curate in the parish of Portsea, working in boys' and men's clubs, he showed a talent for encouraging boys and men in their faith. He wrote an article, 'Lads and Young Men' in C. F. Garbett's book, *The Work of a Great Parish*,[10] which detailed the life of the parish of Portsea in the pre-war years. Tubby's opinion was that, "A parish that neglects its boys is like a country that fails to develop its mineral resources."[11] Tubby seemed to have been remarkably good at running the boys' clubs, gathering large numbers of boys from the area, most of whom also went on to Bible classes,

2   Baron, *The Doctor*, p.11.
3   A. Paterson, *Across the Bridges* (London, Edward Arnold 1911), p.1, cited by Smyth, *Cyril Foster Garbett*, p.141
4   Baron, *The Doctor*, p.14.
5   Ibid., p.207.
6   Ibid., p.208.
7   Ibid., p.208.
8   Henry Louis Nathan was a Liberal, later Labour, politician. He was made first Baron Nathan of Churt in 1940. Harry Nathan was a contemporary of Clayton at St Paul's school and a lifelong friend and supporter of Toc H.
9   The Right Hon. Lord Nathan, in the foreword of P. B. Clayton, *To Conquer Hate* (London, Epworth Press, 1963), p.vi.
10   Garbett, *The Work of a Great Parish*.
11   P. B. Clayton, 'Lads and Young Men', in Garbett, *The Work of A Great Parish*, p.115.

many to confirmation, although it is typical of Tubby's egalitarian and open mind that the officers of the clubs did not have to be confirmed. A colleague of Tubby's at Portsea, E. G. Bucknill,[12] wrote of his talent: "His speciality was the genus BOY. He loved boys for their own sakes, instinctively and sincerely ... they flocked around him, drawn as by a magnet."[13]

In 1915, after declaring that "After the war there will be only two kinds of men, those who had been in it and those who had not",[14] he volunteered as a chaplain to serve on the Western Front and soon became involved in the setting up of Talbot House, a centre which became the famous 'Haven in Hell'[15] through which so many men passed for rest, recreation and if they wanted, religion, during the war. Barclay Baron[16] recounted how his friends from Bermondsey, who were in the Ypres area, called in on Talbot House. "They found him in an infectious atmosphere of gaiety and deep purpose in which the doctor, if he had been there, would have delighted".[17] The house was run on strictly egalitarian lines. The prevailing ethos summed up in the notice above Tubby's study door: "All rank abandon ye who enter here." Julian Bickersteth[18] remembered dining in the house: "We had our meal with Tubby and three private soldiers – the first time I had ever sat down to eat out here in uniform with soldiers."[19] Officers were charged five francs for board and lodging on "the Robin Hood principle of taking from the rich to give to the poor".[20] The Rev W. Muirhead, later on the staff at All Hallows Church, Tower Hill, with Tubby, described the class-less atmosphere:

> Class was forgotten in common fellowship in its rooms. The ranker officer met the non-commissioned nobleman with easy welcome. The one time frequenter of a public school forgot his snobbishness as easily there as the one time frequenter of a public house discovered his worth.[21]

12   E. G. Bucknill, Curate at Portsea 1913-199, *Crockfords*, p.178.
13   Lever, *Clayton of Toc H*, p.32.
14   William Drury, *Camp Follower* (Dublin, Exchequer Printers, 1968), p.13.
15   *Punch Magazine* 1915, cited in G. F. Macleod, 'What is Toc H? The Story of a Light' in P. B. Clayton (ed.), *The Smoking Furnace and the Burning Lamp* (London, Longmans Green, 1927), p.73.
16   Barclay Baron, (1884-1964). Member of the Oxford Bermondsey Mission pre-war. After working for the YMCA during the war he became a member of Toc H. He wrote the early history of the movement *The Birth of a Movement 1919–1922* (London, Westminster, 1946), and served as its vice president and travelling secretary. Snape, *The Back Parts of War*, p.13.
17   Baron, *The Doctor*, p.207.
18   Bickersteth, *The Bickersteth Diaries*.
19   Paul Chapman, *A Haven from Hell: Talbot House, Poperinghe* (Pen and Sword, 2000), p.60.
20   Clayton, *Tales of Talbot House*, p.28.
21   Macleod, 'What is Toc H?' p.73.

Tubby summed up the purpose of the house: "Its whole raison d'être was always to be an Emmaus Inn, a home from home where friendships could be consecrated, and sad hearts renewed and cheered, a place of light and joy and brotherhood and peace".[22] Many soldiers made their way up to the beautiful chapel in the loft and many made their first and last communion there. E. K. Talbot, a Mirfield Father and brother of Neville Talbot, visited Talbot House in December 1916 as part of the National Mission. He described it as: "Much the most Christian institution on the Western Front", and continued: "It is refreshing to get into an atmosphere entirely disinfected of Khaki and saturated with real brotherhood and joy."[23]

Tubby's spiritual and political development was much affected by his experiences in Talbot House. Regular debates were held discussing, for example, the role of women, the nationalisation of the railways, the problem of Ireland and the colour problem in the Empire.[24] These gave Tubby an opportunity to absorb the thoughts and opinions of the wide spectrum of British male society that passed through the doors of the house. The egalitarian rules of the house were popular with the men and prompted Tubby to reflect on equality in state and church at home.

> Glaring inequalities of distribution, whether of safety, leave or pay at home, or of wealth in secular or ecclesiastical life at home have provoked them to sustained indignation: and the fact that within its household the church fails in equality as conspicuously as the state is a running sore to the consciences not only of churchmen but also many bystanders.[25]

The ethos of unstinted welcome and hospitality was one which earned Tubby the names "Boniface" or "The Innkeeper" from his friends. Captain L. F. Browne, in his postscript to *Tales of Talbot House*, "The Innkeeper", described his impression that "Talbot House was to the B.E.F. in the salient what House Beautiful was to the pilgrims in Bunyan's wonderful 'Similitude of a dream'."[26] It was obviously an ethos which it was hoped would pervade the infant Toc H. Browne ended his tribute to Tubby by asking: "Is it too much to hope that London may have its Talbot House with Boniface to welcome all comers and cheer them on their way?"[27] F. R. Barry, writing a review of *Tales of Talbot House* in *Ducdame,* the magazine of Knutsford Test School, in December 1919, wrote:

---

22 Clayton, *Tales of Talbot House*, p.36.
23 London Metropolitan Archives, Ms 30380, E. K. Talbot, letter to the Mirfield Brethren, December 31 1916.
24 Clayton, *Tales of Talbot House*, p.44.
25 Ibid., p.42.
26 Ibid., p.124.
27 Ibid., p.125.

The tale of Talbot House is a radiant story of warmth and light and fellowship and joy breaking into the record of the Salient. To hundreds, to thousands it was holy ground ... the author calls it the Emmaus Inn. Talbot House, in its old form, must be started again in a 'place' in London.[28]

In his history of the Toc H movement, Barclay Baron suggested that many of the principles that the later Toc H was founded upon had their roots in the first four years of the movement, but it can be seen that many of them also stemmed from the work at Talbot House at Poperinghe. The idea that "Christian fellowship" was the whole basis of Toc H, the idea that "active service" was the "essential spring and outcome of fellowship", and "the principle that layman and padre always work hand in hand",[29] all these could be clearly seen in the way Tubby ran Talbot House. Baron also described a scene in the small flat in Red Lion Square which was the first centre of the developing movement which was reminiscent of Poperinghe in the old days: "The same ever-present tea, the same strangely assorted but always enthusiastic collection of men, the same lively conversation which lasted until the small hours".[30] When the Royal Charter of Toc H was granted in 1922 it stated in its preamble that Toc H was founded in order to continue the work initiated in Talbot House during the Great War.[31] Tubby, preaching at Great St Mary's, Cambridge, in 1938, could see that what he had tried to achieve in Talbot House had informed the "four points" of the organisation:

On the ground floor of the Talbot House the open door led straight to rough fellowship. Men of all sorts, born in all kinds of bedrooms, were brothers there. This is our aim today. On the first floor we catered for men's minds. We tried to teach fair thinking, it is needed. On the next floor of the Flanders house, men wrote home. Today men's hearts must learn to love more widely. A steep stair led men in the old Talbot House up to the attic. Here, kneeling they received the source of courage.

He then concluded: "Such was the old Talbot House. I dwell upon it; for if the upper room is ever left beyond the common habit of Toc H, the movement will desert its heritage".[32]

At the end of the war Tubby rescued from Talbot House many scraps of paper with the names of people who had been communicants during the war. These were to be the "foundation members" of an organisation that was crystallising in his mind to

28   B. Baron, *The Birth of a Movement 1919–1922*, p.73.
29   Ibid., p.2.
30   Ibid., p 15.
31   Ibid., p.52.
32   P. B. Clayton, *To Conquer Hate* (London, Epworth Press, 1963), p.197.

perpetuate the work and ethos of Talbot House. At Christmas 1919 he sent out a funny postcard cum invitation, which became known as Tubby's "whizz-bang", in the form of a field postcard to resume contact and establish interest in such an organisation, the starting point being a Talbot House set up in London. There were 4,000 on the roll, 500 of them in London. The replies showed much interest but Tubby was determined to prioritise his work at Knutsford first, and this meant a six-months delay. Barclay Baron thought this was a good thing as "ensuring for it (Toc H) eventually a clearer view of practical problems, a sense of proportion and a vision of the future".[33] However, Tubby continued to plan, writing a series of articles for the *Challenge* during the summer together with an article for *St Martin's Review* to publicise the new venture. In the article he painted a vivid picture of Talbot House as it was in the war, stressing the informality and Christian fellowship. He then asked the question:

> What then is to happen to the fellowship of Talbot House? It is plainly too great to lose. Its lovers have a dream of finding some house … and the rent thereof, of hoisting the old sign board there and taking the consequences.[34]

The Rev G. F. Macleod, writing about Toc H in 1926, recalled Tubby and friends talking in Tubby's room, post-war. He said that their two main "grouses" were, firstly, lamenting the "loss of spirit that had been so glorious in war and had strangely disappeared with the return of peace", and secondly, the realisation that "the real loss of war was in … the terrific loss of the very best men".[35] Regarding the first point they asked the question: "How can we keep alive the spirit of fellowship and service? How can we perpetuate it among the younger brothers of those Elder Brethren … who have gone onwards?" It was the answers to these questions which Macleod argued had encouraged the ideas of the early Toc H.

Tales of Talbot House was published in September 1919. A review in *Punch* is indicative of the opinion that the war had in some cases been revelatory in a positive way: "Those who believe that the war brought its own revelation will find abundant proof in these gaily serious pages."[36]

The first committee meeting of "intimate confederates" was called for 15 November 1919. The agenda for the meeting was set out in army style, and after the "assembly point" and "zero hour" had been stated under the heading of "information" and "the nature of the country", the main business was set out:

---

33   Baron, *Birth of a Movement*, p.8
34   *St Martin's Review*, September 1919, the magazine of St Martin-in-the-Fields, cited in Baron, *Birth of a Movement*, p.71.
35   Macleod, 'What is Toc H?' pp.76-77.
36   Baron, *Birth of a Movement*, p.73.

> The attack on the problem of reopening Talbot House will be carried out by a round table conference ... troops being drawn from Talbothousians, past, present and to come. The attack will be covered by a creeping barrage of expert Londoners and a section of clerical tanks will cooperate.

The aim of the meeting, the agenda went on to explain, was to find ways of "maintaining the old fellowship and extending it to the younger clerks, civil servants and students of London".[37] In a document accompanying the agenda is a report from Tubby which stressed that the organisation was not a backward-looking one: *"Auld Lang Syne* is not our primary object". Plans were put forward to offer a reasonably priced hostel for young working men and students and to "Infuse in them the traditional spirit of the old house and to lighten the loneliness of lodgings". The document emphasised the forward-looking nature of the movement by stating that: "Youth made the greatest sacrifice and it is to this youth that the world owes most in return".[38] The executive committee met again on 19 November and the 17 December 1919. The influence of Bermondsey and Talbot House can be seen by the active participation of Alec Paterson and Neville Talbot on this committee. Writing to George Bell on 23 November 1919, Tubby reported: "I feel tremendously thankful and hopeful over the whole thing. It is quite plain now that T.H. [Talbot House] has more in front of it than behind it".[39]

A poster campaign on the London Underground system in the spring of 1920 showed the crystallisation of the aims of Toc H. It defined the aims of Toc H as:

1. The perpetuation of the active service atmosphere of fellowship.
2. The extension of this tradition to the younger generation.
3. The continuance of the House tradition in service, thought and conduct.

It promised: "First class club premises and hostel accommodation".[40] However the funds of the infant organisation were not at the stage to achieve these aims. An enthusiastic fund-raising campaign continued in the spring of 1920. Two high-profile supporters, the Archbishop of Canterbury and Field Marshal Plumer became presidents. Enough money was raised to set up Toc H Mark One at 23 Queen's Gate Gardens, which was set up as a peacetime replica of Talbot House.

Lieutenant-Colonel Shiner, who was to become the first warden of "Mark One", wrote some recollections of the very early days, firstly at Red Lion Square: "There were five of us in this original team which joined to set up ... a Toc H hostel. Here we lived

---

37   Ibid., p.11.
38   Ibid., p.11.
39   LPL: papers of Bishop Bell, Vol. 248, f.84, letter from P. B. Clayton to George Bell, 33 November 1919.
40   Lever, *Clayton of Toc H*, p.96.

a month or two gathering fragments of the family of Talbot House, Poperinghe round us".[41] After moving to Queen's Gate and being made warden he described how they set about gathering enough members living there to pay for the new house's expenses. He said of the original inhabitants of Mark One: "We were, very properly, an odd crowd – a mixture of young and middle-aged, of professional and manual workers".[42] He recollected how Tubby involved them in the plans and hopes for the appeal then being formulated and asked for their help, but it was his opinion that Tubby had developed very clear plans:

> In reality Tubby wanted about as much assistance from us as the moon needs from man to shed its light, but he accomplished one purpose – he made us feel that our thinking was of use to Toc H.[43]

Tubby's cause for concern was the perceived need for a set of principles which would guide younger members and help make the transition of the movement from one of wartime comradeship and service to one, as Barclay Baron put it, of "Service to society as a whole and to less fortunate fellow beings in particular".[44] He was particularly concerned with the fate of the thousands of young men who left their homes to live and work in the big cities:

> There is no feature of our civilisation more fraught with the gravity of evil than the fact that every city contains young men, unchallenged to the work of any great cause outside their own career.[45]

It was at this time that the custom of inviting experts in their field to speak developed into regular "guest nights". These often resembled a sort of "human zoo" in their variety.[46] The *Guardian* reported on the House at Red Lion Square in February 1920:

> Before the war the London clerk or young businessman who lived in lodgings was the loneliest man imaginable. Now his position is even worse, as he has come to know the companionship of military service. Toc H gives him this companionship and the influence it exerted at Poperinghe will be exerted in London, but in a far wider measure.[47]

---

41   Baron, *Birth of a Movement*, p.96.
42   Ibid., p.97.
43   Ibid., p.97.
44   Ibid., p.23.
45   John Durham, *Talbot House to Tower Hill, A 'Tubby' Clayton Anthology* (London, Toc H Incorporated, 1960), p.104.
46   Macleod, 'What is Toc H ?, p.78.
47   *Guardian*, 6 February 1920, p.142.

As the movement spread out of London it was becoming national. In January Tubby was able to write to Lord Salisbury that there were seventy branches in England,[48] and that some of the regional branches were well on their way to opening their own houses.[49] This created some problems of control and leadership. In response to this Tubby sent out a letter to foundation members in the regions appealing for them to become local leaders:

> The step that we are now taking in the formation of local branches all over the kingdom is vital to the welfare and development of the new work and it is of the utmost importance that Toc H should be represented by a foundation member whose sense of service and fellowship can be relied upon.[50]

The leadership was forthcoming, an example being Pat Leonard, a former chaplain who moved from being chaplain in Cheltenham College to be Staff Padre of Toc H in Manchester. Leonard had been a popular and successful army chaplain, identifying closely with the men of the 3rd Division in which he served.[51] He had won the DSO for bringing in wounded under fire.[52] Gary Sheffield considers that "He clearly played a key role in maintaining military morale in his battalion and seems to have achieved a reasonable balance between his welfare and spiritual duties."[53] The qualities Leonard had shown in the war were clearly ones that were to make him a leading figure in the Toc H Movement. One of his first tasks was to foster the growth of Toc H branches in Lancashire and the Midlands. His success in the Manchester area was "phenomenal".[54] One of his descriptions of Toc H gives a sense of his infectious enthusiasm:

> Toc H then is a family of men seeking to create among themselves such love that it may overflow into every nook and cranny of the social world in which they live. Each group and branch is an infectious hotbed of radiant joy and fellowship – a generating station to which members come that their batteries may be recharged

---

48 James Edward Hubert Gascoyne Cecil, fourth Marquess of Salisbury (1861–1947), politician and prominent lay churchman, trustee of Toc H. Tresham Lever, *Clayton of Toc H*, p.100; *ODNB*.
49 Lever, *Clayton of Toc H*, p.101.
50 Baron, *The Birth of a Movement*, p.81.
51 G. Sheffield, 'Chaplains in Context : British Army Padres and the "Bureaucy of Paternalism in the First World War"', p.118 in E. Madigan and M. Snape(eds.), *The Clergy in Khaki: New Perspectives on British Army Chaplaincy in the First World War*, (Farnham, Ashgate, 2013).
52 University of Birmingham, Church Missionary Society Archives, ACC/18/7/1, Bishop L. H. Gwynne's 'Army Book'.
53 Sheffield, 'Chaplains in Context' p.190.
54 Philip Leonard-Johnson, *Pat Leonard DSO – A Memoir* (2010). http://www.toch-uk.org.uk/documents/Pat%20Leonard%20Memoir%20%28Final%29.pdf. (Feb 2011).

with the divine electricity which they are pledged to use up in the adventure of loving the world.[55]

A report in the *Manchester Guardian* in April 1921 on the opening of a Mark" in Manchester showed that the aims and organisation of the movement were reaching and being understood by a wider audience: "The aim is not merely to perpetuate the old B.E.F. fellowship, but rather to use the goodwill to save the younger generation. It is also felt that such a home would be a very practical war memorial".[56]

Another cause for concern was the perceived need for a set of principles which would guide younger members and help make the transition of the movement from one of wartime comradeship and service to one which would serve society as a whole. In the summer of 1920 Alec Paterson, Tubby and Dick Sheppard met to hammer out the aims and objects which would unite the Toc H movement. The ideas which Alec Paterson and Tubby produced were remarkably similar, and at the meeting the "four points" of the "Toc H compass" emerged. "FELLOWSHIP – to love widely, SERVICE – to build bravely FAIRMINDENESS – to think fairly, THE KINGDOM OF GOD – to witness humbly."[57] At the same time, Tubby was working out the philosophical and spiritual implications of the aims of Toc H. He saw these in terms of reconciliation "of man with God and man with man", and of fellowship in service: "You cannot love men till you work alongside, and know how much you need them. The harder the common task the deeper the common sympathy".[58] Running alongside this was the need for social equality: "The work of Toc H is, therefore to bind in a single tether those who would else be poorer for their ignorance of each other". This should militate against the fact that: "Civilian life sinks us all in one rut or another, according to the bedrooms we were born in or the trades we follow." He was clear on the position of Toc H:

> Toc H thus aims not at the stampeding of the whole social system, but the crea-tion of a place and atmosphere in which the younger generation at least may meet their otherwise unknown contemporaries.[59]

Peter Monie, the honorary administrator of Toc H 1920-1935, wrote in a similar vein in his article, "The Fellowship of the Spirit". He was concerned to explain the meaning of fellowship in terms of Toc H. He spoke of the way in which membership was open to men of all religious allegiances and also the absence of a "test" applied to new members either of Christian belief or practice. People who expressed doubts

---

55   Ibid.
56   *Manchester Guardian*, 21 February 1921, p.3.
57   Lever, *Clayton of Toc H*, p.104.
58   Ibid., p.104.
59   Ibid., p.104.

about the possibility of welding together "Tom, Dick and Harry" into a viable fellow-ship were not taking into consideration the ability of God "To draw all sorts of men into a live and enlivening fellowship, not only with one another but with himself".[60]

As the organisation grew in the early 1920s the principles of service became more established. As well as Toc H Marks One and Two in London, new houses were opened in Manchester and Leicester. Following suggestions from Lieutenant-Colonel A. Murray-Smith, of the Cheltenham Branch of Toc H, the houses acted as centres of supply to the need of local social and welfare associations and the local Toc H members helped out in these according to their time and talents. No new social service organisation was intended or started. He summed up his hopes for the future:

> That in the course of time, as people find that Toc H can furnish willing and capable fellows to help in every town where there is a branch, any organisation that wants a helper for some job or other will, as a matter of course apply first to the Toc H Branch, knowing from common experience that they will not be disappointed.[61]

The Rev G. F. Macleod, writing on "What is Toc H?, and discussing the bonds that held the organisation together, emphasised that "common life giving service that will alone keep human beings together".[62] It is significant that when talking about the social service aspect of Toc H, he related it back to the war: "We seek humbly to create a living war memorial – something alive and eager and outgoing".[63]

In a sermon in 1938, Tubby described how the "Mark" system worked:

> The Marks are residential houses meant to consecrate the mobility of commercial life. ... In London, Marks have much to do. They are not merely lodgings; they are founded to be our college system in the world ... they can be depots of good natured help, dealing with men whom the old parish system is bound to miss.[64]

In 1921 and 1922 the members in the London Marks were making friends with a wide variety of men who became supporters of the movement, among them A. A. Milne and G. K. Chesterton from literary circles, Lord Robert Cecil,[65] Aubrey Herbert,[66]

---

60   Peter Monie, 'The Fellowship of the Spirit', in P. B. Clayton, *A Birthday Book* (London, Toc H Incorporated, 1936), p.13.
61   Baron, *Birth of a Movement*, p.105.
62   Macleod, 'What is Toc H?, p.70.
63   Ibid., p.80.
64   P. B. Clayton, *To Conquer Hate*, p.196.
65   Lord Robert Cecil, politician and peace campaigner, architect of the League of Nations and winner of the Nobel Peace Prize in 1937, *ODNB*.
66   Aubrey Herbert, diplomat, politician and supporter of Albanian nationalism, *ODNB*.

Bishop Gore,[67] and Sir Oliver Lodge,[68] all of whom were respected "for various high-mindedness".[69] Tubby recalled how in the coal strike, pledged to think fairly, Mark Two invited three people with differing viewpoints on the issues to speak at guest night. His comment was, "Politics taught like this improves with telling".[70]

Tubby was proud of the chapel at Mark One, which had been furnished as a replica of the one in Talbot House. In the Annual Report for 1921 he explained the role of the chapel in the life of the Mark:

> Sunday services are rarely held, since it is clearly not the task of the house to offer a substitute for church attendance: worship is here a weekday thing, intended to annul the divorce so common between religion and working life, a point Gilbert Talbot[71] stressed in one of his last letters.[72]

In December 1921 plans were made for a celebration of the anniversary of the opening of Talbot House in 1915. A party was proposed at Grosvenor House, to be preceded by a service of thanksgiving at St Martin-in-the-Fields at which Tom Pym preached. At Grosvenor House, "1,500 members, culled from every class, cheerfully chewed sausage rolls".[73] The enthusiastic celebrations included the signing of a large 'Round Robin' by all present, which was addressed to members who would be present at the centenary of Toc H in 2015. Typically of Tubby, it was written in a light-hearted vein: "To be serious in a document of this character would be unconvincing to the last degree. We therefore content ourselves with wishing all many happy returns of the day and remaining your obedient ancestors at Toc H".[74] It convincingly summed up the optimism felt by the infant Toc H at this time.

1922 was to prove an important year in the development of the movement. In January Tubby embarked on a lecture tour of Canada which was very successful, attracting large audiences and raising funds. Also during 1922 steps were taken to put the organisation on a formal footing by establishing a constitution and being incorporated by Royal Charter. Toc H thereby became an institution, with the Prince of Wales as its patron. Its four objects were stated. The first objective was to preserve and encourage the traditions of service began in wartime, the second was to encourage social service "as between and for the benefit of all ranks of society". The third was

67   Charles Gore, Bishop of Oxford 1911-1919, *ODNB*.
68   Oliver Lodge, physicist and pioneer of the commercial use of radio, *ODNB*.
69   Baron, *Birth of a Movement*, p.107.
70   Ibid., p.107.
71   Lieutenant Gilbert W. L. Talbot, brother of Neville Talbot and son of Bishop E. S Talbot. He was killed at Hooge in the Ypres Salient on 30 July 1915. It is thought that Neville Talbot, instigator of Talbot House, named the house in memory of his brother.
72   University of Birmingham, Toc H Archive, Toc H Annual Report 1921, section 6 G1, p.7.
73   Ibid., p.36.
74   Lever, *Toc H*, p.108.

to promote a wide interest in all people for the needs of their fellow men. The fourth was to mitigate the "evils of class consciousness", in order to "create a body of public opinion free from all social antagonisms",[75] The objectives were phrased in formal and legalistic language, which was felt to be too austere, and at a meeting on December an additional one, known thereafter as "The Main Resolution", was drafted and passed which more accurately summed up what was in the hearts and minds of members. It ended:

> We pledge ourselves to listen now and always for the voice of God, to strive to know his will revealed in Christ and to do it fearlessly. Reckoning nothing of the world's opinion, or its successes, for ourselves or this our family, we will endeavour to think fairly, to love widely, to witness humbly and to build bravely.[76]

The idea of the lamp of maintenance and the ceremony of light that was built around it was partly a result of Murray-Smith's idea that a half minute silence be given at the beginning of meetings to remember old friends "left behind in the Salient", and partly as a result of Barclay Baron and Tubby's desire to come up with a badge or symbol to represent Toc H. In May 1922 Baron and Tubby came up with a design for a lamp with the double cross of Calvary, also part of the coat of arms for Ypres. Each full branch of Toc H was to be presented with a lamp which was a replica of the original lamp presented to Toc H by the Prince of Wales, and each had the inscription *In Luminae Tuo Videbimus Lumen* – In thy light shall we see light, (Psalm 36.9). The ceremony of light consisted of the chairman saying:

> With proud thanksgiving let us remember our elder brethren:
>> They shall grow not old as we that are left grow old.
>> Age shall not weary them nor the years condemn.
>> At the going down of the sun and in the morning
>> We shall remember them.

After the response: we shall remember them, and after a minute's silence, the chairman says:

> Let your light so shine before men that they see your good works.

The branch replies:

> And give glory to our Father which is in heaven.[77]

75   Ibid., pp.127-128.
76   Ibid., p.128.
77   Ibid., p.122.

The symbol of the lamp was to be used in the birthday celebrations of 1922, which were being planned on a large scale. It was held in the Guildhall on 15 December in the presence of the Prince of Wales, the Lord Mayor of London, the burgomasters of Poperinghe and Ypres, Neville Talbot and his father, Bishop E. Talbot. Over 2,000 people were present. The patron, the Prince of Wales had presented a lamp which would be used to light the lamps which were to be presented to the branches. *The Times* gave advance notice in its columns in November of the ceremonial that had been planned:

> From each of the branches taking part there will be a delegation. Each delegation will go to the platform, carrying a lamp, banner and petition. Lord Salisbury … will receive the delegations and present them to the Prince of Wales who will light the lamps. The lamp bearers, when all the lamps are lit, will be grouped on the platform and the lights of the Guildhall will be lowered. The Last Post will be sounded, and after a short silence there will be sung 'God Rest Ye Merry, Gentlemen'.[78]

The Prince, in his address, spoke of his friendship with Gilbert Talbot and his memories of Talbot House. He described the movement as "determined to raise out of a great tragedy a great opportunity for good". He referred to the wide-ranging scope of Toc H's mission: "It has a very great work ahead of it: a work which competes with no other task, but supplements the achievements of all". But he also referred back to the memory of the war when lighting the lamps: "As I light them, let our thoughts be with pledges of service and brotherly love".[79]

In March 1924 Toc H organised a mission in London churches. It was opened by the Bishop of London and led by Edward Keble Talbot, MC, former chaplain and brother to Neville and Gilbert. The mission was run by eight former army chaplains, including Herbert Fleming and Pat Leonard. The mission held services and meetings three times daily in London churches.[80]

In July 1922 Tubby had been offered the living of All Hallows on Tower Hill by Archbishop Davidson. In accepting this challenge, Tubby provided a base for Toc H and also started a pastoral ministry to the financial centre of London, which was to be a large part of his interwar work. All Hallows became a place where city workers could come and eat their packed lunches, and where regular services gradually attracted larger and more youthful congregations. Writing fifteen years later, Tubby acknowledged the debt that Toc H owed to All Hallows but also the debt that All Hallows owed to Toc H:

78   *The Times,* 30 November 1922, p.9.
79   *The Times,* 15 December 1922, p.9.
80   *Church Times,* 7 March 1924, p.263.

Toc H throughout the world has been enriched, assisted and safeguarded from All Hallows ... Without All Hallows it is more than likely that Toc H would now be moribund. ... The debt on the other side is as deep. Without Toc H All Hallows would have had a scope more confined, more conventional.[81]

The idea of putting Tubby at All Hallows was Archbishop Randall Davidson's. Tubby acknowledged his wisdom: "He it was who foresaw that the conjunction of the then frozen life of this great shrine and of the young, impetuous, ardent stream flowing from Christ's re-wounded side in Flanders, would bring to both true life in high measure".[82] Peter Monie, the first treasurer of Toc H, paid tribute to Archbishop Davidson's confidence in Toc H in firmly attaching it to All Hallows. He maintained that Davidson was: "The first person outside it [Toc H] to have a real vision of its possibilities and be willing to take risks".[83] Tubby set about the regeneration of Tower Hill, enlisting the help of the Lord Mayor of London, and gathering around him willing supporters, including Lord Wakefield.[84] They turned the run-down area of Tower Hill into a more attractive place, with space for children to play. Tubby, preaching in 1938 described the significance of the work.

> The guild church of Toc H is on Tower Hill; and since the love of God is not confined within the walls where God in Christ is worshipped, a number of the older city men in Toc H have undertaken to reform Tower Hill and to restore the old promenade to London. Buildings have been both purchased and demolished to give back to East London and to the city, gardens and trees and flowers. More than half a million children have patronised Tower Beach ... Lord Wakefield has placed Toc H on Tower Hill in a position of permanence, bestowing freehold buildings for the erection of a great colony of Christian influence.[85]

In 1927 the relationship between All Hallows and Toc H was formalised by the setting up of a trust fund made possible by a large donation. The aim of the trust fund was to provide funds and training for Toc H chaplains and to place the organisation on a secure financial basis, making sure that the link between them, embodied in Tubby would continue by linking the incumbency of All Hallows permanently with Toc H. A press release exclusively for *The Times* sent out on Friday 2 November stated:

> The Trust owes its origin to a twofold desire to safeguard the spiritual work of the association by the creation of a system of endowed chaplaincies ... to perpetuate

81 Lever, *Toc H*, p.119.
82 Ibid.
83 LPL: the papers of Archbishop Davidson, Vol. 217, ff. 190-191, 'Statement on Toc H and the Denominational Issue', by Peter Monie, 1926 (month unspecified).
84 Charles Wakefield, 1st Viscount Wakefield, oil industrialist and philanthropist. *ODNB*
85 Clayton, *To Conquer Hate*, p.198.

for all time the close associations of the last five years between Toc H and the church of All Hallows Berkyngechriche, which has come to be regarded as the spiritual rallying point for the Anglican members of Toc H. ... All lovers of the great movement, which was born amid the havoc of the Great War ... will read with thankfulness that a further landmark in its spiritual progress has reached.[86]

In 1922 Tubby was invited to Canada to visit and encourage the Toc H branches there. before he went he asked Barclay Baron to put together a short history of the movement which he did in ten days, called *Toc H, Birth of a Movement*. During the tour of Canada and America, he was impressed by the role of women in public affairs,[87] and when he returned he decided that Toc H should have a Women's auxiliary, which became The League of Women Helpers. Its role was described by Barclay Baron. "The undertaking of social service of all kinds for women and girls which would should run parallel to that of Toc H."[88] It gained the nickname of Toc Emma, the initial letters of the trench mortar.

At the beginning of 1925, it was decided that Tubby would set off on a worldwide tour, accompanied by Pat Leonard. The purpose of this tour was to raise funds and also raise awareness of the movement supporting the branches that had sprung up overseas. It also seemed fitting that Toc H should be part of the hopeful internationalism of the 1920s which was manifesting itself in the League of Nations, and via the Edinburgh and Lausanne conferences of that decade would inform some strands of the pacifist movement in the 1930s. Starting in North America and Canada, they progressed to New Zealand and Australia before returning home via Jerusalem. An account of their send-off in the *Toc H Journal* was enthusiastic:

> This ten months of their absence from Europe is more filled with incredible possibilities than at any other time since our re birth in 1920 ... . None of us can foretell what the padre adventurers will be led to accomplish around the world before December.[89]

On his return, Tubby was wary of overestimating the results of the tour, but was encouraged by what he found:

> Everywhere Toc H is still beginning or even beginning to begin. Some units, Adelaide for example, have already found their feet, others, especially in the USA, are just struggling for a foothold. The whole future of Toc H overseas

86 LPL, papers of Archbishop Davidson, Vol. 217, f. 130, press release November 2 1927.
87 M. Harcourt, *Tubby Clayton. A Personal Saga*, (London, Hodder & Stoughton, 1953), p.155.
88 Ibid., p.155.
89 *Toc H Journal*, March 1925, vol.3, p.86.

hangs on the steadfastness of group after group of inconspicuous men going about doing what good they may ... in centres which are more materialistic than cities in England.[90]

The *Church Times* in December 1927 commented on the increasing overseas element in the Toc H organisation: "As it seems to us, Toc H should help towards the realisation of a world citizenship which is no longer an utopian dream but the one object of some statesmanship".[91] Tubby's biographer, Tresham Lever, considered that: "By his travels he had given an international significance to the movement that was his life and of which he was the soul".[92]

The high point of the decade of the 1920s was the purchase by Lord Wakefield of the original Talbot House in 1929 and his gift of it to the Toc H movement. Tubby and Toc H had already been organising battlefield trips to the Ypres Salient, and the provision of a base at Talbot House helped provide a focus for remembrance and a practical help to those who wished either to revisit the scene of their war service, or visit the graves of friends and relatives.

In October 1927 Tubby leased a house from the London port authority to become a conference and retreat centre for clergy and also parish and Toc H workers. The *Church Times* thought this a valuable resource "for the use of weary and spiritually tired men and women".[93] On 5 December 1930 the Prince of Wales outlined a scheme for the organisation and administration of Toc H to be put on a permanent basis, with a paid general staff. For this an endowment of £250,000 was needed and an appeal was launched which was broadcast by the BBC. By December 1930 £140,000 had been raised.[94] An editorial in *The Times* expressed its opinion of Toc H's work in the 1920s: "This strangely named body has become in a single decade of peace to stand for much that is simple, vivid and unpretentious in the whole field of applied Christianity."[95]

By 1930 the annual birthday celebrations and festival of light had grown too large and had to be decentralised. The ceremony at Westminster Abbey was confined to the branches of the Greater London area, as there were now forty-six branches and sixty-four groups nationwide. The *Church Times* reported that there were more than 4,000 members in the London area. The 1930 celebrations included the starting of the World Chain of Light. Tubby and some foundation members had travelled to the upper room in Poperinghe and lit the lamp before the altar the previous evening. It was announced in Westminster Cathedral that:

90 Ibid.
91 *Church Times*, 9 December 1927, p.701.
92 Lever, *Clayton of Toc H*, p.140.
93 *Church Times*, 27 October 1927, p.493.
94 *Church Times*, 12 December 1930, p.755.
95 *The Times*, 8 December 1930, p.9.

This night in the upper room of Talbot House there is lighted a lamp. This begins the world chain of light which by tomorrow will have encircled the globe. To far friends and near, the Flanders household flame shall shine, recalling Christ and true men of his name.[96]

The highlight of the celebration at the Albert Hall was the return of Tubby from Poperinghe and the broadcast of his speech to "the world". The *Church Times* said: "Many branches overseas were awaiting its delivery over the ether". During his speech Tubby read a message from the Prince of Wales:

Many years after the Great War, one shortage at least continues, that is the loss of leadership. It is to help in finding and inspiring leadership that Toc H seems to be so significant; and those who would be leaders must learn to lead through Fellowship and service ... I welcome the solid growth accomplished.[97]

In December 1931 the birthday celebrations were held at Crystal Palace. The Prince of Wales talked about the decentralisation of the movement: "Toc H now has a wide-spread responsibility resting at last on local leadership, discovered among its local membership". He mentioned the two projects that Toc H was then involved in, the expansion of the hostel for sea-going boys in Southampton and the clubs for pit boys in the mining districts of Durham.[98] In 1933 Tubby returned from a trip to British West Africa where he became aware of the extent of the problem of leprosy and made an appeal to members on this behalf. As a result it was reported in *The Times*: "Members of Toc H have volunteered to serve for five years without salary in the Leper colonies under the auspices of The British Empire Leprosy Association."[99]

During the 1930s, more reference was made to the increasingly difficult economic situation and the ways in which Toc H could contribute. The Seventeenth Annual Report of Toc H talked about the work of Toc H in the special areas which had been designated by the government as areas of special deprivation. The editorial In the *Toc H Journal* in October 1931 emphasised the role that the organisation could play in what it called "the national crisis":

It is becoming clearer that success in facing our national emergency will depend ... not on financial matters alone, but on the spirit of the people. It is in this situation that Toc H can play a real part. The spirit it claims is precisely what the

96   *Church Times*, 12 December 1930, p.755.
97   Ibid.
98   *The Times*, 8 June 1931, p.14.
99   *The Times*, 23 January 1934, p.8.

nation needs … there will be much need for overtime in voluntary service this winter.[100]

In 1936 Toc H celebrated its coming of age. Tubby wrote a letter to The *Church Times* asking for the prayers of its readers for the coming week of celebrations. He stressed the importance of the corporate communion being organised for Sunday 29 June, with 4,000 Anglicans communicating at All Hallows throughout the morning, and nearby venues arranged for the other denominations. The *Church Times* reported on the week's activities, mentioning the "great service of dedication" held at St Paul's Cathedral. The order of service was described as "An order of service of great beauty – every word meant something". The text of the Archbishop of York's sermon was "If any man would come after me, let him deny himself and take up his cross and follow me." He said that:

> Toc H was born in a fellowship of death and it handed on to successive genera-
> tions, irrespective of rank and class in a common hope and a common allegiance
> to the captain of their destinies: It comes of age as a movement of youth, to
> whom the older men have handed on the torch.

He went to stress that this common heritage must be expressed in worship as well as action. The Crystal Palace was the venue for the celebrations on the Saturday night. Banner bearers and lamp holders in the long procession were from branches in England, Wales, Scotland, Australia, Africa, India, China and South America. The Duke of Kent read a message from the new King, Edward VIII: "The example of the elder statesman it is now for you to make your own: as Toc H stands tonight full grown it must be ready to light those lamps to shed their light in the paths of the future."[101]

The Effect of the Great War on Toc H.

Toc H had "Its birth far back in the furnace",[102] as Tubby put it and it was natural that the ethos developed in the Great War would have an appreciable effect on the development of the organisation. The yearly birthday celebrations were rooted firmly in the remembrance of wartime experience and the fallen "elder brethren". A review of *Plain Tales from Flanders* in 1929 emphasised Tubby's view of the role of the army chaplains in cementing "The comradeship which is established … the common bond of faith", and continued: "Thus was the spirit of Toc H the secret of its success. It bound men

---

100 *Toc H Journal*, October 1931, Vol. 9, p.393.
101 *Church Times*, 26 June 1936, p.806.
102 P. B. Clayton, 'Two Men's Work', *The Smoking Furnace and the Burning Lamp*, p.36.

together in Christian brotherhood."[103] As Tresham Lever, Tubby's biographer put it: "The bond of fellowship forged in the war remained strong between the old members and was jealously preserved."[104] A. C. Jarvis, wartime chaplain and Chaplain General in the post-war years, wrote in February 1928:

> I am proud to reflect that Toc H is the child of the Royal Army Chaplins'Department. Its founder was one of us, and went forth under our banner and, as such, was the instrument used of God to bring into being an organisation which, I consider, the embodiment of the greatest religious movement of this age, the distinctive glory is that it had won and linked up a vast residuum of young manhood untouched by organised Christianity.[105]

Talbot House, the war-time ethos and the need for remembrance were apparent in much of the development of the new Toc H. As Lieutenant-Colonel A. M. Murray Smith from the Cheltenham branch commented:

> At the front in the war we were extraordinarily happy because we had found our feet for perhaps the first time in our lives in service for others. Now we are civvies, things seem bleak, we miss our objective and we miss the clear sense of working unselfishly together for a common object. Without Toc H we should feel, many of us, desperately lonely.[106]

Barclay Baron felt that there was a distinct sense that this service and comradeship felt during the war should be able to continue in peace time. He wrote: "If these precious things, almost the only credits of war, were suffered to slip away in peacetime, their world they felt would have been hardly worth fighting for."[107] There seemed to be a distinct sense of unwillingness to relinquish the nostalgia for wartime comradeship, of the unacceptability for some of its former inhabitants that the Talbot House atmosphere should fade away.

The ethos of remembrance within Toc H seems to have been clearly understood outside the movement also. The editorial in the *Church Times on* 2 December 1927 reports on the ceremony of presenting original wooden crosses from war graves, these having been replaced by Imperial War Graves Commission (IWGC) headstones, to each newly commissioned branch. The editorial comments that these were "constant

---

103 *Church Times,* 18 October 1929, p.460.
104 Lever, *Clayton of Toc H,* p.102.
105 LPL, papers of Archbishop Davidson, Vol. 217, f.158, memorandum from the Chaplain General, 27 February 1928.
106 Baron, *Birth of a Movement,* p.112.
107 Ibid.

reminders to members of Toc H groups that the spirit of self sacrifice and brotherhood must be preserved and carried on in the tasks and routines of civil life."[108]

In the interwar years Toc H relied to some extent on the cooperation of various groups that had been in the war. Ex-servicemen wanted to retain the sense of comradeship and service experienced and saw in the movement a perfect vehicle for this. As Toc H grew it also benefitted from the work of former chaplains. Pat Leonard DSO,[109] who had been chaplain at Cheltenham College, resigned and became a full-time provincial member of staff and leader of the Manchester branch. Padre Goodwin,[110] formerly of the Little Talbot house at Ypres, who had seen service in Mesopotamia, worked for Toc H in Newcastle and Hugh Sawbridge,[111] who had been a chaplain with the Leicester Brigade, went to Leicester and started a Toc H branch there which resulted in the setting up of Mark XI. Throughout this era also establishment figures with war backgrounds such as Lord Plumer, Lord Salisbury, and Bishop Neville Talbot also played an important role in raising awareness of Toc H. An important source of support was the Prince of Wales, who never failed either to appear at the birthday celebration or send a message. His constant themes in these messages were the links between remembrance and looking towards the future. The abdication of the King in December 1936 came as a blow to Toc H. Lord Salisbury wrote to Tubby on 26 December: "We in Toc H have a great debt of gratitude to the former Prince of Wales, and you probably have been in despair at the blow."[112] The Toc H Annual Report of 1937 placed on record "The debt of affection and gratitude which Toc H owes it first patron, H.R.H. the Duke of Windsor, for his sincere belief in the meaning and purpose of the movement."[113]

However, it was realised that the emphasis on war and remembrance should not be the main one. There was concern that it should not become merely an ex-serviceman's organisation. It was essential that it capture the hearts and minds of a new generation. One of Tubby's major post-war themes, however, was the idea of the younger brother taking on the challenge and having to bear double the burden: "Let the younger brother know that there lies on him not only one man's work but two and sonship and service will be rendered with diligence that will know no rein."[114] This concept cleverly combined reverence for the wartime origins of the movement with emphasis on its post war role. H. Hubbard spoke in a similar vein to a group of public school boys on holiday in Switzerland in 1927.

108 *Church Times*, 2 December 1927, p.686.
109 M. P. Leonard, TCF 1914-1918, DSO 1916, *Crockford's*, p.812.
110 A. R. Goodwin, TCF 1918-1919, *Crockford's*, p.516.
111 H. F. Sawbridge, TCF 1915-1919, MC 1916, *Crockford's*, p.1188.
112 Lever, *Clayton of Toc H*, p.206.
113 University of Birmingham, Toc H Archive, Toc H Annual Report 1927, Section G1, p.7.
114 *The Times*, 29 October 1920, p.15.

It is true that Toc H came out of the Great War, but is equally true to say that today it is no more an ex-serviceman's show than the Red Cross or the Boy Scout movement. On the contrary it is a youth movement and will stand or fall not on the doings of its members who served in the Great War, but on the spirit and vigour of its younger members.[115]

The main principles of Toc H as it emerged in the immediate post-war years were the continuance of the fellowship of the war years and the encouragement of men of all different classes and outlooks to work together in improving society through fellowship, fair-mindedness and service. The *Church Times*, in an editorial written in December 1926, tried to sum up the ethos of the movement:

> The ideal around which Toc H is built is eminently Christian. The movement is a war movement but does not exist to revive old antagonisms or fight old battles again. It is just the simple constant reminder of the fine dead of the fine fellows who marched away … and who never made home again. The fellows who are left behind, inherit a responsibility as they inherit a fine tradition. The idea of Toc H is that this responsibility of service shall be regarded as the jolliest and most splendid of duties.[116]

Always in Tubby's writings and speeches the effect of his war service was apparent. He felt strongly that the ethos of companionship experienced by those who visited Talbot House should inform the service and fellowship of the younger generation, and that their sacrifices should somehow be reflected in the work of their younger brothers and friends.

Toc H and the Social Gospel.

In a report on Toc H in Glasgow in 1926, the Rev G. F. Macleod gave an insight into the many jobs in the community that the ethos of service and job mastery had given rise to:

> Toc H is finding personnel for a boy's club in Glasgow, and scout masters. It had ten men going around the houses of the blind, keeping their wireless sets in order. Once a month it entertains crippled children in the Toc H rooms. Toc H men are running the only Rover troop started among Borstal boys in prison. One member is tutoring another for a forthcoming examination.[117]

---

115 H. Hubbard, 'Toc H What it is and What it Might become', in *The Smoking Furnace*, p.53.
116 *Church Times*, 17 December 1926, p.715.
117 G. F. Macleod 'Toc H, A Report from Glasgow in 1926', in *The Smoking Furnace*, p.85.

George Macleod explained that every man who joined Toc H understood what service is. At the ceremony of initiation he was asked "What is service?" and he replied, "It is the rent we pay for our room on earth."[118] In an article in *Together* magazine in 1957 entitled "How Tubby Pays his Rent on Earth" George Kent recollected some of the activities performed by Toc H members and groups over the years, including the beginning, in Portsmouth, of live football commentary to hospitals by amateur Toc H football enthusiasts, before football games were widely broadcast.[119]

Macleod also commented on the wide-ranging membership of the movement:

> Toc H has never press-ganged men into attendance, but on different evenings during the course of the years it has had within its walls Borstal boys, the leader of a razor slashing gang, an ex-communist, and one of the best known pick-pockets. In each case they have been brought by a friend of Toc H, but the point is that in no case have they failed to return of their own accord. How far we did them any good we do not know. We do know they did us good. The risk increases the fellowship.[120]

In the Toc H annual report of 1927, under a heading of "a few key facts for a new friends of Toc H" the social objectives were described: "It is 'power house' for social services of every kind, directed in each place by a voluntary Jobmaster. Toc H in no way competes with existing societies; it encourages and trains its members to help them."[121]

The practical effects of the movement on the problems of interwar conditions in industrial and disadvantaged areas and population cannot be quantified. It is intangible because of its diversity and individuality. Both the Toc H members and the recipients of the many and various tasks doled out by the jobmasters felt the beneficial effects.

Another theme of Tubby's was the absence of class and social distinction within Toc H. He wanted the egalitarian nature of the original Talbot House to be replicated in the movement and in society as a whole. He was concerned that despite the fact that in the war "a whole manhood dresses in the same colour and had to stand in the same colour mud",[122] post-war society was divided on class lines once more. As G. F. Macleod put it in a Toc H service in Glasgow:

---

118 Ibid., p.82.
119 George Kent, 'How Tubby Pays his Rent on Earth', *Together*, June 1957, p.43.
120 Ibid., p.85.
121 University of Birmingham, Toc H Archives, Toc H Annual Report 1927, Section G1, p.7.
122 G. F. Macleod, 'What is Toc H?', p.71.

The kind of distinctions that men had thought were gone were raising their ugly heads again and the war that was to end war looked very much as if it had succeeded only in creating a new form of strife.[123]

Tubby saw Toc H acting as a series of bridges to cross the gulfs of society:

Toc H is in fact, a fourfold bridge built from both ends at once. It is a bridge to leap the gulf which inherited class hatred makes even more disturbing between the young employer and the young employed, and Toc H spans happily from both sides at once. It is a link which is at last beginning to lessen the alienation between the younger men and organised religion. Now Toc H is spanning the wide seas which separate the young men of the empire, pitifully ignorant of one another and lacking any great unifying force.[124]

The classless and egalitarian ethos of Toc H is perhaps one reason why Toc H made little impact in recruiting from the army in the interwar years. Despite the fact that the movement had been born out of the war, it seemed to have little appeal to regular soldiers. In 1930, Tubby complained to Lord Plumer, an influential supporter of Toc H: "We are faced with the pathetic fact that the army as a whole is ignorant of Toc H, and, if anything, rather averse to playing its part in what is rapidly becoming the biggest and most wholesome men's Society in the Empire".[125] Michael Snape is of the opinion that the results of Lord Plumer's subsequent appeal in an Army Council Circular were disappointing: "No doubt because the movement's ethos was still seen as being incompatible with the hierarchical sensibilities of the army especially if it involved such improprieties as officers and private soldiers calling themselves by their Christian names and slapping each other on the back."[126]

Significantly, Lord Plumer's[127] last words to his friend and biographer, Charles Harrington, were: "Build up Toc H in the army."[128]

Although the Toc H movement was ambitious to reform society, it rarely appeared political. In one sense this was a result of its wide appeal to all sections of society, drawing on support from the church establishment, industrial leaders, philanthropists, ex-servicemen and working men. The occupants of the marks and the members of the branches were drawn from a wide variety of social class. Another reason was Tubby's personal attitude to party politics and class struggle. He had no particular

123 Ibid., p.76.
124 *The Times*, 25 November 1925, p.19.
125 Lever, *Clayton of Toc H*, p.164, cited in M. Snape, *God and the British Soldier, Christianity and Society in the Modern World* (London, Routledge, 2005), p.219.
126 Snape, *God and the British Soldier*, p.219
127 Field Marshal Viscount Plumer had visited Talbot House during the war, and became president of the Toc H Committee in 1920. Lever, *Clayton of Toc H*, p.61.
128 Lever, *Clayton of Toc H*, p.166.

political agenda. One of his biographers says that he had "a political disinterestedness bordering on naiveté",[129] and that he made no worthwhile response to the discussions that followed the General Strike in 1926.

However, Tubby was instrumental in setting up in industrial chaplaincies in big corporations in the 1930s, particularly with Anglo Persian Oil and in the Port of London Authority.[130] Neville Talbot thought this work valuable and in a letter in August 1933 to Mervyn Haigh, then chaplain to Archbishop Lang, he described the success of these industrial chaplaincies: "The chaplains really belong to the family. It is quite in line with what the chaplains did in the war who really got inside and came to belong to the military units".[131]

While some former chaplains were busy trying to reform the church in the Life and Liberty Movement and contribute to industrial harmony through the Industrial Christian Fellowship, Tubby's main purpose was to create harmony between different classes and ages through practical work as a memorial to those who were no longer there to do it.

Conclusion

To what extent then can the work of Toc H and the influence of Tubby's vision be attributed to his role as chaplain and the experiences that he and his fellow chaplains had during the war? How important was the organisation in the post-war life of the church and in society?

Tubby's pre-war career predisposed him to champion those who were oppressed and gave him the ability to inspire men to want to serve God and change society. This was also true of many of the chaplains who served in the Ypres sector, had links with Tubby and were to contribute to Toc H by being full-time or voluntary chaplains in the interwar years. The birth of Toc H and its objectives are clearly rooted in Tubby's war experience. His desire to see a continued remembrance of the dead was combined with a determination to challenge class barriers to continue to build a new sort of society is an example of the change that could be effected out of the "furnace" of war. The Rev J. Derbyshire, preaching in 1927, said: "Toc H is almost unique in its endeavour to make permanent all that was best in the temper of the war, and to apply it to the slow and laborious task of rebuilding".[132] In *Two Men's Work* Tubby said, "Alone among the ex-service clubs of today it [Toc H] had its birth far back in the furnace, before the fire grew cold and now is in free and rapid growth ... Socially it faces foursquare to all parts of the compass."[133] The ethos and values of Talbot House

---

129 Harcourt, *Tubby Clayton*, p.185.
130 Lambeth Palace Library, Archbishop Lang Papers, Vol.117, f. 176, letter from Neville Talbot to Mervyn Haigh 14 August 1933.
131 Ibid.
132 J. H. Derbyshire, 'Lift up your hearts' in *The Smoking Furnace*, p.107.
133 *The Times*, 29 October 1920, p.15.

engendered and encouraged these aims and permeated the thinking of the post-war organisation.

Toc H, although an Anglican institution to begin with, became interdenominational with Nonconformist members and chaplains. However, it retained a strong sacramental emphasis with all its major celebrations being preceded by services of Holy Communion. It never became embroiled in the debates about unity and inter-communion, being content to act together but communicate separately. Its whole ethos in worship, was as in action, was to bring men together in a way that made denomination or class irrelevant. *The Times* commented in an editorial in December 1929: "This strangely-named body has become in a single decade of peace to stand for much that is simple, vivid and unpretentious in the whole field of applied Christianity."[134] B. K. Cunningham in a speech to the Toc H staff conference in 1931 criticised the conferences of "like minded" churchmen as not being of much value as far as the development of fellowship was concerned. He also felt that "undenominationalism is a poor, thin thing." Toc H was able to provide fellowship in direct relation to the variety of people from different religious backgrounds "In a joint sharing of the spiritual wealth of Toc H."[135]

Some contemporary opinions give a flavour of how Toc H was esteemed in the interwar years. Edward, Prince of Wales, said in 1921: "Toc H is plainly one of the best things of its kind emerging from the years of sacrifice."[136] Dick Sheppard said in 1921: "It is one of the very few good things to come out of the war."[137] In 1932 Harry Blackburne recalled: "The question sometimes asked was 'has anything good come out of the war?'" His answer was invariably the same: "Yes – Toc H". He continued: "Toc H stood firstly for loyalty to the past, secondly for loyalty to the present and future and thirdly for loyalty to Jesus Christ".[138] William Temple wrote in the *Manchester Guardian* in 1924:

> Toc H is one of the two good things to come out of the war. I don't know, beside the League of Nations, what else there is that was good came out of the war. I believe it to be the best and possibly the only permanent expression of the fellowship realised in the war that we have in this country.[139]

134 *The Times*, December 7 1920, p.4.
135 *Toc H Journal*, October 1931, Vol. 9, p.434.
136 *The Times*, 16 December 1921, p.7.
137 *The Times*, 27 October 1921, p.8.
138 *The Times*, 27 June 1932, p.14.
139 *Manchester Guardian*, 5 February 1924, p.11.

The Chaplain General, A. C. E. Jarvis, described Toc H in 1928 as: "An outflow of the incarnate life of Jesus Christ. Through no other conception can I account for its initial work or its subsequent appeal and triumph."[140]

Toc H was seen by its members as "the redemption of war".[141] It could be said that Toc H was also unique in that it built upon some good things that had come out of the war, as opposed to other post-war initiatives that had their roots in revulsion at the horror of war. Toc H was born in what Tubby called "the furnace of war" but may claim to have become the "living memorial" he wanted. The movement drew its strength from those who remembered the war and wanted to replicate the good in it: comradeship, fellowship and service, but also did its utmost to recreate this fellowship in an outward-looking and heterogeneous organisation, in which there was room for all classes and all shades of Christian opinion. Although in its "Ceremonies of Light" and birthday celebrations it stressed remembrance, in its work in it society it stressed the future. The Bishop of Manchester, William Temple, speaking in 1926, summed it up:

> Of all the movements that came out of the war, Toc H had the truest vitality, because quite unashamedly it had based itself on a remembrance of fellowship, in endurance and in suffering. Memories, however, tended to grow dim, and unless there was something that perpetually reinforced the vitality of the movement it could hardly grow stronger year by year. With remembrance, therefore was coupled the reality of service.[142]

Tubby summed up the ethos of the movement he created. He spoke on the Christian ethos of Toc H at the birthday celebrations in December 1923:

> It is clear that for many years to come that the earthquake love which flows in every vein of this now far reaching society sprung not from the living nor even from the dead but from the very heart of Christ in Flanders.[143]

---

140 LPL, the papers of Archbishop Randall Davidson, Vol. 217, f. 157, memorandum from the Chaplain General, 29 February 1928.
141 J. Derbyshire, 'Lift up Your Hearts', in *Smoking Furnace*, p.107.
142 *Church Times*, 13 December 1923, p.711.
143 *The Times*, 15 December 1923, p.13.

Figure 1 A wartime portrait of Geoffrey
Studdert Kennedy. (RAChD archives)

Figure 2 A wartime portrait of Pat
Leonard. (Leonard family)

Figure 3 Service candidates of the B.E.F. at Le Touquet Ordination Test School, 1919.
(Toc H archives)

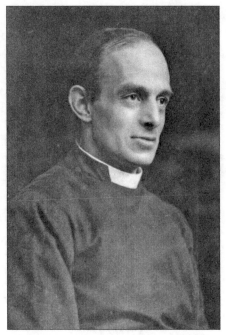

Figure 4 A post-war portrait of F. R. Barry.
(Author's collection)

Figure 5 A post-war portrait of Geoffrey
Studdert Kennedy. (RAChD archives)

Figure 6 Tredegar, South Wales in the 1928 Monmouth ICF Crusade.
(ICF archives)

Figure 7 A wartime portrait of P. B. "Tubby"
Clayton outside Talbot House.
(Toc H archives)

Figure 8 Neville Talbot (left) and P. B.
"Tubby" Clayton outside Talbot House
c.1931. (Toc H archives)

Figure 9 Dick Sheppard at Canterbury
Cathedral c.1929. (Author's collection)

Figure 10 B. K. Cunningham, Principal
of Westcott House 1919-1943.
(Author's collection)

4

Chaplains, Training and Education

The Archbishop of York, Cosmo Gordon Lang,[1] visiting the newly opened "test" ordination school for service candidates at Knutsford in June 1919, was impressed by what he found. He was conscious of the desperate need for more ordinands. His speech was reported in the *Church Times*, and his comments included the opinion that "Unless the services let loose a stream of men to replenish the resources of the church in holy orders", then the church "was done." He said of the prospective ordinands at Knutsford that they were: "Called to the ministry at one of the greatest epochs of the history of the church or the world. They were standing between two worlds, the one gone and the one still to come."[2] The returning chaplains, several of whom were running Knutsford, had, as a result of their war experiences, definite views on the subject and ways of reform.

The role of the Anglican army chaplain came under intense scrutiny from many quarters during and after the war. Criticised by men and officers of the army, chaplains were not immune to criticism also from the church at home and from their own army chaplain leaders. Many chaplains were introspective and critical of their own performance. Many of the more reform-minded chaplains were thinking deeply about the way in which they had been prepared for ordination and the way in which theological colleges in Britain generally prepared their clergy for peace or war. The reaction to C. R. Benstead's denunciation of padres in *Retreat – A Story of 1918*, published in 1930,[3] shows that such a representation or misrepresentation of chaplains was heartily resented and refuted by a wide section of society.[4] The book was criticised

---

1   Cosmo Gordon Lang, Archbishop of York 1909 –1928, Archbishop of Canterbury 1928–1942, *ODNB*.
2   *Church Times*, 20 June 1919, p.755.
3   Charles R. Benstead, *Retreat: A Story of 1918* (Methuen, 1930). One of the main characters in this book, an army chaplain, was portrayed as a weak coward.
4   RAChD, Amport House, scrapbook of press clippings kept by Rev. Dr A. C. E. Jarvis during his time as Chaplain General C. 1930. Section headed: 'Retreat' – C. R. Benstead, controversial letters and criticisms.

by the *Church Times* and the *Guardian*,[5] and P. B. "Tubby" Clayton published a robust rebuttal of the portrayal of the main character in the *Daily Telegraph*, commenting: "Those whom I consulted are agreed with me that the wretched man, if ever selected as chaplain, would have been sent home within two weeks."[6]

The image of the bluff, spiritually incompetent or socially inept chaplain, however, must have had some credence for contemporaries. As we can see by the examples in Bishop Gwynne's and Harry Blackburne's *Army Books*,[7] some chaplains were not cut out for their role. In Blackburne's *Army Book* one chaplain is described as a "rather disappointing man" and another was found "not suitable – rather a grouser".[8] Senior chaplains were well aware of the strains chaplains were under and the need to have a system to ease the situation. Divisional army conferences and retreats, the chaplains' school at St Omer and "chats" with Deputy Chaplain General Gwynne were all part of this system. The difficulties chaplains faced were also to do with the general perception of the clergy in the war and post-war periods. Michael Snape refers to Blackburne's opinion that: "If there was a barrier between chaplains and the other ranks it lay in the fact that the clergy were perceived as remote and aloof figures in civilian life."[9] Inevitably the previous experience and training of some chaplains had not fitted them for their role and returning chaplains could see that the training of the clergy was a question to be addressed. It was Neville Talbot's opinion that: "The church as a society did not set herself either to train or examine closely those who offered themselves for her ministry."[10]

The question of the suitability of the training given to clergy, as with other ideas on church reform and the importance of the social gospel, had been brought into clearer focus by the experiences of chaplains and soldiers in the armed forces. The Fifth Report of the Archbishops' Committee, on *Christianity and Industrial Problems*, maintained that some of the problems clergy faced were because of their social origins: "They should be 'outside class'". To this end the report recommended that: "It is therefore of the first importance that they should possess the pastoral gift of intelligent sympathy to every class in the community the community they are called to serve" and that "clergy should be drawn from every class", being given "training in economic and social science."[11] The report of George Bell on questions posed to chaplains by the Bishop of Kensington in 1916 added its voice to demands for better training for clergy: "Let the theological colleges take a definite line on teaching the clergy to lead and let

---

5   Madigan, *Faith under Fire*, p.15.
6   *Daily Telegraph*, 7 February 1930.
7   University of Birmingham Special Collections, Church Missionary Society Archives, XACC/18/Z/1, 'Army Book' of L. H. Gwynne.
8   RAChD, Amport House, the wartime papers of the Rev H. Blackburne, MC DSO.
9   Snape, *Clergy Under Fire*, p.239.
10   N. Talbot, 'The Training of the Clergy', *The Church in the Furnace*, p.271.
11   The Archbishops' Fifth Committee of Enquiry, *Christianity and Industrial Problems* (London, 1918), p.103.

all the candidates be compelled to go."[12] The Archbishops' Committees' report on *The Evangelistic Work of the Church*, commented on the future training of the ministry: "It is essential that no man should enter upon his ministry without specific training in dealing with souls: this will involve at least some knowledge of moral and ascetic theology and of the psychology of conversion and sanctification."[13]

In a letter to chaplains at the front in 1916, entitled *Ordination after the War*, Archbishop Davidson acknowledged that there were men whose preparation for ordination was suspended by the war and many more for whom "the war has brought for the first time an earnest desire for ordination." This would mean that: "The church of the future recruits for its ministry men of all kinds of upbringing, circumstances and education." This, he admitted, would give rise to "an unusual demand on requirements as to training and examination". The task would not be easy, but the archbishop clearly saw a role for ex-army chaplains in the training process: "It is to this enterprise I invite you when the war is won."[14]

J. C. V. Durrel, the Chief Commissioner of the Church Army in France, wrote in the *Church Times* in December 1918 about the prospect of ordination candidates among ex-servicemen:

> It seems likely that many men, who have passed through the furnace of war and have lived in an atmosphere of motivated self-sacrifice, should find a call to this special consecration of service. They will be men with a message. They will have learnt in such a school as an older generation dreamt of, of what the gospel of Christ crucified means to the world of today.[15]

He reported that, under Bishop Gwynne, "Opportunities have been given for an expression of this vocation with the result that 1600 of the B.E.F. have offered themselves as candidates for Holy Orders." Significantly, Field Marshal Haig had launched an appeal on 14 November 1919 on behalf of a fund for training ex-soldiers for ministry. Durrel concluded: "Near 3,000 men of all ranks have found they have a vocation. They will come to the cure of souls with a firsthand knowledge of every type of man and of the standard of living and thinking which prevail in various classes of society."[16]

Tubby Clayton had been giving some thought to the matter of post-war recruitment since 1915. He admitted that: "Even before the war the number and quality of the candidates for orders had caused grave misgivings." This he blamed on "The miserable

12   The Bishop of Kensington's Report, *The evidence received from chaplains in the Navy and Army in responses they have given to the following letter* (London, 1917), p.31.
13   The Archbishops' Third Committee of Enquiry, *The Evangelistic work of the Church* (London, 1918).
14   RAChD, Amport House, the wartime papers of the Rev H. Blackburne, MC DSO.
15   *Church Times*, 13 December 1918, p.461.
16   Ibid.

penury which the richest church in Christendom was contented to consider adequate for the bulk of its ministers and to the narrow class of society from which they were mostly drawn."[17] Neville Talbot was certainly considering the role that poor training had in the perception of the professionalism of the chaplains at the front in 1917. He was not too critical of the chaplains' role in the war, as he considered that they had won over the troops from a hostile position to one more favourable by a mixture of "devotion, gallantry" and by "methods certainly less reputable such as 'holy grocery'".[18] He held that their experiences in wartime were responsible for their development: "Active service has been a liberal education to them."[19] However, he was critical of the system that produced the chaplains. In his contribution to *The Church in the Furnace*, "The Training of the Clergy", he said: "Unless the Church of England clergy are better trained in the future than in the past, other measures of church reform will be neutralised."[20] Bullock, in his study of ordination training in the era, quoted the former chaplains' opinions:

> Talbot advocated more time, two or three years to be spent by men in theological college, together with a longer diaconate and continued professional guidance. Pym stressed the need to train men as leaders and preachers and as being knowledgeable in practical Psychology and positive Apologetics.[21]

Kenneth Kirk was more robust about the way chaplains performed during the war but also said: "It should be possible in theological colleges to instil more forcibly the avoidance of those tricks, which, both in church and out of it too often make the parson unpleasantly conspicuous. Many chaplains have sloughed them off almost miraculously at the front; cannot they discover some way to scotch them at home?"[22]

In order to gauge the extent to which former chaplains were involved and successful in changing and developing the training of ordinands in the Anglican Church, it is necessary to look at ordination training in the pre-war years and to assess how prepared Anglican priests were, whether for war or parochial life. The supply and training of the clergy had been actively discussed since the end of the nineteenth century, when the recruitment of ordinands was failing to keep pace with industrialisation and population growth. In 1904 the Lower House of Convocation adopted a resolution which recommended that every diocese developed an organisation which would encourage candidates for ordination. The Upper House of Convocation had recommended in 1906 that all clergy should have a degree, but at the Ninth Conference

---

17   Clayton, *Tales of Talbot House*, p.89.
18   Talbot, 'The Training of the Clergy', p.270.
19   Ibid.
20   Ibid., p.269.
21   F. W. Bullock, *A History of Training for the Ministry in the Church of England 1875-1974* (St Leonard's, Home Words Publishing, 1955), p.80.
22   K. Kirk, 'When the Priests Come Home', *The Church in the Furnace*, p.422.

of Divinity Professors, Examining Chaplains and Principals of theological colleges, it was decided that "There is room in the service of the church for persons of very moderate intellectual ability", as long as there was a "wise system of training."[23] In the event, the war resulted in the requirement for degrees to be suspended, initially to 1917, but in practice, indefinitely.

Pre-war ordinands had been ordained after following a variety of training routes. A large number, 57 percent in 1898, were graduates of Oxbridge or Trinity College Dublin, who had been ordained straight from university, or had spent a little time in a theological college such as Cuddesdon and Wycliffe Hall at Oxford or Westcott House in Cambridge. Of 723 chaplains in Gwynne's *Army Book,* 410 were Oxbridge educated.[24] Another postgraduate option was to take part in a more informal training situation in a small group under the tutelage of a bishop or other senior churchman such as J. C. Vaughn at Doncaster, or Samuel Bickersteth at Leeds, both prominent clergy with a reputation for successful training of ordinands. Some ordination candidates had taken theology degrees at the newly emerging and already prestigious universities at London and Durham. Others obtained theology diplomas at Chichester, St Aidans, and St John's Highbury, including Bishop Gwynne and Bishop Taylor Smith. Other possibilities were to obtain an AKC (Associate of King's College,) from King's College London or an LTh from Durham. Mirfield students, after receiving grounding at the College of the Resurrection, usually took a theology degree at the University of Leeds before completing their education at the Community of the Resurrection, Mirfield. Graduates of St David's College, Lampeter, sometimes took a further degree at Oxford or Cambridge, or, after completing a degree at Lampeter, completed their theological and pastoral training at St Michael's College, Aberdare. The Community of the Resurrection at Mirfield and the Society of the Sacred Mission at Kelham stood out, not only because of the young age they took students and the length of their training, but because they took candidates who would have otherwise not have been able to afford to be ordained. Significantly, at Mirfield and Kelham demand for places far outstripped supply. In 1926 Timothy Rees wrote an article in the *Church Times* appealing for funds to build further accommodation for Mirfield students at Leeds University. He commented on the fact that the quality and quantity of ordinands had gone up in the post-war years but that of the fifty candidates selected that year as in theory suitable for training at Mirfield, only twenty could go forward for training because of financial limitations.[25]

Phillip Crick, in his essay 'The Soldier's Religion' in *The Church in the Furnace,* stressed the need to educate the clergy at all levels if the church was to use the "opportunity" presented by the fact that: "Men will be inclined to listen to her [the church's] voice during the process of social reconstruction that must inevitably follow the

---

23   Ibid., p.144-145.
24   Madigan, *Faith Under Fire,* p.67.
25   *Church Times,* 18 January 1926.

war." He continued: "The clergy must be prepared, devotionally and intellectually."[26] He considered that the training of clergy was inadequate, echoing Neville Talbot's complaint that it was too short and not specialised in theology, considering that: "The minimum qualifications for admission to Holy Orders in our church compare most unfavourably with those required in other Churches, or in other callings, such as the medical profession." He called for a "higher level of specialised training even at the cost of a diminution of numbers."[27]

In 1912 the Central Advisory Council of Training for the Ministry (CACTM) was established, to rationalise the different methods of training. However the process of theological training continued to come in for criticism. The Bishop of Liverpool, F. J. Chavasse, commented in the 1901 Church Congress: "There could be no doubt that the present special training of the clergy was often lamentably inadequate. The time is too short and the range of subjects too limited."[28] The charge of non-professionalism was to be one which the chaplains had to face during the war. Neville Talbot was aware of this, and stated his opinion that the chaplains were; "… amateurs. It is not enough. Lack of training, rule of thumb, drift and makeshift will not do. They can only lead to second best."[29] Talbot suggested that more time was needed in theological college, together with a longer diaconate and more time given to professional development. He praised the development of one-year courses in such colleges as Cuddesdon, but thought they were attempting the impossible: "The normal course is only a year long. It is fatally too short", and added: "It is hardly too much to say that the minimum character of training at Theological college create a maximum separation between the clergy and laity. For there is time to contract clerical diseases but not time to get over them."[30] He stressed that the post-war training of ordination candidates would need adequate financing if it was to be successful and that financial provision would be needed for post-ordination training. In B. K. Cunningham's opinion:

> The pre-war theological college system as judged by the padres it produced did not come well out of the experience of war. The devotional training had been along too narrow lines and depended too much on a favourable environment, and when that was no longer given the padre was apt to lose his bearings.[31]

The supply of ordinands declined as a result of the war, as many of those in training had joined up as combatants and prospective candidates had been killed. It was clear to chaplains like Tubby Clayton and Neville Talbot that, as Talbot put it, "The fortunes of the war are going to be vitally bound up with the passing into the ministry

---

26   Crick, 'The Soldier's Religion', *The Church in the Furnace'*, p.365.
27   Ibid., p.366.
28   *The Times*, 8 October, 1901, p.7.
29   Talbot, 'The Training of the Clergy', p.270.
30   Ibid., p.277
31   J. R. H. Moorman, *B. K Cunningham, A Memoir*, (London, SCM Press, 1947), p.103.

of those who have borne arms".[32] Talbot was optimistic about the effect on the church of ex-service candidates for ordination: "Visions arise of a great band of men arising to reinforce the ranks of the ministry – men of tested and grateful faith, experienced in fellowship, converts to discipline. They might be a bridge over the gulf of misunderstanding which divides clergy from laity."[33]

Knutsford

The test school at Knutsford was set up as a response to the growing conviction among both the church at home and chaplains at the front that a way must be found to train the rapidly growing number of servicemen who had expressed a desire to be ordained when the war was over. In 1917, the archbishops pledged to pay for the training of ordinands, many of whom would not have been able to afford it in normal circumstances. R. V. H. Burne said of the scheme:

> It was the first time that the church, acting as a corporate body, officially provided and financed a scheme of training for its ordination candidates. For the first time it was to show that poverty was not a bar to ordination.[34]

Tubby Clayton had carefully recorded the names and nurtured the vocations of many of the possible candidates and, from 1916 onwards, George Partridge of the Central Church Fund had been working on the finances. Chaplain J. V. Macmillan assisted Tubby in devising a school to gather those who had expressed an interest and to test their suitability. E. S. Woods, who had been a chaplain at the Royal Military Academy at Sandhurst during the war, was involved in the interviewing of service candidates coming forward for ordination in 1919.

> One of my main duties was to sift the candidates, in consultation with their own CFs and decide whether they should be demobilised and sent back to begin their training at home, or whether, their vocation being less certain to themselves and less apparent to me, should be kept for a period of training at an army theological school which we hope to get going before long.

Woods was impressed by the quality of the candidates:

> I can't tell you how profoundly I have been touched by many of the men There is truly wonderful material here for the church to train and use ... I can't help

---

32 Talbot, 'The Training of the Clergy', p.285.
33 Ibid., p, 286.
34 R. V. H. Burne, *Knutsford. The Story of the Ordination Test School 1914-1940* (London, SPCK, 1959), p.ix.

feeling that the coming into the ministry of many of these splendid fellows is going to be of one of the factors that are going to renovate the old church.[35]

During his time in France, E. S. Woods covered 2,100 miles and interviewed 280 candidates out of the 400 the church accepted for testing.[36]

F. R. Barry was appointed Chief Instructor at the temporary camp set up at Le Touquet, where there was a dearth of educational equipment and students learnt their Greek alphabet by writing the letters in the sand. Twelve of the assistant instructors under Barry were, or had been, army chaplains. B. K. Cunningham spent a night at the newly opened school and reported in his diary that Barry and his staff had "The institution well in hand – about 70 men – not much to work with but exceedingly happy." Barry, in his foreword to the *Le Touquet Times*, the magazine of the school camp, explained that: "The church has made a big experiment of which there should be a printed record."[37] The magazine also has a report on the Archbishop's message on visiting the school on 5 January 1919. The Archbishop is reported as saying:

> You are sharers with me in the tremendous responsibilities of these days. Each of you has a tremendous responsibility upon you, not only because of the peculiar opportunities of the calling which you are preparing yourselves to follow, but because of the greatness of the times, because of the deep significance of the foundations which must now be laid on the ruins of broken civilisation.

This spirit of optimism and sense of significance was echoed by Barry. "I firmly believe that we have started here a fellowship which will last all through our lives. Years hence we shall look back on Le Touquet as on the watershed of a great river ... we must always remain a band of brothers."[38] The magazine contained a spoof letter purporting to be one mislaid by a student, but actually providing a humorous vehicle by which the reader would be able to become acquainted with the routine at the camp:

> We are a motley crew, from many divisions and every sort of unit ... I was chosen for a "trial spin", and landed here just before Christmas with about seventy others in like case. We now number 170 ... We get up at about 7.00, earlier on celebration mornings. At 7.30 we are summoned ... to family prayers in the chapel. The morning is spent in lectures and classes; sometimes we wrestle with the mysteries of Greek grammar ... Sometimes our Science instructor leads us to the

35   Ibid., p.45.
36   Oliver Tomkins, *Edward Woods* (London, SCM Press, 1957), p.45.
37   Cheshire County Record Office, R. V. H. Burne Collection, *Le Touquet Times*, Jan 1919.
38   Ibid.

heights of scientific enquiry. Sometimes the History man gives us a rapid survey of ancient history from Noah to Nebuchadnezzar.[39]

After physical jerks at 12.00, dinner was served and in the afternoon free time was spent in football matches, or walking by the sea or visiting Le Touquet. More lectures after tea were followed by Evensong and a simple supper. Before lights out concerts or debates were held and prayers at 9.30. The letter was also possibly intended to encourage more candidates for ordination as a section as its end read: "… you would just love this place and all the cheery comradeship of it. Perhaps when you get back from Mesopotamia, you will look us up?" The letter was an alternative and humorous way of explaining and publicising the school and although it was supposed to be from "Bill" to "Dick" it is not hard to see the style of Tubby Clayton throughout.[40]

F. W. Foxley Norris, writing in the *Church Times* in 1921 in response to a letter of criticism about Knutsford, explained:

> In 1918 there were a large number of candidates from the army and navy, about two-thirds of them needed pecuniary help. Most of them had left school long ago and passed no exams since. If a great deal of money was not to be wasted it was essential that we devise some means of finding out whether they were intellectually capable of making good use of the grants. Let it be once and all understood that Knutsford is not in any sense a theological college, neither is it a necessary step in every ordination candidate's training. It supplied and still supplies a want.[41]

Tubby was despatched to find permanent accommodation in England and in March 1919 the school moved to Knutsford Gaol, Cheshire. Barry, who was not yet thirty and very aware of his "vast new responsibility", gathered an eclectic and talented staff around him. Several of the leading figures had been army chaplains. Mervyn Haigh returned from service in East Africa to join the staff; Tubby Clayton was, of course, present and they were joined by former chaplains J. F. Clayton,[42] and F. M. 'Psycho' Sykes. Sykes had agreed to join them for a while before returning to his parish. E. S. G. Wickham was among those army chaplains who were summoned by Barry to take part in the great venture. He recollected in 1938: "I was a chaplain in Germany after the war. I suddenly got a letter from F. R. Barry asking me to join. I wrote back and said 'It sounds very interesting and jolly, but I have not taught anything, and I

39   Ibid.
40   Ibid.
41   *Church Times*, 6 January 1921, p.298.
42   J. F. Clayton, TCF 1916-1919, *Crockford's*, p.251.

am rather deaf.'" He received the answer from Barry: "We have none of us taught anything, and I am deaf too. Come!"[43]

Barry realised that the difficulties of the operation were immense and felt a mixture of apprehension and enthusiasm. Later he recalled: "I shall never forget Evensong on the first night when we assembled in the parish church and sang Psalm 126: 'When the Lord turned again the captivity of Sion, then were we like unto them that dream. Then was our mouth filled with laughter and our tongue with joy.'"[44] In his own memoir, *Period of my Life*, Barry remembered his feelings of inadequacy:

> So we opened our doors and the first batch came in. Now that we had them, what were we to do with them? We might hope to learn methods as we went along, but we had to be pretty clear in our objectives.[45]

The staff, however, were optimistic. R. V. H. Burne, who was in later years to be principal, said: "Under the inspiring leadership of our chief and with the sense of power begotten by fellowship we believed that we should be able to make an impact on the Church of England and bring it new life and a more up to date look. The world was at our feet."

Barry, writing in the first edition of *Ducdame*, the magazine of the test school, was conscious of the roots of the test school as a direct response to the challenges caused by war: "It is into this world, shaken by war from its complacent materialism into a state of uncertainty and self distrust, that school has been launched."[46] Haigh, writing in later years, linked the success of the school to the common experience of war shared by all: "All those at Knutsford had been delivered in varying degrees from the same fiery furnace ... We had been gathered out of the heart of a great tragedy into the heart of a great opportunity."[47]

Burne was in charge of the curriculum and devised, with the help of Fr. Frere of the Community of the Resurrection, a test exam that would be accepted as entrance to university or theological college. Barry kept the religious instruction firmly under his wing and lectured every morning to the whole school. He remembered:

> Ostensibly it was biblical exposition, with the aim of making the bible come alive for them. But in fact I was telling them everything I knew and everything I wanted them to know about the real meaning of Christianity and its significance for the contemporary world.

43   London Metropolitan Archives, A talk on the History of the school given by E. S. G. Wickham at a meeting in London 6 December 1938.
44   F. R. Barry, Preface to R. V. H. Burne, *Knutsford*.
45   Barry, *Period of My Life*, p.70.
46   Cheshire County Record Office, D 3917/32, *Ducdame*, the magazine of the Ordination Test School at Knutsford, Issue one, summer 1919.
47   Barry, *Mervyn Haigh*, p.67.

Tubby Clayton, in his *Plain Tales from Flanders*, gave some idea of the practical difficulties involved in using the prison. He described the buildings. "The elephantine humour of its long-forgotten and forgiven architect built this stupendous nightmare in the shape of a K, each arm of which contained upon 4 floors about 200 cells." For a while study in the cells, which had become bedrooms and studies was impossible because the gas lights were situated outside the cells. He recounts, however, that the practical difficulties were soon overcome by men who had been used to the trenches. A cartoon pinned up on the notice board at one point depicted a man with head in hands in a prison cell with the caption: "What has brought him to this?" Beneath it was written "The Church of England".

The school was divided into houses each bearing the name of a prison wing. Tubby's house was B.1V and consisted of members, including a colonel, a naval commander, several junior officers, some NCOs and some riflemen and privates. The strict daily regime, which began at 6.45 a.m. and ended at 9.30 p.m., was leavened by an atmosphere of gaiety and sometimes horseplay, often at the instigation of Tubby or Mervyn Haigh. Plays and operettas were devised and performed. The atmosphere can be deduced from the title of the magazine, *Ducdame* being "A Greek invocation for the calling of fools into a circle."[48] The mixture of academic improvement, riotous enthusiasm, non-judgmental fellowship and a deep spiritual core to be found at Knutsford can have come as no surprise to those who had spent any time at Talbot House during the war.

On 5 December 1919 a letter to the editor of the *Church Times* from a "Knutsfordian" referred to previous criticism in the paper about Knutsford's reputation for levity and jollity engendered by its magazine *Ducdame*. He responded: "You state that *Ducdame* gives the impression of riotous confusion and that preparation for the priesthood is taken as great jest. This you feel does the school an injustice." He went on, "Would you suggest we drop the joyous jesting and adopt funeral seriousness?" He explained that: "Just as the army was a collection of civilians in uniform, so Knutsford is a collection of soldiers in civvies. They are just ordinary beings who feel called to the priesthood."[49] He went on to describe his own experience at Knutsford. "The day was beautifully balanced without ostentation. Every morning there was a half hour silence, followed by a daily celebration and a set time for meditation. Every evening saw the church full." This view of Knutsford is supported by a report in the *Challenge* in May 1920, which comments on the fellowship and common life of the school.

> Conceive of a body of 300 men, all with the same experience behind them, consecrated to the same tremendous aim, men of all types. All kinds of upbringing

---

48   *Ducdame,* Issue One, summer 1919.
49   *Church Times,* 5 December 1919, p.538.

sharing the common life ... and you will realise something of its intensity. ... It is perhaps the closest fellowship that exists in England at the moment.[50]

Mervyn Haigh wrote of his experience there: "Nothing can qualify my own conviction that in the community of faith, worship and work ... of which I was a member at Knutsford had a part in such a manifestation, such a living embodiment of fellowship of spirit, as I have never had part of before nor have I ever had part in since to the same extent."[51] When Tubby left to start the post-war Toc H organisation he took the school prayer to adapt as the Toc H prayer. In his sermon to the Toc H Festival in June 1931 he commented on the fact that the prayer had been designed for those who would be rejected for training for ordination, as well as those hoping to go forward:

> I want you to remember that the prayer was written for the most part for men hoping to be ordained, but it had much for the rejected candidates. 'Rejected' did not mean at Knutsford what it ordinarily means. It did not mean that they were less good candidates. It simply signified that they could not get through the examinations and degrees. They were better suited to serve God in other ways.[52]

The school at Knutsford was not immune to controversy and criticism, not least from the colleges who had been struggling with the financial implications of training men who had not the educational or financial means to go forward for ordination without benefit of the central fund. There were regular advertisements in the *Church Times* from Mirfield and Kelham appealing for funds for their work in training ordinands who were without means. It was realised, however, that Knutsford in due course would provide theological colleges with candidates to be trained. An article in the *Manchester Guardian* in April 1920 defended the record and usefulness of the school:

> Some of the theological colleges complained that Knutsford was a wasteful system of education, carried on while they themselves remain empty. This was only temporary. These same colleges are now practically full and partly with Knutsford men. The suggestion of a 'wasteful system' also falls to the ground since the colleges could not have done ... the preliminary work as cheaply as Knutsford, where the cost is down to the minimum.[53]

The *Challenge* newspaper also praised Knutsford in May 1920, commenting on its role as a successful pre-university and ordination institution. It reported that so far there were sixty Knutsford students at Oxford or Cambridge, fifteen at Durham, seven

50   *Challenge*, 7 May 1920 p.3.
51   Barry, M*ervyn Haigh* p.66.
52   *Toc H Journal*, Vol 9, 1931 p.329.
53   *Manchester Guardian*, 30 April 1920, p.434.

at Leeds, thirty-five at Manchester, seven at Bristol and twenty at King's College London. There were Knutsford men at some Welsh universities and at Cheshunt, Salisbury, St John's Highbury, and Kelham. Six hundred and seventy-five men passed through Knutsford, out of which 435 were eventually ordained. The report in the *Challenge* commented: "There is no doubt that it saved the church from serious disaster, especially in the years 1921-24."[54] Of the men ordained during this time 40 percent were ex-servicemen, mostly from Knutsford. The *Manchester Guardian* summed up their contribution:

> The insistent call of the clergy for increased salaries is accompanied by an equally insistent cry for help from the churches and parishes. Were it not for Knutsford there would be no immediate hope of supplying any but the smallest part of that help.[55]

An editorial in the *Manchester Guardian* on 20 February 1920 commented on the dropout rate of ex-service candidates. "There is little room for surprise that out of the 3,330 men on the list of the service candidates committee, 1,421 have abandoned the desire for ordination or have been found unsuitable." But it also made the point that: "Discouragements from entering the priesthood are many and sore: only burning zeal or a private income is likely to outweigh the drawbacks."[56] After numerous debates in the National Assembly, It was decided that the test school should continue at Knutsford until 1921 and Barry was able to announce this in the July 1920 edition of *Ducdame*:

> This astonishing voyage has not ended. Again the church has had the big vision. The school will continue in existence till December, 1921 and lads from the generation after ours ... are to be made free of our brotherhood. It is, admittedly, an experiment and it is for use to justify it. But it marks a real turning point in the official policy of the Church of England. Kelham and Mirfield have been doing it for years. But for the first time since the reformation the church in her corporate capacity has given boys of every section of society ... to realise a vocation to the ministry.[57]

Barry recalled a reunion of Knutsford men in 1969. In that year there were 450 priests in active work or recently retired who began their training at Knutsford. These figures probably included ex-students of the college at Harwarden, where the college moved in 1926 after several years based in a house near Knutsford. The Knutsford students

---

54   *Challenge,* May 1920, p.3.
55   *Manchester Guardian* 30 April 1920, p.434.
56   *Manchester Guardian,* 20 February 1920.
57   *Ducdame,* editorial, July 1920.

had gone all over the world, several becoming bishops, including Bishop Leonard Wilson of Birmingham, Bishop Ambrose Reeves of Johannesburg and Bishop George Clarkson of Pontefract.[58] Despite the difficulties that could have arisen when ex-servicemen of widely differing backgrounds were placed in the hothouse atmosphere of Knutsford in less than ideal conditions, Barry had felt from the beginning that all would be well:

> For the salient fact about life in Knutsford prison was that it was a *Koinonia* experience. With a tragedy shared in common behind them and a common hope and expectancy before them, the pattern of the resurrection, they could hardly avoid being welded into a close and exhilarating friendship … no ground could possibly have been more favourable for building up a dynamic community."[59]

The initiatives at Le Touquet and Knutsford and the success of the test school bear witness to the desire of the chaplains to build on the more successful aspects of their work during the war and to ensure that the Church of England was provided with clergy who, despite their social or educational background, would bring their wartime experiences to the work of post-war reconstruction.

B. K. Cunningham

The work of B. K. Cunningham at Westcott House was another strand of the former army chaplains' concern with the training of the clergy, different from, but complementary to, the work at Knutsford. Cunningham had been warden of an intimate and elite theological hostel at Farnham. At the time of the reunion of the Farnham Hostel men in 1913, 105 men had been trained there. Cunningham's biographer, Moorman, said of these years: "His genius for friendship and his faculty of winning the affection and loyalty of his men has resulted in a new kind of community".[60] The war resulted in the closure of the hostel and Cunningham became the much admired and loved leader of the "Chaplains' Bombing School" – the retreat centre for army chaplains at St Omer. Between the school opening in February 1917 and its closing in March 1919, 873 chaplains visited the school and gained spiritual refreshment and intellectual stimulus under Cunningham's benign direction.

At the end of the war, Cunningham was asked to talk to the chaplains who were just about to embark on the Knutsford adventure. He spoke of the "common life" which had been such a feature of Farnham: "Our part is to be careful nurses of the common life, to keep that healthy and strong, and to see that no individual is allowed to stand apart from it." He continued by emphasising the need to develop priests with their own distinctive personality. "First the making of the man and then the priest

---

58   Barry, *Period of my Life*, p.77.
59   Ibid., p.71.
60   Moorman, *B. K. Cunningham, A Memoir*, p.48.

must be built on the man."[61] He reminded the new staff of Knutsford of the influential nature of their task:

> Reverence and individuality work from within outward, and when we correct a man it is better, when possible to let it be self correction ... you will be terrified at the extent to which these boys look to you. You will have tremendous power; be careful not to use it. Influence yes, but power, no.[62]

In 1919 Cunningham was asked to be the principal of Westcott House in Cambridge. Unlike Talbot, he did not value professionalism in the clergy, preferring to concentrate on the individuality of the priest. In his first Embertide letter at Westcott House he wrote:

> I am anxious too, that men ordained from this place, to whatever school of thought they belong, should be above all else *real* in character and belief and worship. It is, as those of us who have been chaplains know well, the strong and wholesome demand of this generation.[63]

He was determined that the college should have no church party bias and made sure that men from all kinds of churchmanship were included among the students. He did not want his students to be exclusive and only mix with like-minded men. Moorman commented: "To B. K.'s way of thinking, such men were losing something fundamental to true Anglicanism, and he was determined that while they were at Westcott house, if never afterwards, they should learn to mix with men of a different churchmanship from their own and understand something of the other's point of view."[64] An example of his fair-mindedness on issues of churchmanship was the fact that when vestments were to be introduced into the chapel in 1929, they were to be used three times a week but no one was to know in advance when those times would be.

Cunningham chose H. E. Wynn as his vice-principal, an ex-chaplain whom he had got to know in France. As at many of the theological colleges, the candidates after the war contained a large contingent of ex-servicemen who had faced the reality of life and death on the battlefields. However, during the 1920s the intake of the college became more varied. These were not the "English gentlemen" who had dressed for dinner at Farnham Castle and, according to Moorman, Cunningham had difficulty adjusting. In his diary in 1924 he wrote:

---

61   Ibid., p.52.
62   Ibid., p.53.
63   Ibid., p.96.
64   Ibid., p.100

I rather think our "Knutsford" element is too numerous and out of proportion to public school men. I come to the end of term with some sense of relief and a deepening feeling that that I am much to blame for not being able to care for those who are not by birth gentlemen.[65]

However, he adjusted eventually and was able to work well with the changed conditions. He continued to supervise several generations of ordinands until his retirement in 1943.

Christopher Chavasse

In 1922, Christopher Chavasse was invited to return to his roots and become rector of St Aldates in Oxford. The living was augmented by the overseeing of the Oxford Pastorate, which catered for the needs of evangelical Christian students. The Bishop of Oxford, at Chavasse's institution and induction, spoke of his war record: "Without exaggeration, for gallantry in the field, service and self-sacrifice there is none who has shown greater powers of leadership and has given a nobler example of gallantry, endurance and self-sacrifice than your new rector."[66]

At the Islington conference[67] on 18 January 1926, Chavasse's father, Bishop F. J. Chavasse,[68] spoke about the vision he had for a new Oxford college where students could be trained for ordination in an evangelical atmosphere and tradition. The donations he received as a result of this speech enabled his tentative plans to go ahead. It was proposed that St Peter's Le Bailey become the college chapel and Christopher Chavasse was invited to become the incumbent, holding it in plurality with St Aldates. Bishop Chavasse died in February 1928 and Chavasse decided to resign from St Aldates and dedicate himself to the task of setting up St Peter's Hall, establishing it as a memorial to his father. He put the scheme to the vice chancellor, stating:

Its primary objects are to promote religion and education generally and especially to assist students of limited means, to encourage candidates for Holy Orders and missionary work abroad, and to maintain the principles of the Church of England as set forth in the Book of Common Prayer.[69]

The first provisional council of trustees met during the Trinity term of 1928 and even though the new buildings would not be in place by the Michaelmas term, Chavasse put an advertisement in the press announcing an entrance exam. Thirteen students were accepted as a result and St Peter's rectory was used as a hostel, the aim being to achieve

---

65 Moorman, *B. K. Cunningham, A Memoir*, p.105.
66 Gummer, *The Chavasse Twins*, p.86.
67 Annual Evangelical Conference instigated in 1860 in Islington but taking place in Church House Westminster from 1920.
68 Francis Chavasse, evangelical Bishop of Liverpool 1900-1923, *ODNB*.
69 Gummer, *The Chavasse Twins*, p.114.

the status of a permanent private hall as quickly as possible. As a result, the arrangements for academic studies of the new students had to be supervised by the censor of non-collegiate students. The decree which was to be presented to Convocation in January was published in the *University Gazette* in December 1928. When, in January 1929, the application for a licence granting private hall status came before the university convocation, the discussion did not proceed as smoothly as hoped. The new college had come under attack from some Anglo-Catholic academics, led by Dr K. E. Kirk, as it was feared that the hall would have too much of an evangelical influence in the Tractarian stronghold of Oxford. However, a vote was taken and the application for a licence to become a university private hall was granted by 260 votes to 60.[70]

By the end of its first year St Peter's had forty students with three resident tutors and their master, Chavasse. Chavasse realised that St Peter's would not attract students of high academic ability as it had no scholarships and no fund to provide them. Therefore in order to raise the profile of the college he offered place to students of outstanding sporting ability. As well as making its mark in the sporting life of the university, St Peter's became, as Chavasse had hoped, a focus for evangelical students and ordinands. A group of students meeting at the college, constituting what Gummer called "a wave of religious enthusiasm", organised a meeting at Oxford Town Hall in November 1933 in which: "The town hall was packed, whilst half the university listened in complete silence to the personal testimony of five undergraduates, who were prominent leaders at the union or in different branches of sport."[71] Chavasse reported his feelings to the council after this event. He regarded the founding of St Peter's Hall, which went on to become St Peter's College, as one of his greatest achievements. "You can do things in Oxford ... which have results all over the world. And what can be more influential than shaping the lives of young men who are to be the leaders of the future?"[72] These were poignant words from a man who had seen his own twin brother and so many other potential leaders of the twentieth century die in the trenches.

Throughout the interwar years former chaplains continued to concern themselves with the next generations of clergy. At a Kelham College's anniversary in London in 1935, C. Salisbury Woodward, by then Bishop of Bristol, made some criticisms of the existing system of training ordinands: "The Bishop felt that the time has come to overhaul her machinery in order to ensure men shall be properly prepared for the work of leading souls." He thought that the system of selections of ordinands was haphazard, especially in the case of the 40 percent who did not apply for financial help. In their case the decision was left up to themselves and the heads of theological colleges. Salisbury Woodward advocated the setting up of regional selection boards: "Composed of one or two bishops and heads of theological colleges and one or two laymen, before everyone who offers himself for holy orders must appear." His second

70   Ibid., pp.116-117.
71   Ibid., p.123.
72   Ibid., p.128.

point dealt with the actual training, which he considered to be too intellectual and not practical enough. He thought that the training given to an ordinand overlooked the fact that :"His chief work will not be to give reasons for the faith that is in him, or argue with atheists, but to live among simple souls, going about doing good and building up the Kingdom of God." He advocated also training in Christian psychology and more time to be given to pastoral work: "Training that will equip them for preparing lads for confirmation, for dealing with the spiritual difficulties of visiting the sick and dying".[73] He concluded by asking for a longer period of training. This emphasis on pastoral and psychological training, emphasising the practical aspects of relation-ships with people has an echo of the lessons learned by many of the chaplains from their wartime experiences. In a slight contrast, Kenneth Kirk, speaking at the same occasion dwelt on the necessity of ordinands to be trained to take on the "Platonists" in society who thought of the church "as a sort of celestial Rotarian society", and were inclined to take the jolly and pleasant parts of the Christian gospel, ignoring the "unpalatable sterner aspects". Kirk deplored this trend and commended the more "Monastic training centres such as Kelham", to fight the trend of materialism and "Keep alight the Christian lamp of learning and civilisation."[74]

In 1929 William Temple chaired an ecumenical conference, the Conference on Preparation for the Ministry, at York. The conference received letters from a wide spectrum of clergy from all denominations, including some former chaplains. B. K. Cunningham wrote that although the training in devotional matters in Anglican theological colleges was good, the standard of intellectual and theological ability of the students varied considerably. However, he pointed out that this posed questions and a dilemma:

> Of the ten men ordained from this college at Advent, four had taken first class in their respective Triposes. The ten are now working … in typical English parishes, and it can hardly be claimed that the honours men appear to function more efficiently than the pass men. Is the system at fault? Ought there to be a differentiation of ministry from the start?[75]

Charles Raven also warned against a complacent attitude: "It is dangerous to suggest that no really radical changes are needed." He considered that: "It is not enough to study Theology in terms of Bible and Creeds and then to get a smattering of popular Science and Sociology: we must somehow relate our Theology to the actual outlook and circumstances of today: and this we have hardly began to do."[76]

---

73   *Church Times*, 20 September 1935, p.336.
74   Ibid.
75   Nottinghamshire Record Office, DD 1332/112/4, pamphlet, *Conference on the Preparation of the Ministry*, (month unknown) p.2.
76   Ibid., p.1.

Academic Theology

As some former chaplains were concentrating on the training of ordinands others were making contributions to education by breaking new ground in theological thinking, both in doctrinal matters and moral and pastoral issues. Robert Keable, writing about a discussion he had with another chaplain during the war on religious reading material, said:

> There is not a shadow of a doubt that the body of religious men who, before the war, thought that religion wanted restating, and the religion of the Church of England, especially, refining, have come into their own. They have found an excuse for articulation and an opportunity such as no reformers of our day have ever had.[77]

Charles Raven had returned from the trenches with his life view altered and some of his theological assumptions challenged. Like Studdert Kennedy he was critical of the concept of the impassibility of God, and in his article, *The Holy Spirit*, written at the front, he emphasised this, basing his argument on Romans 8, v v.18-28, with its language of cosmic struggle. In 1923 his book, *Appolinarianism*, which was an attempt to rehabilitate the reputation of the early Christian heretic, Appolinarius, earned him a Cambridge DD. This book was well received by the critics as an important contribution to English theology. Meanwhile he had been developing his ideas on how the church and society needed to change. In an essay called "The New Reformation", which was first published in the *Challenge* and later published in *Anglican Essays*, he set out his ideas both for the post-war world and for the incorporation of the physical sciences into theology. He wrote of "The tyranny of materialism", and the task of the church to act to create a revival of "life in all its aspects". He continued, "The new physical sciences have rendered as untenable the traditional ideas of authority, of the supernatural, of miracles, and in fact the whole matter of God's operation …".[78] His attitude was one of acceptance of the modern scientific methods of observation, experiment criticism and verification. He was critical of the theology taught at university, commenting: "As if a detailed study of the authorship of Isaiah or the manuscript evidence for a few verses in the gospels ever helped a man to see God or to preach Christ."[79] From 1920-22 he edited the *Challenge*. Dillistone considered this editorship an important aspect of Raven's contribution to the post-war ideological and theological climate of opinion:

77   R. Keable, *Standing By*, p.42.
78   Ibid., p.113.
79   Dillistone *Charles Raven*, p.114.

Within a short space of time he had brought to the attention of thoughtful church members some of the issues which were to assume increasing importance in the next twenty years. Reunion, Christianity and war, religion and science, the new relationship between the sexes, the ministry of women, planned parenthood, Christianity and Eastern cultures, Christ and modern philosophy.[80]

Raven was responsible for the organisation of the 1926 Church congress at Southport on the theme of "The Eternal Spirit". He had been working on the themes of the relationship of Christian doctrine to biological and psychological sciences in preparing for giving the Noble lectures at Harvard and the Hulsean lectures at Cambridge and they were combined in his book *The Creator Spirit* published in 1927. The preface states:

> The purpose of this book is simple, if its scope is ambitious. It is an attempt to show that the work of the Holy Spirit is to be traced in the creative as well as the inspirational energies of The Godhead; that creation, incarnation and inspiration reveal the same eternal values, that biology and psychology bear witness to love rather than to will.[81]

Dillistone considered that: "Raven's aim was to set forth afresh the splendour of the Divine unity in terms of creation, incarnation and inspiration."[82] Michael Ramsay, in his overview of the theology of the Church of England, *From Gore to Temple* said that: "Within the field of Incarnational theology a special place belongs to C. E. Raven".[83]

As a result of his appointment as Regius professor of Divinity in 1932, Raven realised that he would be expected to contribute largely to the contemporary theological debates. His book *Jesus and the Gospel of Love*, published in 1932, had not made much impression in academic theological circles and he was aware of criticism that he was a populist author. In his inaugural lecture, *Signs of the Times: Some Reflections Upon the Scope and Opportunity of Theology* he commented on the current theology. Firstly, he dealt with the criticisms of theology and concluded that: "Its concentration upon biblical criticism and ... ecclesiastical order had prevented it from being a steady witness to Christ himself."[84] Secondly, he promoted the need for unity through political and educational developments and power to transform dreams into reality. In his conclusion he returned to the theme that: "The time is over-ripe for a new unfolding of the doctrine of the spirit by the aid of our new knowledge of the history and psychology of religious experience."[85]

80   Ibid., p.128.
81   Ibid.
82   Ibid., p.129.
83   A. M. Ramsay, *From Gore to Temple: The Development of Anglican Theology between Lux Mundi and the Second World War, 1889-1939*, (London, 1960) p.25.
84   Dillistone, *Charles Raven*, p.203.
85   Ibid., p.204.

It can be seen that Raven's efforts towards working out his theological position contain in them the fruit of the seeds that had been planted in his evolving the concept of a "New Reformation" based on his experiences during and after the war. Although Raven's was an academic understanding of the problems of the meaning of the war for belief and society, his thoughts are echoed in the writings and actions of other former chaplains as they struggled to apply their experience to life in the interwar years.

Kenneth Kirk had been senior chaplain of the 66th Division. His contribution to *The Church in the Furnace*, "When the Priests Come Home", contained his views on the relationship which he believed had sprung up between priests and men in the front line and quoted from a soldier's letter in which the man said that long talks in the huts had "done him more good than if you had preached a sermon every day." Kirk commented: "I doubt if in their parish at home the same lads and the same chaplain would have ever got on speaking terms at all."[86] This breaking down of social barriers prompted Kirk to think deeply about the education of the working class. As a result he wrote *The Study of Silent Minds*,[87] in which he advocated a more comprehensive education, including the study of great literature, institutions, psychology and logic. His experiences of dealing with men's theological questions at the front by asking another man to answer and explain led him to stress the cooperative nature of learning. "No spiritual activity, however great its triumphs may appear, is on the road to ultimate success unless it is adding to the corporate wealth and friendship of a city of friends."[88] Although this book disappeared from later lists of Kirk's work, his biographer is of the opinion that the book constituted "a clear exposition of principle which guided his thought and work in later years".[89] It also gives a clear idea of how his views on education had been shaped by his experiences in war.

On returning to Oxford to resume his academic career, Kirk turned his attention to the comparatively new field of moral theology. He had already spoken in his essay, "When the Priests Come Home", of the practical application of moral theology.

> Moral Theology has been much abused yet it is exactly what is needed – the science of applying the broad principles of Christianity to particular cases … it is pathetic that too often the vicar or curate is the last person in the parish to detect a hypocrite or rebuke an impostor; pathetic, also, that he is the last to recognise excellence in an outward pagan.[90]

In 1918 he had given lectures to temporary chaplains at Catterick and Ripon army camps and from these lectures wrote his *Some Principles of Moral Theology and their*

---

86   Kirk, 'When the Priests Come Home', *The Church in Furnace*, p.414.
87   K. Kirk, *A Study in Silent Minds, War Studies in Education* (London, SCM, 1918).
88   Kemp, *The Life and Letters of Kenneth Escott Kirk*, p.46.
89   Ibid.
90   Kirk, 'When the Priests Come Home', p.434.

Application in 1920, followed by *Ignorance, Faith and Conformity* in1925, and *Conscience and its Problems* in 1927. Kirk's work put moral theology on the academic agenda.[91] In 1925, the chair of Pastoral Theology at Oxford University was changed to the Regius professor of Moral and Pastoral Theology and in 1933 Kirk was appointed to the position. In 1937 he was consecrated Bishop of Oxford.

In 1927 *Essays Catholic and Critical* appeared, edited by a former chaplain, E. G. Selwyn.[92] Ramsay considered it to be representative of the "newer catholic liberalism", which he thought was written in "conscious succession to *Lux Mundi*".[93] The aim of it contributors, according to Roger Lloyd, was to find "A synthesis between critical scholarship and catholic tradition".[94] Since 1920 E. G. Selwyn, as editor of *Theology*, had given the new liberalism a platform.[95] Eric Milner-White, former wartime chaplain, contributed an essay entitled "The Spirit and The Church in History'".[96] Edwyn Hoskyns' contribution, "The Christ of the Synoptic Gospels" condemned liberal modernist theology, speaking against negative criticism of the New Testament. Hoskyns had been a chaplain to a Lancashire Territorial regiment during the war, had won a Military Cross and had returned to become a popular and respected lecturer in theology at Corpus Christi College. Charles Smyth, in his introduction to the Cambridge sermons of Hoskyns, said of his teaching: "It was through these lectures ... that he left an abiding mark upon the Church of England; for through them he exerted an unrivalled influence on the younger clergy."[97] Ramsay said that the writers of these essays "had a considerable influence in the years between the wars", and added, "this school could reach out eirenically towards the Liberal evangelicals and fulfil in many way a mediating role".[98] He remembered "Hoskyn's lectures on the Theology and Ethics of the New Testament were an exciting experience for us who heard them in the 1920s."[99]

Oliver Quick, who had been trained by B. K. Cunningham at Farnham Hostel, had been working with his former principal at the chaplains' school at St Omer during his time as an army chaplain. His main contributions to analytical theology were *The Christian Sacraments* (1927)[100] and *Doctrines of the Creed* (1937).[101] According to Ramsay, Quick was gifted in creative exposition and was "able to draw together

91   K. Kirk, *Some Principles of Moral Theology and their Application* (London, Longmans, Green & Co., 1920), *Ignorance, Faith and Conformity* (London, Longmans & Co., 1925), *Conscience and its Problems* (London, Longmans, Green & Co., 1927).
92   E. G. Selwyn, TCF 1918-1919, *Crockford's*, p.1201.
93   Ramsay, *From Gore to Temple*, p.102.
94   Lloyd, *The Church of England 1900-1965*, p.272.
95   Ibid.
96   Ramsay, *From Gore to Temple* p.103.
97   Lloyd, *The Church of England 1900-1965*, p.274.
98   Ramsay, *Gore to Temple* p.107.
99   Ibid., p.132.
100 Quick, Oliver, *The Christian Sacraments* (London Nisbet 1927).
101 Quick, Oliver, *Doctrines of the Creed* (Nisbet, 1938).

different elements in the understanding of the Atonement and present the doctrine with a fresh inventiveness." Ramsay claimed that Quick expounded "a liberal orthodoxy" but was not linked to any particular party within the church.[102]

Quick was one of several former chaplains, including F. R. Barry and E. G. Selwyn, who were appointed to the Archbishops' Commission on the Doctrine of the Church of England in 1921. Its brief was to "Consider the nature and grounds of Christian doctrine with a view to demonstrating the extent of the existing agreement within the Church of England, and with a view to investigating how it is possible to remove or diminish existing differences."[103] As the commission did not report until 1938 it was, as F. R. Barry remembered, a little out of date. "By that time the whole situation had changed and the questions that were being asked were different questions."[104] William Temple, Chairman at the time of the Commission's reporting, said of the Commission: "If we began our work again today, its perspectives would be different."[105] However Barry, writing in his memoirs, considered the report: "Still well worth reading, and if anyone reads it today might be surprised to discover how 'liberal' it was and what a width of interpretation it allowed as legitimate in the Church of England."[106]

A book that Dean Inge hailed as: "The evangelical Lux Mundi" was produced by a group influenced by the Brotherhood Movement of the evangelical party. Rogers was the editor of this volume, called *Liberal Evangelicalism* and contributed an essay on "Religious Authority". Later, he described the genesis of the volume as "a group of men brought up in evangelical tradition ... who endeavoured to formulate the evangelical message anew for the age in which they lived."[107] In the preface Rogers put forward the group's ideas on the atonement. "The modern evangelical is dissatisfied with some of the older and cruder penal and substitutionary theories of the atonement ... The modern evangelical finds salvation for himself and society at the cross of Jesus."[108] A further volume of essays published in 1932, *The Inner life*, was edited by Rogers and contained contributions by E. S. Woods on "Witness and Service", Charles Raven on "The Indwelling Christ" and a contribution from G. C. L. Lunt, another former chaplain, on "The Individual and Fellowship". In his introduction Rogers examined the purpose of the new book of essays: "The second volume directs itself more particularly at the inner Christian life ... it seeks to show how God works through the evolutionary purpose which the history of the world reveals". He continued, "We have been at some pains to deal with conversion in relation to modern Psychology and to explain what the doctrine of the indwelling Christ means in our own spiritual experience."

---

102 Ramsay, *Gore to Temple*. p.107.
103 Ibid., p.156.
104 Barry, *Period of My Life*.
105 Ramsay, *Gore to Temple* p.159.
106 Barry, *Period of My Life*, p.88.
107 T .G. Rogers(ed), *The Inner Life. Essays in Liberal Evangelicism* (London, Hodder & Stoughton, 1925), p.v.
108 Ibid pp.168-167.

He emphasised the meaning of the title of the book of essays. "There *is* an inner spiritual life which crates the power and sets the standard for conduct."[109]

The discoveries and theories of Sigmund Freud regarding the unconscious and primitive forces controlling minds were being developed in pre-war Austria and Germany and slowly developed into the practice of psychoanalysis. The main British proponent of Freudian theories was Dr Ernest Jones, who set up the London Psycho-Analytical society in 1913.[110] Cases of shell shock and mental damage in the war led to increased interest by doctors such as W. R. Rivers, but it was not until the 1920s that "complexes and repressions, transference and sublimation, entered the drawing rooms of the English speaking World".[111] The increased interest led to an increase of publications about psychiatry and psychoanalysis. The ideas of Freudian psychoanalysis seemed to go against ideas of free will and rationality, which had implications for the clergy in their spiritual and pastoral work, so it was perhaps inevitable that some clergy would investigate and comment on the use of psychology in the work of the priest. It was also perhaps to be expected that former chaplains should have been prominent in this, given their increased insights into the character of men in the trenches.

Tom Pym was among the first clerics to write on psychology and its impact on practical and pastoral theology. His aim was "to provide something of the nature of and a summary of psychological theory, in so far as it bears on Christian faith and ethics."[112] He recommended that every diocese had an expert trained in psychological approaches to pastoral work and that all ordinands should receive some training, perhaps some having the opportunity of "a short medical course" and some time spent on studying psychoanalysis.[113] These ideas seem very advanced for their era but received some encouragement from a review in the *Guardian* in 1921. In its review of *Psychology and the Christian life* it said, "Mr Pym is not among those who are afraid of applying the methods of Psychology to the individual soul. His book is distinguished by the deep personal faith, a sincere reverence for holy things and definite belief in the power of Psychology to deepen the faith of reverence of others."[114]

F. R. Barry entered the field in 1923 with a book entitled *Christianity and Psychology* in which he attempted to survey the most recent thinking on the subject and consider its implications for ministry. In his introduction he asserted: "I am convinced that nothing but added strength and depth and range of our religious lives, and even still more in ministerial work, can come from a careful study of psychology."[115] In the

109 Ibid., p.vii.
110 Richard Overy, *The Morbid Age Britain and the Crisis of Civilization 1919-1939* (London 2009) p.142.
111 Ibid., p.143.
112 Tom Pym, *Psychology and the Christian Life* (London, SCM Press, 1921), p.8.
113 Ibid., p.111.
114 *Church Times*, 18 November 1921.
115 F. R. Barry, *Christianity and Psychology* (London, SCM Press, 1923), p.14.

chapter on "Instinct" he summarised some of the Freudian theories, and said: "It must be recognised that the instinctive and non rational forces deeply colour and affect the rational." In Chapter Four, 'Psychology and the Religious Life', he explained that "It is in the power of anyone who will read the Gospels eagerly and without prejudice to see how the cardinal teaching of Christianity fits in with the facts which psychology brings to light, and answers the need of the soul."[116] He considered that: "It goes without saying that to know a little about the way in which our minds work cannot fail to be useful to every one of us in trying to make the best of our lives and to live in a right relationship with God."[117] He dealt with the problem of free will in his last chapter, "Psychology and the Christian Faith", and concluded:

> It remains true that the whole lesson of psychology warns us that we are not born free. All of us are selves in the making. Freedom is not something to be realised: it is not an axiom, but an achievement. We become free only when our whole selves are caught up into a harmonious controlling purpose ... and that, in the fullest sense, is love.[118]

In his book *St Paul and Social Psychology*, Barry drew upon St Paul's epistle to the Ephesians to make a point about how civilisation could be improved, drawing on the "New Psychology" to show how the "group mind" postulated by psychological learning, could be used in the cause of Christian unity.

> Modern Psychology has demonstrated the "group mind", and it is beyond doubt that when people are organised in a group or a society they behave, under certain conditions differently and far better than their normal behaviour as individuals. Hence the latent power of organised Christianity and the imperative duty for Christians to achieve some external unity whereby this power might be effective.[119]

Although Geoffrey Studdert Kennedy has not been remembered for his contribution to academic theology, Stuart Bell, in his examination of the theology of Studdert Kennedy, has said that he was "arguably the most original thinker to emerge from the Great War and its immediate aftermath."[120] Studdert Kennedy was the main advocate of the idea of divine passiblity in the interwar years. Bell is of the opinion that it is strange that this aspect of Studdert Kennedy's reputation has been ignored and that his fame rests on his role as an army chaplain and his work for the ICF. He quotes the

116 Ibid., p.21.
117 Ibid., p.94.
118 Ibid., p.286.
119 F. R. Barry, *St Paul and Social Psychology*, quoted in *Church Times*, review July 1923.
120 S. Bell, 'The Theology of "Woodbine Willie" in Context', *The Clergy in Khaki*, p.153.

obituaries for Studdert Kennedy to prove this point, e.g. the opinion expressed by D. F. Carey: "Studdert Kennedy was the last to make any claim to be a theologian in the exact sense of the word."[121]

Some former chaplains were prominent in academic theological circles in the post-war years but, as Bell points out, the theological opinions of an army chaplain with "a colourful reputation" were not likely to have achieved prominence in a field dominated by the intellectual elite. The publications of Studdert Kennedy in the last year of the war and the first years of peace show clearly that his ideas of a suffering God had developed as a result of his wartime experiences,[122] exemplified in *The Hardest Part* which was written in response to the question asked him by many soldiers, "What is God like?" He wrote: "I don't know or love the Almighty potentate … my only real God is the suffering Father revealed in the sorrow of Christ."[123]

The idea of a suffering God was one with which other former chaplains engaged, for example, F. R. Barry and Timothy Rees. Barry, in his contribution to *The Church in the Furnace,* "Faith in the Light of War", writing before the end of the war, said of God: "He is not outside the struggle against evil, He is in it, in the turmoil and the pain, sharing with us in the toil and the conflict."[124] Bell has pointed out that Timothy Rees's most famous hymn *God is Love, Let Heaven Adore Him* contains the lines:

And when human hearts are breaking
Under sorrow's iron rod,
That same sorrow, that same aching,
Wrings with pain the heart of God.[125]

Although Studdert Kennedy and his fellow chaplain colleagues' ideas were not acknowledged in the interwar years by the mainstream academic theologian elite, Bell makes it clear that they were a forerunner of changes in theology prompted by the sufferings of the Second World War which made the idea of divine possibility more pertinent.

---

121 D. F. Carey, 'G .A. Studdert Kennedy – War Padre', *G. A. Studdert Kennedy – By His Friends*, p.149.

122 G.A. Studdert Kennedy, *The Hardest Part* (London, Hodder & Stoughton, 1918); *Rough Rhymes of a Padre* (London, Hodder & Stoughton,1918); *More Rough Rhymes of a Padre* (London, Hodder & Stoughton, 1920); *Peace Rhymes of a Padre* (London, Hodder & Stoughton 1920); *The Sorrows of God and Other Poems* (London, Hodder & Stoughton, 1921).

123 Studdert Kennedy, *The Hardest Part*, pp.xiii-xiv.

124 F. R. Barry, 'Faith in the Light of War', in *The Church in the Furnace*, p.49.

125 T. Rees, *Sermons and Hymns Collected and Prepared for Publication by John Lambert Rees* (London and Oxford, A.R. Mowbray & Co., 1946), p.110.

Education

Another educational field in which former chaplains were to be found in the interwar years was that of secondary education, particularly in the development of the Woodard schools. The movement, which promoted the formation of public schools with a distinctly Anglican Christian ethos, was founded by Nathaniel Woodard in 1848 for:

> The promoting and extending education in the doctrine and principles of the Church of England ... by means of colleges and schools, but that no such college or school should be opened without the permission of the bishop of the Diocese.[126]

By 1914 the administration of the schools had been organised into four regional chapters. The largest of these was the Western Area, the college of Saints Mary and Nicholas. In charge of this area, including the schools of Hurstpierpoint, Bloxham, Ardingly and Lancing, was the Provost of Lancing. In 1914 there were sixteen schools in different parts of the country. H. K. Southwell became the Provost of Lancing in 1902. He continued this responsibility, interrupted by service as a chaplain until his appointment as Bishop of Lewes in 1920, but returned in 1926 when he retired from this position. His obituary in 1937 stated, "He will chiefly be remembered for his services to the Woodward Schools and for his work as Assistant Chaplain General during the war."[127] On Southwell's death, in 1937, the responsibility of Provost of Lancing was given to Kenneth Kirk, then Regius Professor of Moral and Pastoral Theology at Oxford University, and soon to be made Bishop of Oxford.[128] In the same year Kirk wrote *The story of the Woodard Schools*. R. C. Freeman, clerk to the Woodard corporation, commented that this book was: "The only really well-written book on that foundation in 100 years."[129] Despite many other commitments, Kirk seemed to have taken this responsibility seriously and visited many of the schools regularly. His biographer, Kemp, said of him: "For the Woodard Corporation, he was above all the right man in the time of need".[130]

E. C. Crosse had left for New Zealand after his service as chaplain and had taken up an appointment as headmaster of Christ's College, Christchurch. He returned in 1934 to become headmaster of a Woodard school, Ardingly, at a time when its numbers were low because of the financial problems of prospective parents caused by the economic depression, and its future was uncertain. He set about restoring its viability. In a history of the school his achievements are described: "In six and

---

126 Extract from founder's statutes quoted in *The Times*, 11 March 1914, p.9.
127 *The Times*, 11 March 1937, p.18.
128 *The Times*, 7 April 1937, p.18.
129 Kemp, *The Life and Letters of Kenneth Escott Kirk*, p.191.
130 Ibid., p.193.

a half years of hard work, Ardingly had been restored to prosperity and was full to overflowing."[131]

Crosse's first step, a bold one under the circumstances, was to lower the fees. This allowed parents to send their boys, paying, including travel and books, under £100 a year. He achieved this by cutting down on luxuries and the amount spent on administration. In a report of speech day at Ardingly in June 1934 he was quoted as saying in explanation of the economies: "He did not think that it hurt any boy to black his own boots and wait on himself far more than was often done and generally learn to do with a minimum of personal service."[132] He drew on his experience in New Zealand, encouraging students from poorer homes to take up scholarships.

Conclusion

Former chaplains had drawn on their experiences of the way in which they had coped under wartime conditions to inform their concerns and actions in the field of training for ordination. They had been in a prime position to witness occasions on which a chaplain's training had not equipped him for his task. Knutsford had given many men an opportunity of turning their wartime ambitions of entering the church into reality unfettered by financial constraints. The presence of men such as Haigh, Barry and Clayton ensured that the atmosphere reinforced the sense of vocation that the candidates experienced in France, ensuring that it was not lost on their return, and eased the transition of the men with vocations to a peacetime career in the church. Chavasse, with St Peter's College at Oxford, expanded the opportunities of a Christian-based university education and Cunningham presided over several generations of ordinands with the wisdom he had shown in running the chaplains' school at St Omer.

The interwar years saw vital developments in modern theological thinking, especially applying the evidence provided by natural and scientific knowledge to the understanding of contemporary theology. Raven was instrumental in developing incarnational theology, while Barry and Pym sought to apply psychology to the Christian faith. Kirk broke new ground in the fields of moral and pastoral theology while chaplains from different traditions contributed to volumes of essays expounding both new ground in Liberal Catholicism and Liberal Evangelicalism. In their contributions to the training of ordinands they were very significant in ensuring that the Church of England continued to be served by a sufficient number of well-trained clergy. In the development of theological scholarship in the interwar years former chaplains seem to have been very much at the centre, and sometimes at the forefront of contemporary developments, and it is clear that many of their arguments stem from the intellectual and emotional turmoil they experienced in the trenches.

---

131 R. Perry, *Ardingly 1848-1946, A History of the School* (London, The Ardinians Society, 1951), p.237.
132 *The Times*, 18 June 1934, p.9.

5

"Revival not Reformation" – Former Chaplains and Reforms in the Church of England in the Interwar Years

---

Kenneth Kirk, in his contribution to *The Church in the Furnace*, "When the Priests Come Home", was optimistic that disagreements and church party strife would not have a large part to play in the post-war church:

> Even though much remains difficult and uncertain and at cross purposes in the future of the church, we shall have to secure a sense of her divine mission and her supernatural strength to trouble over much. Peevish controversy and ill tempered denunciation will lose much of their present vogue.[1]

This seems an optimistic opinion in view of the controversies and changes which developed in the Anglican Church during the 1920s and 1930s. Many of the chaplains from all fronts in the Great War returned with both a sense of the church's inadequacy and a desire to reform it. Often their personal theology had been challenged, and also their understanding of the way in which the church must relate to its people if it was to go forward. There were internal conflicts regarding the whole order and future of the church's liturgy and doctrine, which caused controversy and change in the 1920s and in which the former chaplains were to be involved. The chaplains, who have left the most detailed record of their thoughts, and those whose actions can be traced in contemporary sources, belonged to the evangelical, catholic and liberal wings of the church and so their influence can be seen to be operating throughout the whole church.

The Life and Liberty Movement

On the occasion of Archbishop Randall Davidson's visit to the front in May 1916, he had some detailed and fruitful discussions with the chaplains he met there. At a

---

1   Kirk, 'When the Priests Come Home', p.420.

conference of Fourth Army Chaplains, the topics under discussion were: "The National Mission, ordinands, new plans for services after the war, the nature of the impression made on the men, the sort of service that suits best and so on."[2] There was considerable interest in the state of the church and its role in the future among chaplains at the front, and this pressure continued with the ideas expressed to Archbishop Davidson on his next visit in January 1919. Many questions were asked and suggestions made in the discussions that took place at the time of the Archbishop's latter visit, on subjects such as church parties, clergy pensions and grouping of the country parishes, the nature of church government, disestablishment, unity with other denominations and the role of women. A particular issue with Tom Pym was that of advowsons.[3] He was on the extreme wing of the chaplains in France and not many of his ideas were accepted by his fellow chaplains, but he stuck to his principles, not accepting a living or appointment paid for by the church but returning to work post-war as warden of Cambridge House, a Cambridge University settlement in Camberwell. The discussions which took place among the Anglican army chaplains, however, were in tune with developments on such issues on the home front led by William Temple and Dick Sheppard, who had in 1917 initiated a "ginger group" to press for more urgent and far-reaching reform in the church and was to grow into the Life and Liberty Movement. At an inaugural meeting in March 1917 at St Martin-in-the-Fields vicarage they agreed that: "The first thing to press for was self-government", so that "the church, when set free, may really tackle the great problems that perplex men, and be a source to which men can turn for inspiration."[4]

The problems being highlighted by the chaplains and by the emerging Life and Liberty Movement were not new ones. There had been a movement for church reform from the 1890s when the Church Reform League was founded, which called for "self-government by means of reformed houses of Convocation."[5] As a result of this increasing concern the Representative Church Council was set up.[6] It had little power, but provided a template on which future reforms could be based. Roger Lloyd said of it: "If there had been no Representative Church Council, there would certainly have been no Enabling Act in 1919."[7]

---

2   M .F. Snape, 'Archbishop Davidson's Visit to the Western Front, May 1916,' in M. Barber, S. Taylor and G. Sewell (eds.), *From the Reformation To The Permissive Society* (Woodbridge, Boydell Press, 2010), pp.480-481.
3   Advowsons put the disposal of livings in the hands of patrons who could sell this right if they desired.
4   LP L: the papers of Archbishop William Temple, Vol. 46, f. 23, Minutes of a meeting on 29 March 1917.
5   *Reform of the Church. The proposals of the Church Reform league*, quoted in *The Times*, 10 August 1896, p.7.
6   The Representative Church Council made up of the two convocations and the two houses of laymen, had met together in Church House for the first time in July 1904, http://www.churchhouse.org.uk/.
7   Lloyd, *The Church of England*, p.234.

Discussion about reform had gained the support not only of liberal Catholics and the English Church Union, an Anglo-Catholic body, but also liberal evangelicals such as Guy Rogers and E. S. Woods, both former chaplains. The Life and Liberty Movement was to press for more urgent and far-reaching reform. The intentions of the group were stated in their letter to *The Times* on 20 June 1917, describing themselves as: "A vigorous forward movement." The letter continued: "Those who are promoting this movement are convinced that we must win for the church full power to control its own life, even at the cost, if necessary, of disestablishment and of whatever consequences that may possibly involve."[8] Keith Thompson argues that one of the factors which influenced the creation of this group on the home front was the discovery by the chaplains of the "alienation of the working classes from the church".[9]

The organisers were aware of the support for change in the church from chaplains at the front and from its inception were encouraging input from chaplains. Harry Blackburne wrote about his summons to speak at the first Life and Liberty conference: "Dick has asked me to say a few words at the Life and Liberty meeting at Queen's Hall."[10] He was also asked to be on what Sheppard called his "revolutionary committee", but sounded a word of caution: "We have to construct as well as destroy: the latter easy enough, but the former mighty hard."[11] He recounted a meeting that Bishop Gwynne had arranged at the chaplains' school. Among those present were "Neville and Ted Talbot, Tom Pym, B. K. Cunningham, Sykes, Barry and myself. We had a great talk about Life and Liberty and what we ought to do out here in regard to it."[12] Bishop Gwynne was of the opinion that these opinions held by chaplains stemmed from positive ideas, not from negativity: "I firmly believe that the discontent to which they gave expression is not a sign of weakness, but on the contrary, a sign that we are willing to face the facts."[13] William Temple had received a letter from chaplains of the 7th Division in France in July 1917, which put forward their fears:

> No matter what type of party we belonged to of old, we are all now haunted by the fear that the Home Church cannot see and will not rise up meet the needs which have shocked each of us on entering, as ministers of Christ, this huge intermingling of all sorts and conditions of our countrymen.

They continued expressing concerns that matters would not change "having seen with our eye the vanity and harmfulness of many old grooves, we are about to return to

---

8   *The Times*, 20 June 1917, p.10.
9   Thompson, *Bureaucracy and Church Reform*, p.157.
10 Blackburne, *This Also Happened on the Western Front*, p.97.
11 Ibid., p.120.
12 Ibid., p.153.
13 Gwynne, introduction to *The Church in the Furnace*, p.xi.

them".[14] In December 1917, the council of Life and Liberty issued a letter asking: "Could church reforms really wait until peace came?"[15]

It is possible that the speed at which Life and Liberty got off the ground might have been helped by the outburst of reforming opinions from chaplains at the front. Temple, writing to Davidson in February 1917, informed him that:

> The group that Dick Sheppard has got around him are people who are really keen on what the church stands for and want to be really keen on the church. But the war and the mission have brought them to boiling point.[16]

Charles Raven, writing in the *Challenge* in November 1918, suggested that the chaplains "refuse, if need be to take any part in organised and traditional religious life unless certain things which are now just topics for debate are carried out."[17] Neville Talbot, writing to his father, Bishop E. S. Talbot of Winchester, early in 1918, was impatient: "So, before we come back, make a fundamental change. Act on the Life and Liberty appeal. I feel that the church is kind of ditched like an old vehicle without wheels. So, put wheels on the bus."[18]

At the first anniversary of the Life and Liberty Movement at Queen's Hall a resolution was put forward for an Enabling Bill. This was seconded by E. S. Woods. The *Church Times* reported the meeting: "E. S. Woods said that there were a great deal of men who maintained a connection with organised religion. They had, however, given up expecting that the official representative of Christianity would do anything. They demanded reality."[19] He continued, "The church spoke of itself as an army, but it was more like an ambulance. It should be a sort of expeditionary force of the Kingdom of God." On the occasion of his visit to the Western Front in January 1919 Archbishop Davidson faced questions and discussions on the church and society in the post-war world. The report of that occasion in the *Church Times* gave more details on the nature of the topics. His aim was: "To gain from them [the chaplains] any light which their experiences have to throw on the equipping of the church for the tasks which lay before her." Another question was that of the future organisation of the Church of England and in particular the movement towards self-government. Many questions and suggestions were asked and made in the discussions that took place at the time

---

14   LPL, papers of Archbishop William Temple, Vol. 46, f.23, letter from the Church of England chaplains of the 7th Division to William Temple, July 1917.
15   A. Wilkinson, *The Church of England and the First World War* (London, SCM Press, 1978), p.372.
16   LPL, unpublished letter, Temple-Davidson 4 Feb 1917. Quoted in Thompson, *Bureaucracy and Church Reform*, p.159.
17   *Challenge*, 29 Nov 1918, p.12.
18   F. H. Brabant, *Neville Stuart Talbot 1879-1943, A Memoir*, p.71.
19   *Church Times*, 19 July 1918, p.43.

of the Archbishop's visit, on subjects such as church parties, clergy pensions and grouping of country parishes. On the question of unity the report said:

> There can be no doubt that as the archbishop listened to the discussions he must have been aware that among the great number of the chaplains of all schools of thought of the Church of England in France, there is a willingness to explore new paths toward the ultimate goal of unity.[20]

Archbishop Davidson had already expressed some exasperation at the impetuosity of the chaplains, implying that they were in fact unwilling to return to the routine of parish life. Archbishop Lang, on a visit to the front in 1917, was pleased in some ways with the opinions of the chaplains: "It is good to see the discontent which prevails with the conventional ways of the church … Life and Liberty were moving and the chaplains were outspoken", but also, like Davidson, he was critical. He thought that they had: "Not much sense of proportion … and are very ignorant of the position and problems of the church at home", and that they were: "In some danger of adjusting the church to the army rather than of lifting the army to the church."[21] George Bell commented on the answers received from serving chaplains to a questionnaire in 1916 as part of the Bishop of Kensington's Report. He seemed aware of the contribution the ideas of the chaplains could have to the post-war church:

> As men who are face to face with reality they are insistent in that the task of renewal and reconstruction must be taken in hand by the church herself if she is to win a hearing from the nation.[22]

The enthusiasm for church reform and Life and Liberty was not, however, one that was shared by all members of the church establishment. Archbishops Lang and Davidson may have been alarmed at the militancy and impatience of the chaplains at the front, but Bishop Hensley Henson was outspoken in his criticism of the whole movement. In a letter to the *Church Times* he commented on the stress of the Life and Liberty Movement on immediate action. He asked:

> Is the religious settlement which was slowly hammered into shape in the course of 130 years … to be hustled out of existence in a few months, during the desperate distraction of a great war, by a handful of enthusiasts who really have little title

20 *Church Times*, 31 January 1919.
21 J. G. Lockhart, *Cosmo Gordon Lang* (London, Hodder & Stoughton, 1949), p.257.
22 *The National Mission of Repentance and Hope*, 'A report on the chaplains' replies to the Lord Bishop of Kensington', p.21.

beyond their enthusiasm to put to the task? It is unfair to the Church of England. It is outrageously unfair to the English people.[23]

He was also scornful of the role of the chaplains. Writing to Archbishop Davidson on 17 July 1917 he referred to the Life and Liberty meeting being addressed by: "a returned chaplain in khaki", who assured the audience: "That great numbers of officers and men are eagerly longing for the prompt and drastic handling of the Church."[24] On the general theme of the value of the former chaplains to the work of the church, Henson wrote some scathing comments in his New Year letter of 1919 to his diocese of Hereford:

> I have read a great many books by chaplain or groups of chaplains and though some of them have considerable merit. I cannot say that I have found much which seems to assist us in the difficult problems of ecclesiastic reconstruction. Mostly the books have impressed me by their frank ignorance of the ordinary religious condition of the English parishes ... which is of course explicable enough if one remembers that clergymen were selected for chaplains not on the grounds of knowledge and experience, but because they were young, generous, enthusiastic, adaptable and physically strong.[25]

An article by Clifton Kelway, secretary of the Church Reform League, in the *Church Times* pointed out that these chaplains would soon be returning to their parishes to put their ideas into action:

> Although credible prelates like the Bishop of Hereford may resist an attempt on the part of the chaplains to dictate the policy of the church, I should be greatly surprised if those of us who are fighting the Church's battle for a measure of self-government do not speedily find ourselves reinforced by thousands of these 'Young, generous, enthusiastic, adaptable and physically strong men', clerical and lay who have already helped save England.[26]

The role of Life and Liberty was underestimated, in the opinion of Roger Lloyd. He argued that although the advocates of reform were merely calling for legalising "the long established but voluntary Representative Council,"[27] it was their insistence on the reforms happening at once that was revolutionary. The refusal of the Life and Liberty members to allow the church hierarchy to wait until after the war was essential to the

23   *Church Times*, 26 July 1917, cited by Lloyd, *The Church of England*, p.236.
24   Thompson, *Bureaucracy and Church Reform*, p.153.
25   *The Times*, 15 January 1919, p.6.
26   *Church Times*, 19 July 1918, p.63.
27   Lloyd, *The Church of England*, p.237.

passing of the Enabling Act, which had become law by the end of 1919 and which gave the church the ability to pass important reforming legislation without having to have each act referred to parliament. A Church Assembly would be set up which had the power to legislate on church affairs. Lloyd described the achievement thus: "The Church of England had become a tempered democracy. It had been in fetters and a framework allowing Life and Liberty to flow had been constructed."[28]

The Enabling Act was passed by the end of 1919 and the Church Assembly met for the first time on 20 June 1920. It began its huge task of reorganising the structure and government of the church. Much-needed legislation on patronage, clergy pensions and dilapidations, to cite just a few, was now able to be formulated and passed; established councils and conferences regulating diocese, deaneries and parishes. Notably, parochial church councils were set up. With the passing of the Enabling Act and the setting up of the Church Assembly, the Life and Liberty Movement set itself new projects including reform of the Prayer Book and supporting moves toward church unity. A meeting of Life and Liberty in July 1923 continued the forward-looking approach by discussing a resolution supporting the development of a revised Prayer Book. A report in *The Times* described their aims: "They wanted to try a few experiments under authority and an alternative Prayer Book was the way to do it."[29] At this meeting Studdert Kennedy was outspoken in criticism of the existing Prayer Book. He thought that, "All their teaching about God would fall upon deaf ears while the Prayer Book contained unchristian ideas. The whole practice of baptism was as rotten as it could be and needed radical alteration."[30] In a meeting in October 1926 the chairman, E. S. Woods, spoke of Life and Liberty in the years since the advent of the Church Assembly as having achieved: "A steady growth in practical work ... especially in advising and assisting Parochial Church Councils all over the country in beginning to carry out church reform." At the same meeting, Mervyn Haigh, by now chaplain to the Archbishop of Canterbury, said: "He believed that the Life and Liberty Movement was more needed than ever. They had to do much hard thinking and to set before men the great hope and new ideas that lay before them."[31] Percy Dearmer[32] believed that: "The sectarian spirit would pass away and already was much

---

28   Ibid., p.238.
29   *The Times*, 3 July 1923, p.11.
30   Ibid.
31   *The Times*, 18 October 1926, p.12
32   Percy Dearmer was the pre-war incumbent of St Mary's Primrose Hill and wrote the popular *Parson's Pocket Book*. This outlined his ideas about Anglo-Catholic practices in the liturgy, which were nevertheless well inside the rubrics of the Anglican Church. During the Great War he served as chaplain to the British Red Cross ambulance unit in Serbia, where his wife died of enteric fever in 1915. In 1916 he worked with the Young Men's Christian Association in France and, in 1916 and 1917, with the Mission of Help in India. Donald Grey, *Percy Dearmer, A Parson's Pilgrimage* (Norwich, Canterbury Press, 2000), *ODNB*.

lessened in the nation at large, where the relation between free Anglicans and Free Churchmen were improving every month."[33]

However, major figures in the Life and Liberty Movement, such as Dick Sheppard, were soon disillusioned by the result of the Enabling Act, that is, the Church Assembly. Alan Wilkinson considered that Sheppard: "... was bitterly disappointed by the actual results of all the enthusiasm and idealism which had gone into the movement."[34] However, he added: "The act was a necessary step along the way as the church began to search for the right relationship with an increasingly secular and pluralist society."[35] After William Temple became Bishop of Manchester in 1920 the movement seemed to lose impetus. Alan Wilkinson is of the opinion that the results of the movement were bound to disappoint, as "The issues raised by the war were more theological and ethical than administrative." F. R. Barry, in a pamphlet based on a series of sermons given in Cambridge in 1922, echoed the sense that the administrative reforms of the church had not been enough to revitalise it: "What we need most and need undeniably is liberation of spiritual forces to sweep across our petrified efficiency and awaken it ... into singing life."[36] He continued, "We need revival not reformation."[37]

Despite much evidence that the Life and Liberty Movement still considered it had work to do, in December 1926 E. S. Woods announced its dissolution. In doing so he said: "It is not for us to estimate the extent of the service it has been able to render. We believe that though the body dissolve itself the spirit that has animated the movement has so permeated the church that it cannot die." He continued:

> We desire to put on record the happiness of the fellowship with which men and women of widely differing views have worked and prayed together within our movement ... and have thus promoted, as we hope and believe the cause of unity within the Church of England.[38]

The Chaplains' Fellowship

On 26 July 1918 an article appeared in the *Church Times* about a proposed "Chaplains' Fellowship." Its committee included C. S. Woodward, F. B. Macnutt, Guy Rogers, Eric Milner-White and E. S. Woods. They were appealing for names and addresses of chaplains who had already returned home: "It has increasingly been felt by many ex-temporary Church of England chaplains who have served in the army and navy

33 *The Times*, 18 October 1926, p.11.
34 Wilkinson, *The Church of England*, p.273.
35 Ibid., p.274.
36 F. R. Barry, *One Clear Call – An Appeal to the Church of England* (Cambridge, W. Heffer & Sons, 1922), p.7.
37 Ibid., p.7.
38 *The Times*, 9 December 1926, p.13.

since the war began that some fellowship be formed in which they may unite to consult and act together when they have left the services."[39] In October another meeting, "long desired", was organised. Fifty chaplains were present and another 100 had expressed the wish to enrol. Guy Rogers was in the chair. A report in the *Church Times* described the atmosphere: "The fellowship bids to be a very lively body especially when peace reinforces it with the chaplains now serving". The objects of the fellowship were introduced by F. B. Macnutt and Eric Milner-White. The suggested objects were:

1. To conserve and apply the results of our experience on service.
2. To maintain the bond of fellowship which already exists between us.
3. To press for such reforms in the life and work of that church as our common experience has proved to be urgently required.
4. To discover the right lines of immediate action ... and to follow them without regard to personal cost.

The "lines of action" included support for social reform, but also involved the "cause of self-government", the adaptation of services "to fit our present needs", the cause of "cooperation and reunion with nonconformists" and aid of discharged soldiers and sailors. They therefore seem to have engaged with many of the major preoccupations facing the church in the post-war era.[40]

On 1 December 1918 the fellowship met again at St Martin-in-the-Fields. The morning session was devoted to discussions on how to promote church unity and in the afternoon self-government for the church was the topic. However, according to the report in the *Church Times* "No hasty or anarchic action was advocated." Significantly, at this meeting it was regarded as "inevitable that the fellowship would as soon as possible make non-Church of England chaplains free of its life and comradeship".[41] In October 1919 the *Church Times* report on a meeting said that the chaplains were already, "without any view to religious propaganda", helping the associations of returned soldiers and sailors, implying that evangelising work done would be non-denominational. However, the feeling was that the fellowship was not to degenerate into a "talking shop." The report concluded: "If the Padres' Fellowship finds its corporate voice this defect should be remedied."[42] The *Church Times* commented that often:

Chaplains and others, dismayed at the apparent indifference of the men to the appeal of the church have evolved schemes for presenting the faith in such a

39   *Church Times*, 26 July 1918, p.63.
40   *Church Times*, 11 October 1918, p.259.
41   *Church Times*, 6 December 1918, p.241.
42   *Church Times*, 11 October 1919, p.318.

way as to appeal to the ordinary man. Such schemes are often alluring in their simplicity, but a closer examination reveals blemishes.[43]

One of the main preoccupations of the Padres' Fellowship, and one which was to also cause much controversy in the post-war years, was that of church unity. The Manchester Guardian reported in May 1920 on the Padres' Fellowship:

> One of its aims is to attempt some constructive contribution to 'The healing of the divisions in Christendom', and its members, having had the privilege of being thrown into close touch with the most representative manhood of the Empire and with one another in common service, feel that they cannot shirk such a responsibility.

The padres had concluded that if practical steps "approved by authority" were to be taken it would be in the spirit of "friendly personal interchange" enjoyed on active service in the army.[44]

In March 1920 the editorial of the *Church Times* launched an attack on former army chaplains and the Padres' Fellowship:

> The returning army chaplain frequently came back with revolutionary ideas ... a rebel against what is left of the Sunday proprieties, against the vestiges of clerical dress, against what he called the whole stupid business. He is usually a sacramentalist of some kind but disposed to regard all ministers of religion as ... holding equally a commission from the Divine King.

The editorial went on to report that members of the fellowship "are in favour of giving liberty to practice within the fellowship, intercommunion in connection with its meetings for worship". This was criticised as something that went beyond "the advocates of a mere interchange of pulpits."[45]

Guy Rogers described some of "the new ideas fermenting" among returning chaplains:

> To many who had never hesitated to give the Holy Communion under conditions of war to anyone of a good heart who sought for it, it seemed intolerable to return to a barbed wire kind of life where Christians could not gather round the one table of their Lord.[46]

---

43   Ibid.
44   *Manchester Guardian*, 21 May 1920, p.506.
45   *Church Times*, 5 March 1920, p.241.
46   Rogers, *A Rebel at Heart*, p.130.

Rogers went on to add that the Padres' Fellowship had for a time been in "general sympathy" with the objectives of intercommunion but that B. K. Cunningham, "With his immense influence saw to it that sympathy did not go too far". It was Rogers' opinion that the fellowship gradually lost momentum. This meant that: "One possible instrument of progress was blunted and finally broken."[47] References to the fellowship are certainly few and far between in the church press after the early 1920s.

Church Reunion

Church Reunion had become a topical and controversial topic by 1920. Charlotte Methuen has explained how the impetus towards unity arose out of a sense that the Paris Peace Conference was flawed and that as Bishops West, Woods and Linton Smith put it: "It was becoming more and more apparent that any true internationalism must have a spiritual, that is, a Christian foundation."[48] Missionaries and mission churches abroad also added to the pressure, concerned that: "Denominational division rooted in the processes of European history could be damaging for the gospel when it was preached in Africa, or India or the East."[49] An example of this had been the attempts of Anglican and Nonconformist churches in East Africa to come to the basis of an agreement on union. Conferences at Kikuyu, in Kenya, in 1911 and then in 1913, had not reached an agreement, but at the conference in 1913 an understanding permitting a certain amount of intercommunion in special circumstances had been reached, and the Bishop of Mombassa had celebrated communion at a joint service in the Presbyterian church at Kikuyu. This had resulted in Frank Weston, Bishop of Zanzibar, denouncing this action as heretical. Roger Lloyd commented that this issue "involved the whole Anglican communion in bitter controversy, which only the opening of the First World War stilled".[50]

At the beginning of 1920 a group of Anglican and Free Church ministers met in Oxford at a nonconformist college (Mansfield College), to discuss church unity. They produced the Mansfield Resolution, which stated:

> The denominations to which we severally belong are equally, as corporate groups, within the church of Christ. We believe that that all dealings between then should be conducted on the basis of mutual recognition which is fundamental to

---

47 Ibid., p.130.
48 F. Woods, F. Weston and M. Linton Smith, 'Lambeth and Reunion, An Interpretation of the Mind of the Lambeth Conference of 1920', cited by Charlotte Methuen, 'Lambeth 1920: The Appeal to all Christian People. An Account by G. K. A. Bell and the Redactions of the Appeal' in Barber. M., Taylor, S., and Sewell, G. (eds) *From the Reformation To The Permissive Society* (Woodbridge, Boydell Press, 2010), p.524.
49 Rogers, *A Rebel at Heart*, p.524.
50 Lloyd, *The Church of England*, p.434.

any approach towards the realisation of the reunited church for which we long and labour to pray.

It called for "interchange of pulpits", "mutual admission to the Lord's Table, subject to authority," and "acceptance by ministers of authorisation as shall enable them to minister freely in the churches of other denominations."[51] The resolution was signed, among others by no less than nine former Anglican army chaplains: Harry Blackburne, Pat McCormick, J. V. Macmillan, F. B. Macnutt, Charles Raven, Guy Rogers, Dick Sheppard, E. S. Woods and C. S. Woodward.

In April 1920 Neville Talbot weighed into the debate on unity with his book *Thoughts on Unity*. Talbot had been one of the first Anglicans of a high church persuasion to be active in the Student Christian Movement before the war and in his preface acknowledged the impact the ecumenical nature of the movement had had on him. He showed how the war had increased the urgency for worldwide reunion: "If the war has done one thing, it has driven home on the common consciousness the sense that the world is one."[52] A review of the book in the *Manchester Guardian* described how Talbot stressed the need for episcopacy: "For all the scattered churches he sees one bond of unity – 'episcopacy'",[53] and quoted from the book: "I am sure that those who have repudiated episcopacy will not and cannot return to it as an exclusive channel of grace: will they return to it and accept it as an organ of the unity of the one church of Christ?"[54] Talbot looked at the question of unity from a more global aspect than many of his contemporaries, but saw the role of the Church of England at home and abroad as vital to the progress of unity:

> The position of the Church of England is remarkable. It holds within itself two traditions, catholic and evangelical. Its strength lies in the combination of a mutually contributing influence in the practical working of the church and its thought. It contains men who are both priestly and prophetic.[55]

Talbot agreed with the principle of interchange of pulpits, on the basis that "The churches have precious things to give to each other",[56] but thought it would work much better on special occasions rather than as guests in each other's churches. He commented on the possibility that the right place to start intercommunion was at ecumenical conferences and when members of different denomination were working

51   *Manchester Guardian*, 27 February 1920, p.218.
52   N. Talbot, *Thoughts on Unity* (London, SCM Press, 1920), p.1.
53   *Manchester Guardian*, 30 April 1920, p.431.
54   Ibid.
55   Talbot, *Thoughts on Unity*, p.65.
56   Ibid., p.13.

together in united service.[57] In the last pages of the book he referred to the war as a factor which had emphasised evil and therefore should give impetus to efforts at unity:

> The fires of a world war seem hardly at all to have consumed the elements in civilisation which cried out for purgation. The violence of war seems to have reinforced the idolatry of force ... all the more therefore do we hope that it shall be given to the church of Christ to be saved from blindness and hardness of heart to know the things which lead to peace.[58]

The interest and expectation that the forthcoming Lambeth Conference engendered can be seen in a letter published in *The Times* by Dick Sheppard on 29 June 1920, calling for: "Authoritative guidance on what surely are the most urgent problems that now confront the catholic church." He explained:

> We desire now, for a variety of reasons, the chief of which is that what we have learned during the war of the mind of our master, to receive as communicants at the altar in our churches all lovers of our Lord Jesus Christ who are able to say 'Lord I believe, help thou my unbelief'. Further, we desire that those clergy who are of our mind should not be regarded as disloyal to their own church or to their belief on the subject of episcopacy if they accept from time to time, the invitations of Free Church ministers to receive communion in their churches.[59]

The opinions of discussion and controversy over reunion both at home and abroad in the 1920s and 1930s need to be seen in the context of the Lambeth Conference of 1920. Unity was a major theme of the conference and the committee discussing it produced the *Appeal to All Christian People* which provided the backdrop to considerations of unity in the following decade. Charlotte Methuen, in her introduction to G. K. Bell's account of the conference, has said of it: "Looking back on the Lambeth Conference of 1920 most participants and observers agreed that the *Appeal to All Christian People* was its most significant result." On 30 July the report of the Committee on Reunion, containing the substance of the *Appeal to all Christian People*, was put to the whole conference and despite Archbishop Lang's worries was accepted wholeheartedly.[60] Although Randall Davidson felt that uncertainty about the necessity for non-Episcopalian ministers to be ordained might cause difficulties in the Anglican Church, he was on the whole satisfied with the results. By 1923: "A whole series of discussions between Anglicans and non-Episcopalian churches all over the world had begun and

---

57   Ibid., p.119.
58   Ibid., pp.121-122.
59   *The Times*, 29 June 1920, p.12.
60   Methuen, 'Lambeth 1920: The Appeal to All Christian People', p.524.

were proceeding in an atmosphere of cordiality and friendship."[61] However, by the Lambeth Conference of 1930 not much more had been achieved, the main stumbling block being Episcopal and non-Episcopal orders.

A letter to the *Church Times* signed in March 1930 by, among others, Raven, Woods, Rogers and Woodward, explained how the original conception of an apostolic succession had developed as a way of promoting doctrinal unity:

> The Anglican view of orders since the Reformation has not been bound in theory or practice to such an idea of validity as denies to those not episcopaly [*sic*] ordained a true ministry of word and sacrament.[62]

This seemed to imply that the writers of the letter were willing to accept non-Episcopal orders as valid. F. R. Barry in *One Clear Call*, written in 1922, asked that Christians put aside their differences in a "New truce of God" in which they were not asked to "Sink our differences, but may be fairly ordered to transcend them, in a common endeavour of discipleship."[63] E. S. Woods, writing in 1926, shared the concern over the question of ordained ministry: "The negotiations have reached what for the time being seems to be an insuperable barrier in the question of the Christian ministry."[64] He also considered that one of the problems was a lack of enthusiasm of the "rank and file" of various religious denominations, who lack "momentum and drive". He reached the conclusion that: "When the churches really want to unite, questions of faith and order will suddenly cease to be as intractable as they are now."[65] He also, personally, wanted nothing less than "organic union".[66]

During the interwar years Guy Rogers became a leading advocate of church unity and intercommunion. These were to be topics on which he was vocal in meetings and in the press during the 1920s and 1930s. In his autobiography, *A Rebel at Heart*, he went into some detail on intercommunion:

> In relation to the immediate access of all God's people to the Holy Communion, approaching Him through Christ, I have had what I can only call 'a revelation'. Christians should come together to the Lord's Table as members of one church and no individual church has the right to set up barriers to prevent them. There is one Lord and one Holy Table; not a number of different tables nor a number of Lords of separate churches. To refuse intercommunion is to live in sin. It is not

---

61   Ibid., p.411.
62   *Church Times*, 19 March 1930, p.15.
63   Barry, *One Clear Call*, p.15.
64   E. S. Woods, *Getting Ready for Reunion* (Cambridge, W. Heffer & Sons, 1926), p.12.
65   Ibid., p.5.
66   Ibid., p.9.

a coping-stone of a church to be organically united a millennium hence, but a stepping stone today to a deeper experience of fellowship and prayer.[67]

Rogers was protected by the controversial Bishop of Birmingham, Ernest Barnes, who had Protestant views on the sacraments and modernist ideas. Rogers described how Barnes was prepared to give him leeway to promote "causes already dear to me, such as intercommunion with free churches, the ministry of the laity, and the application of Christian principles to social and international life."[68]

Rogers believed that one of the main results of the ICF crusade in Birmingham was to show the virtue of churches working together to the people of the city: "The moral effect of a United Church constantly striving to come into being, acting as if it existed wherever and whenever possible, would gradually force the solution of the traditional barriers which keep us apart."[69] Writing to *The Times* in March 1931 he defended what he called: "The great act of witness to the necessity and value of Home Reunion."[70] He had evidently been criticised for allowing intercommunion and stated: "When Christian fellowship has reached the stage that desire for sacramental fellowship is insistent and sincere, to refuse to give expression of it seems to us to be a refusal of to follow the leading of the Holy Spirit." In a chapter in *The Church in the Twentieth Century*, published in 1936, Rogers summed up his opinions on unity and intercommunion. He reminded his readers that the Lambeth Conference of 1920 had suggested that full intercommunion was inconsistent with the "present will and intention of Christians to perpetuate separately organised churches".[71] However, a statement of the Lambeth Committee of Anglicans and Free Churchmen, set up after the conference, and on which both the Archbishops sat, had affirmed the conviction that "non-Episcopal ministers are real ministers of Christ's word and sacraments in the universal church".[72] Writing in his book *The Church and the People* in 1930, he said that, for himself: "an unbroken succession of bishops neither adds nor diminishes my confidence in my own ministry."[73] He looked forward to the day when there was a world church: "Something larger than Anglicanism and other than Rome, as we know it at the present."[74]

---

67   Rogers, *A Rebel at Heart*, p.152.
68   Rogers, A *Rebel at Heart*, p.211.
69   T. G. Rogers, *Church and People* (London, Sampson Low, Marston & Co.,1931), p.64.
70   *The Times*, 18 March 1931, p.12.
71   Harvey, G. L. H. (ed.), *The Church in the Twentieth Century* (London, Macmillan, 1936), p.162.
72   Ibid., p.163.
73   Rogers, *Church and People*, p.6.
74   Ibid., p.8.

Another priest who was pushing the boundaries on intercommunion was Dick Sheppard. The *Church Times*, in an editorial criticising Sheppard's book *The Impatience of a Parson*,[75] said:

> If Mr Sheppard has his way he would turn the Church of England into another protestant sect without creeds and apparently without sacraments. He definitely repudiates the doctrine of baptismal regeneration and the doctrine of apostolic succession … Sheppard pleads that the next Archbishop of Canterbury be a reformer, but it is a destroyer not a reformer that he really demands.[76]

In an interview given in October 1926, reported by the *Church Times*, Sheppard said that St Martin's stood for "diffused rather than sectional Christianity" and that he would not refuse Holy Communion to nonconformists. However, in the same article, on the occasion of his leaving St Martin's, the *Church Times* concluded:

> There is nothing of the protestant in Mr Sheppard. That he has disregarded many of the rules and safeguards by which the holy church … has hedged around the sacraments is not due to his undervaluing the importance of holy things, but to the intense love of souls that had moved him to bid all and sundry to enter and share the feast.[77]

Charles Raven, also writing a chapter in *The Church in the Twentieth Century* in 1936, considered the problem of the interchange of pulpits. In his chapter "Intercommunion", he felt that the war had given great opportunities for better interdenominational relationships and was disappointed that the Lambeth Conference had not resulted in any great changes: "The sequel was disappointing. Organised and influential opposition to any advance began to make itself felt."[78] However the sanctioning of the interchange of pulpits and the growing practice of inviting preachers of other denominations had "revealed to congregations how much in common the various churches possess." He recommended the spread of collaboration between various denominations in the field of rapidly changing theological understanding and that this cooperation should "touch the mass of church people".[79] He supported this argument by commenting: "The divisions between the reformed churches are mostly concerned with matters of little interest to the laity." He continued "Those who accept the new outlook find

75   H. R. L. Sheppard, *The Impatience of a Parson: A Plea for the Recovery of Vital Christianity* (London, Hodder & Stoughton, 1927).
76   *Church Times*, 21 October 1927, p.296.
77   *Church Times*, 1 October 1926, p.357.
78   Harvey, *The Church in the Twentieth Century*, p.195.
79   Ibid., p.197.

themselves drawn into a real unity with those in other churches who share their convictions, a way unaffected by church order or other superficial divergences."[80]

It is clear that Raven's theology predisposed him to the concept of church unity. Dillistone commented on his attitude in the 1920s and 1930s. "No one had been more eager to break down the barriers that divided Christendom. He preached in churches of other communions in Britain and America when such action lacked official approval. He strongly advocated the united communion as a means towards achieving unity."[81]

In 1927 the World Conference on Faith and Order took place in Lausanne. The Anglican Church sent a delegation which included E. S. Woods. Any resolutions of the conference were not to be considered binding on the Anglican Church. E. S. Woods was one of the thirty-five delegates chosen to make up a continuation committee to continue the work of organising for church unity after the conference. The long-term results of the conference inspired what was has been called an "ecumenical theological conversation", which according to a speaker at the 2002 World Conference on Faith and Order "provided building blocks on which the churches have been able to build new relationships".[82]

In 1932, a conference took place between representatives of the Church of Scotland and the Church of England on unity. The Anglican representatives included the former chaplains E. G. Selwyn, Dean of Winchester, R. G. Parsons, Bishop of Southwark, Oliver Quick and J. W. Hunkin.[83] It was agreed that the statement of the 1920 Lambeth Conference be used as a starting point to their discussions and their aim was to look for common ground in their beliefs. The meeting was reconvened in May 1933, and reports given to the Church of Scotland assembly and to the Archbishop of Canterbury. In May of that year an organisation called "Friends of Reunion" was launched from the headquarters of the ICF. It was "A representative group of leaders of the churches", who had plans for "a popular movement."[84] The council of members for this new non-denominational group to discuss unity included Selwyn, Quick, Haigh, Woods, Rogers, Raven and Parsons.

Services

From the beginning, the experiences of trench warfare challenged the chaplains' ideas and preconceptions of Anglican worship. Priests who insisted on fasting communion at home realised the impracticality of this concept in the changing conditions that

---

80 C. Raven, 'Intercommunion' in Harvey (ed.), *The Church in the Twentieth Century*, p.194.
81 Dillistone, *Charles Raven*, p.276.
82 Mary Tanner, speaking at 75th Anniversary of Faith & Order, Lausanne, 25 August 2002. www.oikoumene.org/en/who.../faith-and-order/history. (Accessed May 2012).
83 J. W. Hunkin, TCF 1915-1919,*Crockford's*, p.1366.
84 *The Times*, 19 May 1933, p.20.

obtained at the front.[85] Clergy of a lower church inclination who abhorred the practice of reservation realised its value in administering Holy Communion in difficult and dangerous positions. Those who disapproved of decorations saw the value of some candles and flowers in brightening up a barn or dugout for a service. There seemed to be a consensus of opinion among Anglican chaplains that Holy Communion was the service that meant most to the troops as they prepared for battle and faced the loss of comrades.[86] Robert Keable commented on the way that controversies over the way services were conducted at home seemed irrelevant at the front:

> We have long since largely scrapped the Prayer Book and a great deal of traditional ritual in France. The official parade service has secured at a blow all that Prayer Book reform has been fighting for and no one dreams of sticking to the Athanasiun creed ... Kikuyu happens every week in France somewhere ... People in England are prepared to act as if they lived in a century in which people attached importance to these things.[87]

Many chaplains began to concentrate more on voluntary services rather than on the compulsory parade services, which were resented by many soldiers. Informal services held in barns and dugouts became an increasing part of a chaplain's work. Eric Milner-White described his feelings, "an immense spontaneous amicable anarchy has sprung up and this has been the Church in the Furnace."[88] The difficulty that the chaplains faced in providing suitable and appropriate services at the Front was that Mattins and Evensong were the only forms of service well known to the congregations at these informal services. The chaplains condensed the main elements of the Apostles' Creed, the Lord's Prayer and the confession around the singing of hymns, which Milner-White found were particularly useful: "Singing has a worth impossible to exaggerate ... careful watching has convinced me that a hymn mediates to an Englishman another country ... it is his chosen sacrament of approach to God."[89]

Some chaplains who had come from industrial parishes were well aware of the limited appeal of the Anglican Church and its services to the majority of the population, but to many the depth of ignorance about God and religion that they found among the officers and men at the front came as a shock. The report, *The Army and Religion* thoroughly examined the state of religion and the army and found it wanting. Much of the blame was placed on the failings of organised religion in Britain before the war and some ideas given about the solutions after the war.[90]

---

85   Blackburne, *This also happened on the Western Front*, p.16.
86   Birmingham University, CMS Archives, XACC/18/Z/1, the Rev Wyteland: IWM, H. Spooner Papers (1/51/94), Julian Bickersteth, *The Bickersteth Diaries* (London, 1995) p.82.
87   Keable, *Standing By*, p.42.
88   E. Milner-White, 'Worship and Services', *The Church in the Furnace*, p.175.
89   Ibid., p.196.
90   Cairns, *The Army and Religion*, Chapter Five.

In their contributions to *The Church in the Furnace*, Eric Milner-White and C. S. Woodward dealt with services, their role at the front and suggestions for improvements post-war. Milner-White stressed that the nature of providing services in all types of condition in the war had given chaplains "new ideas and ideals as to the scope and wealth of public devotion."[91] He warned that changes were inevitable "when those who for three years have almost forgotten the ordered progress of the Prayer Book return to their altars".[92] He commented on the need to abbreviate and change Mattins and Evensong to suit local conditions, but stressed that they had remained distinctly faithful to the Church of England template, based on the Confession, the Lord's Prayer and the Creed. He called for "more and wider schemes of devotion that shall have a place in the Prayer Book."[93] On the subject of the funeral service, he commented on the vast variety of the committals performed by different chaplains in difficult circumstances, and appealed that these variations and changes should be incorporated. Considering the service of Holy Communion, he reported changes that had evolved in the length and structure of the service, and also talked about the experiments with non-fasting communion and the use of reservation. Significantly, he mentioned the effect this might have on "the controversies of three generations", but stressed that: "They do not cause one breath of controversy at the front."[94] Milner-White then went on to criticise the Prayer Book in its present form as being too intellectual and of being off-putting to "the simple ardent Christian". He stressed the need to make the Prayer Book the church's servant, not its master, and of the need to experiment. His suggestions included the reduction of the role of the conductor in intercessions, and that the congregational participation be increased. He suggested that the framework of service be kept simple so they it can be learned from childhood and pleaded for "a more intimate, human understanding, a pictorial, worshipful manner of prayer."[95] He also advocated that the Holy Communion service could be made more "homely" if special collects, epistles and gospels were provided for "church, national and family occasions".[96] Throughout his essay, Milner-White constantly referred to the circumstances at the front that had led to his conclusion and ended with a plea for forgiveness from the church for times when "in the pitifulness of our impotence as priests we have turned in France to blame her or improve her ways as those that know the spirit better".[97]

In his essay on *Worship and Services*, C. Salisbury Woodward set out to add the voice of "average men and women"[98] to the debate which had been taking place among

---

91   Ibid., p.175.
92   Ibid., p.175.
93   Ibid., p.179.
94   Ibid., p.182.
95   Ibid., p.195.
96   Ibid., p.203.
97   Ibid., p.210.
98   C. Salisbury Woodward, 'Worship and Services', *The Church in the Furnace*, p.215.

"experts" about the services of the church. He made the point: "We are far too ready to ignore the uncomfortable fact that of late years churchgoing … has steadily declined almost in proportion as services have been multiplied and elaborated."[99] He made the suggestion that many services were too difficult and complicated to a new church-goer, and that the church should provide a variety of services based on the Sunday services of the church. Like Milner-White, he criticised the forms of Mattins and Evensong, in particular the general nature of intercessions and the inaccessibility of the psalms. He recommended the development of a "simpler and more elastic form of service for the time when the men come home."[100]

One of the results of the National Mission had been the setting up of the Archbishops' Committees to examine the role of the church in various respects. On the committee looking at worship, chaplains were represented by being invited to attach a report to the findings. The chaplains involved were Neville Talbot, F. B. Macnutt and H. Southwell. They had also canvassed the views of a "considerable number of chaplains who have, we believe a right to speak owing to experience."[101] The views of the chaplains were that there should be changes to the services of the church in the light of their experiences of taking services at the front. They called for "bold and wise experiment." They explained that they did not want to do away with the Prayer Book services, as there were both priests and laymen who "are deeply attached to the Prayer Book". They echoed the ideas of Milner-White in suggesting that the psalms and lessons needed to be modified and the lectionary chosen carefully. Morning and evening prayer, Mattins andEvensong, were described as being like "cakes which are too rich, indigestible and even repellent",[102] and ideas for extending what was described as "a narrow range of method" were given. It was suggested by the chaplains that new sentences and proper prefaces should be made available and that there should be alternative, shortened and simpler forms of exhortation, confession and absolution. There should be a revised Psalter with retranslations of obscure passages. It was recommended that services should be as congregational as possible, "without intoning, without wide use of anthems and with the development of hymn singing."[103] The experience and disappointment of the chaplains concerning the relative unpopularity of Holy Communion at the front led them to suggest changes here also: "All chaplains will return from the Front anxious to make this service the main, corporate, family, congregational act of worship and fellowship." Other suggestions included the abolition of Mattins and the regular circulation of prayers and thanksgivings dealing with current affairs by the bishop. More contemporary relevance would,

---

99   Ibid., p.216.
100 Ibid., p.223.
101 The Archbishops' Second Committee of Enquiry, *The Worship of the Church* (London, 1918), Appendix, p.33.
102 Ibid., p.34.
103 Ibid., p.34

they felt, ameliorate the fact that they had found "striking evidence that many men feel that the Prayer Book as at present used is remote from common life".[104]

Writing in 1922 F. R. Barry criticised the fact that many religious people kept outside institutional religion as they could not find expression in the services: "The whole atmosphere is charged with unreality, people pass by and look elsewhere. Much of our worship is so restrained as to be almost a barren formality. It lacks colour and spontaneity ... Our worship, like the life of the church tends to be something merely institutional."[105] He was not impressed by the 1928 Alternative Prayer Book:

> We cannot meet the demands of the Christianity which is emerging in the new age by inserting a few more 'prayers for special occasions' or by rearrangement of existing offices. What is needed is a courageously new approach to the meaning of worship in the Christian community. Urgently we need to recapture the 'experimental' stresses in public prayer.[106]

Harry Blackburne had much to say in his book *This Also Happened on the Western Front* about how the attitudes of the chaplain to service had to adapt to wartime conditions. After leaving full-time chaplaincy and becoming a parish priest at Ashford in Kent, he seemed to have kept up this flexibility and maintained a middle of the road kind of churchmanship. Speaking on the particular problems of country parishes at a meeting of Church Congress in 1927, Blackburne said:

> Our object should be to make services helpful to those who come to them and not just satisfactory to ourselves. In the parish of which I am speaking we aim at making our service English and not continental in character. ... We venture to hope that those who love the church Eucharist and value the statement of penance are as well thought of as those who prefer Mattins and plain celebrations of the Holy Communion. Many would call us wishy-washy simply because we aim at being comprehensive. It is because of this that we welcome the new Prayer Book.[107]

Guy Rogers, writing in 1930, considering the way forward in bringing in what he called "the outsider" thought that the church services were not suited to encouraging a person "of a vigorous mind, untrained in our apologetic". He suggested:

> A summary of the creed similar to the summary of the Ten Commandments which should be sanctioned for alternative use and that further encouragement

104 Ibid., p.34.
105 Barry, *One Clear Call*, p.5.
106 Ibid., p.313.
107 *Church Times*, 28 October 1927, p.387.

should be given to service resting on a simple creedal basis to which the outsider could be freely invited.[108]

Although he considered that the preaching of the church had improved, "The more thoughtful of our preachers do not always assume a formulated faith on the part of their hearers", he still thought that the services would pose a problem to the visitor. "The services are less elastic than the preaching and there are too many fences for the sincere inquirer." He concluded, "We need a touch of modern realism."

Former chaplains had been determined to make a difference to the way that services were taken and saw this as a way to rectify the drift away from church attendance to a more "diffusive Christianity". Men of varied churchmanship were all agreed that the inclusion of up-to-date language and experimentation in services were essential to the encouragement of new congregations and the deepening of faith in existing ones. They were to have opinions on the new revised Prayer Book, which as we shall see raised more issues than simply the wording of the services.

Chaplains and the Prayer Book Controversy

The revision of the liturgy of the Church of England had been on the agenda before the war. The Royal Commission on Ecclesiastical Discipline had reported in 1906, recommending changes aiming to accommodate the development of Tractarian practices. The war had both delayed revision and complicated the issues surrounding it. The rise of ritualism, including the formation of the English Church Union in 1860, had resulted in reaction in the form of the Public Worship Regulation Act of 1874, which allowed for prosecutions of ritualists in the church courts.[109] The Royal Commission of 1906 had taken into account the desire of many priests to have a more Tractarian approach to the liturgy but also considered what Maiden has described as the "ritualistic lawlessness that affected the church as the Anglo-Catholic movement rose to prominence".[110]

The war had brought key issues to the foreground, for example how the sacrament was reserved increasingly for practical purposes. In 1919 Archbishop Davidson sanctioned the use of the reserved sacrament for the use of administration to the sick only. Another aspect of the changes which could be attributed to war was the sense of increasing resentment, at the front and at home, of the role of Parliament acting as what Maiden called "The lay synod of the church", resulting in the development of Life and Liberty. This attitude was shared by liberal evangelicals and English

---

108 Rogers, *Church and People*, p.44.
109 Maiden, J. *National Religion and the Prayer Book Controversy, 1927–1928* (Boydell Press: Suffolk, 2009), p.4.
110 Ibid., p.11.

Catholics. Together they made up the "centre-high consensus", part of the mainstream of Anglican thought in the 1920s: they were epitomised by William Temple.[111]

The aims of Prayer Book revision were to "widen the latitude of acceptable practices and set in stone the limits of Anglican ritual."[112] Anglo-Catholicism had been
increasing in influence in the years since the Royal Commission and the bishops were
concerned that ritualistic practices were taking hold and would be beyond their power
to control. However, the proposals came under criticism from the evangelical wing of
the church as being too catholic, from the catholic wing for not going far enough in
sanctioning Tractarian practices, and also from those clergy and laymen who saw the
revision as taking the church too far away from the idea of a Protestant church bound
to national identity. Maiden described how this issue was bound to be problematic:
"This 'national' dimension to the revision controversy would feature widely in the
rhetoric and polemic of the Protestant campaign against the bishops' book."[113]

Some of the chaplains had a wider view of church services than just the communion
service and their proposals dealt with the larger question of making the liturgy of the
church accessible to more people. The matter of Prayer Book revision was discussed
at the sixth anniversary meeting of Life and Liberty in July 1923. Studdert Kennedy
explained that the movement "asked that the Prayer Book should be Christian in the
fullest sense of the word. All their teaching about God would fall on deaf ears, while
the Prayer Book contained unchristian ideas." He criticised the services of baptism,
marriage and burial of the dead on the grounds that they were unintelligible to ordinary people and considered that "the whole practice of baptism was as rotten as it
could be".[114]

Percy Dearmer had been involved in discussions about the nature of the services
of the Anglican Church for many years before the war. He had written *The Parson's
Pocketbook* in 1899, which had given advice on the use of vestments, incense and
Church furnishings. His biographer considered that *The Parson's Pocket Book* was
Dearmer's attempt to remedy what he saw as "the lamentable confusion, lawlessness
and vulgarity that are conspicuous in the church at this present time".[115] In 1904 he
was appointed to the Royal Commission on Ecclesiastical Discipline.

In 1923 a proposal for a new Prayer Book to work alongside the 1662 one started
to be discussed in Church Assembly. A group of youngish clergy, most of whom had
seen war service, produced an alternative Prayer Book. Donald Grey stated that the
book, called "The Grey Book" (to distinguish it from other alternatives, namely the
green and orange books), was mainly the work of F. R. Barry, Percy Dearmer and R.

111 Ibid.
112 Ibid., p.12.
113 Ibid., p.13.
114 *The Times*, 3 July 1923, p.11.
115 D. Gray, *Percy Dearmer, A Parson's Pilgrimage* (Norwich, Canterbury Press, 2000), p.43.

G. Parsons.[116] Barry remembers it as involving also Dick Sheppard, Mervyn Haigh and Leslie Hunter. He described it as "A liberal proposal for a new Prayer Book".[117] William Temple wrote the foreword and described the compilers as "drawn from all parties of the church".[118] Barry's biographer, West, commented that the final version showed "The mark of Russell's [Barry's] hand throughout".[119] West was also of the opinion that it was Barry's experience of devising suitable services among the troops in Egypt and France during the war that had stimulated his interest in Prayer Book revision. The group concentrated on improving the intelligibility of the lectionary and weeding out archaic expressions. The marriage service was modified with expressions such as "followers of holy and godly matrons" removed, along with the requirement of the bride to "obey".[120] The baptism service was a cause of concern to the group as they realised that this was the service where non-church-goers were most likely to come into contact with the liturgy of the church. They proposed replacing "born in sin", and substituted it for the statement: "It is plain that human nature as we see it ourselves and in the whole race of and mankind is not what God our father intends it to be".[121] Tom Pym, also a member of the Grey Book group, was concerned with the reform of the occasional offices and thought that: "People who never entered a church except for christenings, weddings and funerals, should at those important times be met with language which would enter their hearts because it was simple and intelligible to them."[122]

In the Church Assembly meeting in 1923, R. G. Parsons made a statement about the Grey Book: "Those responsible for the Grey Book had endeavoured to construct an order of the liturgy which would conserve things beloved by both Catholics and Evangelicals."[123] In October 1923 members of the group that supported the Grey Book wrote to *The Times* to publicise it and commend it to "members of the Church of England as a whole." They went on to describe it as:

> … loyal to the doctrines of the Church of England. We consider that in many important particulars a revision of the church services on the lines indicated in it would make them more real and intelligible and so help many people to discover the value of public worship.[124]

---

116 D. Gray, *Earth and Altar: The Evolution of the Parish Communion in the Church of England to 1945* (Norwich, Canterbury Press, 1986), p.55.
117 Barry, *Period of My Life*, p.86.
118 William Temple in the Foreword to *The Grey Book*, cited by Gray, *Earth and Altar*, p.55.
119 F. West, *F. R. B.: Portrait of Bishop Russell Barry* (Bramcote, Grove Books, 1980), p.34.
120 Ibid., p.35.
121 Ibid.
122 Pym, *Tom Pym, A Portrait*, p.60.
123 *The Times*, 3 July 1923, p.19.
124 *The Times*, 26 October 1923, p.8.

This letter was signed, among others, by ex-chaplains Harry Blackburne, B. K. Cunningham, J. V. Macmillan, Charles Raven, Geoffrey Studdert Kennedy and Guy Rogers. Guy Rogers and R. G. Parsons were on the consultative committee of the House of Clergy of the Church Assembly and Parsons was lobbying for the inclusion of the ideas put forward in the Grey Book.

Guy Rogers described how he had started off an "ardent" supporter of the revised Prayer Book, believing that here was: "much in our way of thinking about God which was imperfectly expressed in 1662." He became disenchanted with the proposals when he found out how little change could be expected in the baptismal service: "The task became more and more wearisome as the years went by and it became evident that the need to keep the balance of doctrine 'fairly' as between Catholic and Protestant elements was distorting and disturbing all our business."[125] The matter that most disturbed Rogers was the perpetual reservation of the sacrament, not for the purpose of communicating the sick, but in an aumbry or tabernacle for the purpose of adoration. In the Church Assembly meeting in February 1927 he spoke out against continuous reservation. Although wanting the sacred elements taken to the sick with as little delay as possible, he did not want the elements used in worship. Despite having voted in the end for the Deposited Book,[126] he was relieved when it was rejected by Parliament. He remembered that, according to his wife he "danced about in my underclothes with relief or joy."[127] When the Church Assembly was making revisions to the Deposited Book to present it again to Parliament in February 1928, he again spoke out against continuous reservation.

When the revised Prayer Book was ready to go to Parliament, the Grey Book group issued a statement expressing support for the final version or Deposited Book, especially the alternative order for the Holy Communion service. When the Deposited Prayer Book was rejected by the House of Commons on 18 December 1927, F. R. Barry and others, including Tubby Clayton, Pat McCormick, Tom Pym, E. S. Woods and Studdert Kennedy, wrote to The Times in indignation: "We are certain that many of those who voted in the majority in the House of Commons on Thursday night will awake to the fact that what they have achieved is a setback for the cause of true religion."[128] When the second attempt was being made to get the slightly altered book through Parliament in June 1928, the former chaplains who had supported the Grey Book made an appeal to the readers of The Times based strongly on their war-time experience. After having pointed out that the shortage of ordinands was not, as the Home Secretary believed, due to a rise in Anglo-Catholicism, but by the fact that 5,000 graves contained the bodies of English ordinands, they went on to dismiss the controversy of reservation, claiming that reservation was carried out naturally

125 Rogers, A Rebel at Heart, p.160.
126 This was the version eventually decided upon which was to be presented to parliament.
127 Ibid., p.161.
128 The Times, 20 December 1927, p.15.

on the battlefield and never gave offence. The letter made a plea on behalf of "those who fought and fell in the B.E.F.". They would say: "that active service sifts out ruthlessly the essential issues from the secondary ... they would urge us not to weaken the Christian cause by perpetuating controversy on matters of secondary importance."[129]

The Grey Book and its compilers did not appear to have a marked effect on the course of Prayer Book revision, but its existence does shed some light on the effort of former chaplains to make sense of their experiences in the war to inform their ideas on the services of the church in the 1920s. Their concerns about the intelligibility of the services to ordinary people had an echo of their concerns about both the future and the nature of the church in the war era expressed during and just after the war. The revised Prayer Book, despite having been passed by the Church Assembly with a majority was twice defeated in the House of Commons, by a combination of evangelical feeling that it compromised the Protestant tradition too much, a high Anglican party feeling that it did not go far enough to condone Anglo-Catholic practices and a feeling in conservative circles that it compromised the national and established nature of the Church of England.

Conclusion

In their eyes and those of contemporary observers, army chaplains had returned from the war with an expertise in dealing with the problems of encouraging men touched with "diffusive Christianity" into the full life of the church. They had clear opinions on the ways in which the church had to change, and these opinions influenced leaders of change, such as William Temple. The objections that chaplains like Tom Pym, Ben O'Rorke and F. R. Barry had to the way in which the Church of England was managed bore fruit in the independence gained by the Enabling Act of 1919, even though this was in some ways a disappointment to them.

The Chaplains' Fellowship provided a forum for chaplains adjusting to peacetime ministry, and their meetings produced some interesting suggestions about the role of the church in society and the role of such a fellowship in attaining these goals. However, under peacetime conditions, and possibly hostility from other clergy who could see it as an exclusive organisation, it faded away, with some chaplains who were serious about its principles attaching themselves as chaplains to Toc H and becoming involved in the Industrial Christian Fellowship. The Fellowship's interdenominational nature, however, and its stress on continuing the freedom of action on unity found in the trenches, gave impetus to the movement for unity in the church.

Historians have differed in their judgement on partisan splits in the Church of England in the interwar years. Callum Brown painted a picture in which: "Splits

---

129 *The Times*, 13 June 1928, p.17.

between evangelicals, ritualists and liberals became severe."[130] Roger Lloyd sees these arguments dying down after the controversy about the revised Prayer Book:

> The last really discreditable outbreak of such sectarian strife was on the occasions of the debating of the revised Prayer Book in 1928. It was most violent while it lasted, but it subsided with remarkable speed and it is doubtful whether we shall see any revival of it.[131]

The chaplains came to the discussion from all parties, and any partisan feeling had been lessened by their experiences in war. During the Prayer Book controversy, and with the exception of Chavasse, they managed to focus on the liturgical changes they were advocating and not become too embroiled in controversy of a party nature.

Many of the former chaplains had clear views on the necessity for church unity and did much to encourage this process. This was an aspect of interwar religious life which was clearly a result of the chaplains' experiences in taking services in wartime, as was their insistence on supporting moves towards unity, both within the Anglican Church and with Non-conformists. In this respect they did become controversial, with men such as Rogers, Talbot, Barry and Sheppard challenging boundaries on intercommunion, preaching and joint services. They would not accept that issues that had seemed simple in the trenches could cause so much division in the years to follow. However, by their words and actions they made a clear contribution to interdenomi-national unity in this era.

An aspect of the former chaplains' contribution to the church, which can be directly attributed to their war service, was their reforming attitude towards the services of the church. During the war they had many opportunities to reflect on the relevance of the liturgy of the Church of England to men in time of war and had resorted to adapting the service as best they could, using what Milner-White called "mangled matins" as an example of this improvisation. They contributed substantially to war and post-war reports on services and they continued to push for reform and experimentation in their individual ministries. Although Donald Gray in his study of the genesis of the family communion movement does not directly attribute it to the attitude of the chaplains to services of Holy Communion, their actions and ideas on the subject clearly formed one of the strands leading to the modern concept of family communion.

---

130 Brown, *Religion and Society*, p.50.
131 Lloyd, *The Church of England*, p.280.

6

Controversies in Wider Society

The question of divorce was one which was increasingly on the public agenda in the 1920s. It also became a focus of feminist pressure, due to the inequality of the grounds for divorce as applied to men and women. In the Matrimonial Causes Act of 1857 men were allowed to divorce their wives on grounds of adultery, but wives who wanted a divorce had to cite another reason in addition to adultery. A bill introduced as a private member's bill in 1927 to enable a woman to obtain a divorce on the grounds of adultery alone was passed without serious opposition. However, it was still only possible to obtain a divorce by proving adultery, and this led to countless cases of people perjuring themselves in court by arranging false proof of adultery in order to expedite a divorce. The law therefore condoned and encouraged immorality. In the Convocation of Canterbury of 1931 Dr Donaldson made the point that: "The present position of the state law was practically an encouragement to deception."[1]

The position of the Church of England was that people who had been divorced could not be remarried in church while the former spouse was still alive. The resolution of the Lambeth Conference of 1930, as reported in *The Times,* had recommended that: "The marriage of one whose former partner is still living should not be celebrated according to the rites of the church, making no distinction between innocent and guilty parties." However, *The Times* report added: "This year's conference has struck a new note by further suggesting that the church is bound to concern itself with the moral welfare of the guilty in place of merely regarding them as outside the pale."[2] The resolution also provided for the bishops' discretion to be used in deciding whether to admit divorced people to communion. Although this was the official line of the Church of England there was controversy, with modernist churchmen like Hastings Rashdall and Bishop E. Barnes of Birmingham calling for a more lenient and understanding approach. Mainstream Anglican policy was, however, firm on the remarriage of divorced people, in many cases forbidding them to receive Holy Communion.

1   *The Times,* 5 June 1931, p.11.
2   *The Times,* 15 August 1930, p.13.

Guy Rogers served on the Archbishops' Commission on Marriage and Divorce, which reported in 1935 and described how, as usual, he signed the minority report along with Bishop Barnes. It argued that in some circumstances divorcees should be admitted to Holy Communion and stated: "Admission to communion is a confirmation of need of moral help, not a certificate of moral excellence."[3] In his book *The Church and the People*, he wrote at some length about how marriages could be saved by the transforming power of prayer, but also spoke of "marriages which had been 'desecrated' by such events as cruelty, desertion, unfaithfulness and venereal disease."[4] He stated that: "I have no doubt that there is in extreme cases a necessity for divorce, and I have no feeling of disloyalty to the teaching of Jesus in thinking so."[5]

He sympathised with the efforts of the Church of England to "maintain the standard of marriage as set by our Lord", but did not find them "wisely directed". He stressed that Jesus was a "saviour and friend of sinners", rather than a rigid lawgiver. He asked several questions:

> Is a second marriage, while one of the partners is still living, never to be sanctioned by the church, or is it all things considered in some cases the best way out of the catastrophe? Is a first marriage indissoluble from a Christian point of view? If not, can there be a blessing on a second after the dissolution of the first, out of the reservoirs of divine love and mercy and compassion?[6]

Rogers considered that the parish priest had the right to use his discretion, and related how he had "several times celebrated such marriages. Not out of pity or of friendship alone, but because I felt that in doing so I was acting in the spirit of Christ." He added: "some of them are the happiest marriages I know".[7] Rogers also advocated the admittance of divorced persons to communion: "Presumably the divorced person comes, as we all ought to do, in a spirit of repentance and faith ... who are we to cut off others from possible sources of blessing?"[8]

F. R. Barry, writing in 1931 in *The Relevance of Christianity*, also condemned the necessity to commit perjury or adultery to end a marriage: "On no grounds can it be held that this situation is morally healthy in any society."[9] Although acknowledging that marriage should be lifelong and indissoluble he added: "We must recognise that

---

3   John Barnes, *Ahead of his Age – Bishop Barnes of Birmingham* (London, Collins, 1979), p.327.
4   Rogers, *The Church and the People*, p.153.
5   Ibid., p.154.
6   Ibid., p.155.
7   Ibid., p.156.
8   Ibid., p.157.
9   F. R. Barry, *The Relevance of Christianity* (London, Nisbet & Co., 1932), p.223.

there are bound to be cases where a marriage proves morally unworkable."[10] He went on:

> There yet remain the 'quite exceptional circumstances'. If despite all faith, hope and love, the marriage proves to be morally unendurable or even destructive of spiritual health, or if it has ceased to have any moral content (as through unrepentant infidelity), then I cannot believe the Christian church will be really be serving the cause of Christian marriage by a rigorist … attitude.[11]

He was against excommunication of divorced persons who remarried, denying that they were "living in sin" and said therefore, if the church recognised the remarriage by admitting the parties to communion, there seemed no logical justification for refusing its blessing to the wedding ceremony. He completed his section on the question of divorce by asserting: "The essential interest of the Christian ethic is not to prevent people from getting unmarried but to help them to get married in the best way and to make the most they can out of marriage."[12]

Both Rogers and Barry, along with Linton Smith, encouraged marriage preparation classes. Rogers stressed that the sense of the vocation of marriage should be emphasised. He acknowledged the need for teaching the "physical facts and social obligations" of marriage, but also thought that here was: "the constant need for the deepening of the sense of vocation and of presenting marriage as a new field for service, a new state full of the most glorious possibilities into which God is leading his young friends."[13] Another strong advocate of marriage preparation was Tom Pym. He had attacked the absence of such preparation strongly. In August 1931 he gave a paper to the annual meeting of the British Medical Association, entitled: "The need of education in questions of sex", and two similar talks to a diocesan synod caused much consternation among the clergy. The bishop of the diocese: "felt that the plain outspokenness [of the talk], though it appealed to and helped some, upset others".[14] According to Dora Pym, Tom Pym felt that the consideration of questions about divorce was not useful unless: "a picture of a Christian home, which included every feature of marriage plainly expressed, was given by the clergy with the same thoroughness with which candidates were prepared for Confirmation."[15] He wrote a letter to *The Times* in December 1934, urging the "proper education and preparation of people before they are married".[16] He reminded the congregation that four years previously the Lambeth Conference had emphasised this need, and continued:

10   Ibid., p.235.
11   Ibid., p.241.
12   Ibid., p.241.
13   Rogers, *Church and People*, p.140.
14   Pym, *Tom Pym, A Portrait*, p.90.
15   Ibid., p.90.
16   *The Times*, 29 December 1934, p.6.

Yet the clergy of the Anglican Church who have to deal with so many at the time of their weddings, have no instruction or training whatever in the material which they should offer as a preparation ... marriage remains the only sacrament for which people are unprepared."[17] He brought together his ideas on showing a positive slant on preparing for marriage in his book published in 1938, *Sex and Sense*.[18]

Kenneth Kirk, who had become a leading moral theologian, held opposing views on the sanctity of marriage and dissolution of marriage vows. Speaking in a lecture at Oxford in October 1935 he talked of the sanctity of marriage as a vocation:

> If marriage is rightly thought of as a 'vocation to an allegiance', then the vows should hold for the two persons concerned the force of an unconditional promise. Even though the person to which the promise was made proffered to give a release from it this in fact did not in itself constitute a release.[19]

He spoke in the newly revived Church Congress in 1935 on "The New Morality" and stated that "The new morality was, in the realm of sex, very much like the old immorality under a new disguise." He commented on how psychology had stressed the importance of happiness, leading to "liberty of sex experiment among the unmarried and almost complete liberty of divorce among the married". He went on to explain that:

> The short cut to a perfect morality by way of the principle of material happiness is a disastrous one ... in a very short time were given to the new morality by the whole of society, without any of those restraints which traditional Christian thinking would lay upon it, it would prove ... a disastrous failure.[20]

Although mainstream Anglican opinion was against divorce it was realised that these beliefs contrasted with the changing morals of British society, and at the Canterbury Convocation in 1936 a resolution accepted the fact that: "the Christian standard may not always be possible in a state that comprises all sorts of people, including many who do not accept the Christian way", and that therefore the Convocation should support some demands in the change of the divorce laws.[21] According to Machin, many leading Anglicans were prepared to go further and consider altering the church's

---

17   Ibid.
18   T. W. Pym, *Sex and Sense* (London, 1938).
19   *Church Times*, 20 September 1935, p.309.
20   *The Church Times*, 12 October 1935, p.382.
21   Canterbury Convocation 1936, (CCC i, 2, pp.243, 246-7), cited by G. I. T. Machin in *Churches and Social issues in Twentieth-century Britain*, (Oxford, Clarendon Press, 1998), p.101.

teaching on marriage. Speaking in this debate R. G. Parsons, former chaplain and Bishop of Southwark from 1936, spoke in support of the motion that: "It is the sacred responsibility laid upon the Church of England to enact such discipline of its own in regard to marriage as may time to time appear most salutary and efficacious."[22] Parson's opinion was that "there were circumstances in which its [marriage's] disso-lution might be recognised by the church at any rate to the extent of admitting, if the church thought fit, to its communion people who had contracted a second union during the lifetime of the former partner."

The question of contraception was another aspect where the traditional teaching of the church was at variance with developments in society. Throughout the interwar years the question was controversial in society generally, with pioneering advocates of contraception like Marie Stopes often in conflict with those who worried about the prospect of a population fall and those who advocated the encouragement of smaller families in the working class and larger families in the middle and upper classes. Eugenics enthusiasts looked to birth control to stem what Overy calls "the potential biological crisis" which "was a central element in the morbid culture of the post-war years."[23] Eugenics extremists discussed solutions including compulsory sterilisation of the unfit. The Dean of St Paul's, Ralph Inge, speaking to the Royal Institution in May 1931, wanted an ideal British population of only twenty million, all "certificated of bodily and mental fitness."[24]

The mainstream Anglican opinion was again quite clear, that sexual intercourse without the intention to procreate was contrary to the will of God. P. T. R. Kirk, writing in 1931, although admitting to the fact that family limitation would give chil-dren more chance to have a healthy upbringing, advocated primarily abstinence as a way to achieve this, considering that after a while, in a marriage, "the comradeship of man and wife has become so fine an experience that love can continue to grow without further sexual intercourse."[25] However, in 1930 the Lambeth Conference for the first time admitted to some exceptions. *The Times* reported in its round-up of the confer-ence news: "The outstanding fact remains that for the first time the practice of birth control in certain circumstances is allowed by the Lambeth Conference."[26] F. R. Barry argued that undue limitation of families involved "grave moral symptoms," being espe-cially scathing of motives to do with "needlessly high" standards of living and "social snobbery". His opinion was that: "From the Christian standpoint a human baby is of more value than a Baby Austin." However he also considered that: "The procreation of children is bearable only as the crown and delight of joy", and asked, "shall we fill the

22 G. I .T. Machin, 'Marriage and the Churches in the 1930s: Royal Abdication and Divorce Reform 1936-37', *Journal of Ecclesiastical History*, Vol. 42 (1991), p.70.
23 Overy, *The Morbid Age*, p.100.
24 Speech reported in *Nature*, 6 June 1931, cited by Overy, ibid., p.106.
25 P. T. R. Kirk, *The Movement Christwards* (London, A.R.Mowbray, 1931), p.72.
26 *The Times*, 15 August 1930, p.13.

world with unwanted babies?"[27] He was sympathetic to the needs of the modern young mothers not to be trapped into years of childbearing and suggested that if a woman's full-time childbearing and nurturing years could be limited to ten years, then: "it seems therefore to be undesirable that a woman who has her own profession should abandon it on marriage."[28] He thought that abstention was not necessarily the answer, causing tension and unhappiness, and that in the right circumstances "to brand the recourse to contraceptives as morally reprehensible ... might seem to betoken a lack of moral realism." In his opinion the counter-arguments to contraception were: "A rationalisation of repugnance ... rather than morally impressive reasons".

In his advocacy of contraception as in some cases morally right, rather than an unfortunate necessity, Barry went beyond the contemporary thinking on contraception as expressed in Convocation and the church press.

A *Church Times* report in January 1935 criticised the decision of Birmingham Council to open a birth control clinic. It praised the efforts of some local Anglican and Roman Catholic clergy to prevent this, and then added, "The Bishop of Birmingham supported by Canon Guy Rogers had previously been in the field, urging the establishment of a clinic."[29] In May 1935, the *Church Times* contained a long article by the Bishop of Ely condemning the use of contraception and forecasting disastrous population fall.[30] It is clear that former chaplains were prepared to speak out on this controversial matter, not always in agreement with each other but showing the interest of the church on a moral issue, debates on which had reached their climax in the interwar years.

Religious Broadcasting

The British Broadcasting Company was founded in 1922, and was given its royal charter, becoming the British Broadcasting Corporation (BBC) in 1926, under the chairmanship of John Reith. Its remit then as now was public service broadcasting, with an obligation to educate, inform and entertain. The corporation had a monopoly and decided what was fit for the British public to hear. Although Reith was a strong Scottish Presbyterian and wanted the BBC to be involved in religious broadcasting it was not until the middle 1920s that this began. Catriona Noonan has explained the slow start:

> Despite Reith's own conviction, religion was not initially seen as key to the BBC's output. When religion was acknowledged, it was seen as primarily recreational with little concerted effort made to formalise output. Slowly, teaching became

27 Barry, *Relevance of Christianity*, p.227.
28 Ibid., p.228.
29 *Church Times*, 18 January 1935, p.67.
30 *Church Times*, 3 May 1935, p.531.

part of the objective, with conversion and evangelism tied to this objective. This reticence can be attributed to the fact that few believed the BBC could bolster the place of Christianity in British culture. Furthermore, the recruitment and development needed to begin such a process of spiritual engagement was beyond the resources of the corporation at the time. Therefore, it was not until the mid 1920s that the strategic place of religion in radio was re-examined.[31]

Radio audiences grew rapidly, reaching over 9 million by 1939.[32] It was not a medium the churches could afford to ignore.

The broadcasting of religious services was controversial on several counts. The churches were afraid that it would lead to loss of congregations. They also questioned the suitability of radio as a secondary medium, where people could move about and perform other tasks. There was concern that an unsuitable atmosphere would prevail in the home of the listeners when the programme was being broadcast:

> Therefore, the churches had to accept that the benefit and support to religious adherents would be greatly outweighed by the occasions a broadcast was heard in a public house or when someone kept their hat on![33]

The first religious broadcast was transmitted in 1922 from the aerial works at Blackheath, to a radius of 100 miles. Alexander Fleming, of St Columba's, Port Street, initiated the Sunday evening religious address, which took place in the interval of the Sunday evening symphony concert.[34] Reith thought that former army padres were suited to this platform, and well-known figures such as P. B. Clayton and Geoffrey Studdert Kennedy were featured in these concert interval addresses. John Wolfe, in his study of religious broadcasting, commented that: "Many speakers had a reputation from the First World War ... they had been tested amid bombs."[35]

An advisory committee, "The Sunday Committee" was set up in May 1923 under Cyril Foster Garbett. C. S. Woodward was included and Dick Sheppard was asked by Sir John Reith to be on this committee. After returning to St Martin-in-the-Fields following a spell as a chaplain to an Australian hospital on the Western Front, Sheppard had built up the church to become a popular and controversial symbol of Christianity in London. It is not surprising that he should have been one of the first priests to welcome and encourage the new medium. According to his biographer, Ellis

31 Catriona Noonan, *The Production of Religious Broadcasting: The Case of the BBC*, Glasgow University PhD thesis (2008), p.55.
32 A. Briggs, *The History of Broadcasting in the United Kingdom, Vol. 1* (Oxford, OUP, 1961), p.82.
33 Noonan, *Religious Broadcasting*, p.56.
34 K. M. Wolfe, *The Churches and the British Broadcasting Corporation 1922-1956: The Politics of Broadcast Religion* (London, SCM Press, 1984), p.5.
35 Wolfe, *The Churches and the BBC*, p.7.

Roberts, Sheppard was not convinced at first of the advisability of allowing the evening service from St Martin's to be broadcast. He wrote to both St Paul's Cathedral and Westminster Abbey to suggest that the service be broadcast from one of these well-known centres of worship. R. J. Northcott,[36] sometime curate of St Martin's, remembered that this suggestion was "treated as being almost blasphemous."[37] When St Paul's and Westminster Abbey refused he went ahead and the first broadcast service from a place of worship was broadcast on the feast of the Epiphany 1924. Ellis Roberts commented on the appropriateness of this first service being taken by Sheppard from St Martin's:

> Nothing could have been more appropriate than St Martin's should have been the first Church and Dick Sheppard the first priest to use the radio for religion. St Martin's under his leadership stood for service to sick in mind and body … a flaming desire to leave the well-fed sheep in the fold and go out after the lost and strayed.[38]

Part of Sheppard's motivation lay in the concern over what may have filled the airways instead. He wrote in the *Manchester Guardian:*

> I admit I took the plunge with great trepidation, but if we had not started it the evening might have just been given over to secular entertainments and it seemed just one of those things … that the church could claim and use to the utmost. I wonder how far it is realised that the gospel is brought to the homes of millions who would otherwise not hear it, and that it is an unmixed blessing to thousands who are bedridden or invalids, and to whom the sound of public prayers and the hymns they remember and love are looked forward to with joy from week to week.[39]

Another biographer of Sheppard, Scott, described how, "On the last Sunday of 1923, Dick kept his congregation behind after the evening service and rehearsed them."[40] Technically, the first service went well, Reith commenting: "From what came to our room that night, no one would have realised that this was a first and rather startling experiment."[41] The first words announcing the service were spoken by Dick Sheppard:

36 R. J. Northcott, TCF 1917-1920, curate of St Martin-in-the-Fields 1936-1938, *Crockford's*, p.990.
37 R. J. Northcott, *Dick Sheppard and St Martin's* (London, Longmans, Green & Co., 1937), p.6.
38 Ellis Roberts, *H. R. L. Sheppard,* p.112.
39 Ibid., p.113.
40 Scott, *Dick Sheppard,* p.130.
41 Ibid., p.130.

It is our singular privilege tonight and in future on the second Sunday in each month to be allowed to say prayers, to sing hymns and to preach Christ in the presence of any of you who are willing to listen in. We count it a great happiness.[42]

Wolfe is of the opinion that 6 January 1924, the date of the first service from St Martin's, marked "the real beginning of religious broadcasting."[43] The service at 8.15 pm from St Martin's became a monthly occasion. At the first regular service Sheppard explained his policy of: "Arranging the service so that it was acceptable to Free Churchmen as much as Anglicans, and also possible to be understood by those who did not go to church."[44] Nonconformist ministers were asked to preach on a regular basis to give an ecumenical dimension to the broadcasts.[45] After the first broadcast Sheppard received a thousand letters,[46] which gave some idea of the varied places and situations in which the broadcast had been received. A woman in Compton fixed a loudspeaker outside her house so that the rest of the village could hear it, and men in Lewisham joined in with the hymns in the village pub and then stayed to discuss the sermon.[47] Pat McCormick explained the technique of broadcasting: "You must never read or preach your broadcast sermon, but just talk it, visualising, if you can, the fireplaces with listeners sitting round in twos or threes, although you may have two thousand people before you in church."[48]

In the *BBC Handbook* in 1929, Sheppard explained further the motivation behind religious broadcasting:

A lack of interest in churches and church affairs may be perfectly compatible with a genuine and sincere enthusiasm for Christianity: It is hoped that religious broadcasting has an opportunity which probably none of us yet realises.[49]

However, the enthusiasm shown by listeners was not matched by the church and clergy as a whole. Another early broadcaster, W. H. Elliot, considered that it was due to the persistence of John Reith that religious broadcasting got off the ground.

The church was dead against it. A resolution came before Convocation calling for its prohibition. Dick and I tucked our toes in and said that whatever the church

42   A. H. Grey, F. A. Iremonger et al., *St Martin-in-the-Fields Calling, Broadcast Addresses* (London, Athenaeum Press, 1932), p.14.
43   Wolfe, *The Churches and the BBC*, p.9.
44   Northcott, *Dick Sheppard*, p.ix.
45   Ellis Roberts, *H. R. L. Sheppard*, p.113.
46   Scott, *Dick Sheppard*, p.130.
47   Ibid., p.131.
48   *St Martin in-the-Fields Calling*, p.9.
49   *BBC Handbook 1929*, p.208.

might say or do we would go on. However, it did not come to that, mostly, I believe, because Reith was such a rock that nobody could move him.[50]

The initial doubts and arguments are shown in two letters to *The Times* in April 1926. There is a letter of complaint from the Rev R. C. Griffith about a service broadcast from Norwich Cathedral taking place on Sunday evening at normal service time: "A Cathedral nave service when broadcast at the same hour as the parish churches must of necessity exist at their expense." He continued with the second regularly rehearsed objection to religious broadcasting: "The broadcasting of such a service leads to encourage gross idleness on the part of able-bodied people content to sit at home and make no effort to attend in person an act of worship."[51] The position of the BBC was defended by a letter from J. C. Stobart. He pointed out the difficulties of a coherent policy: "it is not an easy question, nor are the clergy unanimous." He explained that the majority of the services broadcast took place outside service times, but that it was also necessary occasionally to broadcast service in real time so that the listener could experience being part of an actual service. He moved on to the crux of the matter:

> Is the wireless service to be regarded as a formidable competitor to the actual service in the church, rather than as a powerful ally? Finally, is it not advisable to take the largest and broadest views in regard to a new medium which is bound to effect changes in the habits and outlook of rising generations?[52]

The first Daily Service was broadcast from Savoy House on Monday 22 January 1928. Former chaplain H. J. Johnson conducted a simple service, accompanied by hymns sung by the BBC Singers. 7,000 letters of appreciation for the fifteen-minute service were received within a few weeks of its launch,[53] and it still continues today. The success of this tentative step into daily religious broadcasting showed the appetite for such broadcasting by the public. The proportion of radio time devoted to religious output also increased. In 1927 2.25 hours of religious broadcasting per week contrasted with 16.4 hours devoted to dance music. By 1930 there were 5.2 hours of religious broadcasting compared to 11.48 hours devoted to dance music.[54]

By 1931 religious broadcasting had become more accepted by the church. Convocation met in January 1931 and heard the report of the committee on "The religious value of broadcast services." A vote of gratitude was suggested for the BBC. Former chaplains Guy Rogers, Pat McCormick and E. G. Selwyn had been appointed

50   Scott, *Dick Sheppard,* p.129.
51   *The Times* 9 April 1926, p.17.
52   *The Times,* 10 April 1926, p.15.
53   Daily service website: www.bbc.co.uk/radio4/features/daily-service/history/, *(accessed 2/2/2011).*
54   A. Briggs, *The History of Broadcasting in the United Kingdom: Volume IV: Sound and Vision* (Oxford, OUP 1978), p.82.

to this committee. The committee reported that in its considered judgment, "The effect has been exceedingly valuable ... it had recalled to the acknowledgement of God many thousands who had been out of touch with sacred things." However, the benefits of religious broadcasting were not evident to all, as the committee added: "It wished that far more clergy would realise that broadcasting has come to stay and is one of the most potent factors in the nation's life."[55] Acclaim was not universal. Arthur Kearney, former navy and army chaplain, reckoned that "Wireless services give inoculation of the mildest form of Christianity yet discovered."[56] E. G. Selwyn, although admitting that: "There is no question of competition between the BBC and the church" went on to suggest that the broadcast services of the church: "were in danger of creating a passive type of worshipper, who obviously grasped only a small part of what true worship meant."[57]

An article in *The Times* reporting the convocation meeting congratulated the BBC on avoiding the dangers of doctrinal controversies, providing "Impartially for various denominations and for various shades of opinion." The article asked that it might consider more variety in their choice of preachers: "The type of sermon euphemistically described as 'breezy' probably does appeal to a large section of the public ... yet it is apt to occur too often." What invalids value, it continues, "is the quiet devotional type of address with some real thought in it."[58]

In July 1931 the Bishop of Rochester, Linton Smith, invited another former chaplain to his Diocesan Conference. H. J. Johnson was a curate of St Martin-in-the-Fields and had been involved in the broadcasting from that parish. The topic of the conference was "The effects of broadcasting on religious life." Johnson bemoaned the lack of initiative on the church's behalf: "In regard to the church services broadcast, all the initiative has come from the BBC and not the Church of England." The report of the conference in *The Times* goes on: "He could not imagine why the Anglican authorities did not set aside their best brains to study the new media."[59]

Significantly, former chaplains were well represented in the clergy that did take advantage of the new medium. John Reith asked C. S. Woodward to be responsible for coordinating services for children and to develop a style of service which involved children. Woodward started broadcasting children's services from his London parish, and by 1929 a children's church service was broadcast on the first Sunday of each month. Percy Dearmer conducted services in a Broadcasting House studio, bringing a group of children with him who asked questions which he answered. He designed the services with suitable hymns, which could be learned and sung by children at home.

55   *The Times*, 22 January 1931, p.19.
56   Machin, *Churches and Social issues in Twentieth-century Britain*, p.83.
57   *The Times*, 14 February 1914, p.16.
58   *The Times*, 24 January 1931, p.13.
59   *The Times*, 10 July 1931, p.12.

C. S. Woodward continued to preach on air throughout the 1920s and 1930s as Bishop of Bristol. In July 1935, the Bristol diocesan branch of the Church of England Men's Society was discussing "Religion and the Radio" under his chairmanship. He asserted that the religious activity of the BBC showed a noble record. He admitted that in a small parish on a wet day religious wireless services served as a temptation to stay home but: "on balance – that there were tens of thousands of people who would not, and many who could not, go to church, who had the advantage of broadcast service". He did concede that listening to a service from an armchair demanded far less from a man than church attendance. He advocated fewer broadcast services from churches and more studio services with sermons. In subsequent discussions the delegates agreed that: "religion was helped rather than hindered by wireless".[60] E. S. Woods, similarly, was regularly found in the radio schedules. From his church in Croydon, the first morning service, a Harvest celebration, was broadcast in October 1935. Wolfe commented that Croydon became "a sort of morning St Martin's."[61]

When Pat McCormick became the incumbent of St Martin's in 1927, he continued the tradition of broadcast services from the church. He seems to have been a popular radio personality, with a natural and sincere manner He was particularly adept at radio appeals for the St Martin's Christmas charities, as the first year he did this he received double the amount that Dick Sheppard had received the previous year. In the preface to his book of Lenten talks, published in 1930, McCormick admitted that they are very much based on his broadcasts. He asked his readers to forgive him:

> If they read very much the same thing as they have heard; but I cannot do otherwise as my whole soul is burning with the desire to present the good news of Jesus Christ to the man in the street in a way that he can understand; and one fact that emerges from my vast correspondence seems to be that they do understand.[62]

In a letter to *The Times* in 1933 he had some suggestions to make in the light of the proposed talks, which were to take place twice a month on "God and the world through Christian eyes". He emphasised some points which "seem vital to the value of these addresses". Firstly, he advised the speakers to speak simply and to avoid using theological terms without defining them. He added, "The failure of an opportunity of this kind will be appalling if it arises through neglecting this fundamental fact in broadcasting." Secondly, he suggested that the people who listened to the broadcast get together in groups to discuss it with the aid of the printed version in the *Listener*. He spoke about the vast numbers of people listening who were interested in religion but did not know what Christianity was about. He hoped that the talks would encourage them to "make an effort to learn what it means". This, he hoped, would

60   *Church Times*, 12 July 1935, p.735.
61   Wolfe *The Churches and the BBC*, p.81.
62   P. McCormick, *Be of Good Cheer* (London, Longmans, Green & Co., 1934) p.x.

work against the secularism in the works of such writers as George Bernard Shaw. He saw these discussions as an opportunity to "discuss problems frankly even if it only came to agreeing to differ on the individual interpretation of events."[63] McCormick was conscious that the success of religious broadcasting would only come to fruition if the men and women encouraged to go to church by broadcasts found a welcome in their parish churches. In his talk "The value of broadcasting",[64] he stressed, "It depends on whether they are going to welcome and make a home for – yes and adjust their services to suit – the ordinary men and women who are brought to a new vision of the religion of Jesus Christ." He continued: "A dead church, a Pharisaic congregation, a minister not abounding in humanity nor a lifeless service will stultify the work which broadcasting can accomplish." He also placed the responsibility on the listener to act: "If religious broadcasting is going to have its proper value for you, and for the world, you must not think that that you can follow Christ by merely listening."

The predominance of St Martin-in-the-Fields was sometimes resented by those of different religious standpoints within the Church of England. A comment in "Journalists' Jottings" in the *Church Times* in May 1935 hinted at this: "They have quaint ideas at Broadcasting House. Until recently they were persuaded that St Martin-in-the-Fields was the Church of England."[65]

Despite the initial opposition and scepticism of some clergy, and fears of the possible competition posed by religious broadcasting, the whole concept proved popular with radio audiences. In the 1930s the BBC was broadcasting regular services on Sunday, talks for children, the Daily Service and the epilogue. It was perhaps unfortunate that the growing popularity of religious broadcasting coincided with a decline in actual attendance. Wolfe indicated that this suggested "Something wrong."[66] Former chaplains were perhaps in a better position to realise what was needed to appeal to an "unchurched" audience, and seized the opportunity of the new medium to extend the means of catering to diffusive Christianity in the country as a whole.

Cinema

The growth of cinema also exercised the opinions of the church in the interwar years. Cinema attendance had grown during the 1920s and expanded with the coming of sound in 1929. By 1939 cinema attendances had reached 1.5 million, representing attendance at least once a week by 40 percent of the population.[67]

In the 1920s, the effect of cinema on young people had been investigated by an inquiry inaugurated by the National Council on Public Morals, under the presidency

---

63   *The Times*, 6 January 1933, p.8.
64   McCormick, *Be of Good Cheer*, p.22.
65   *Church Times*, 29 March 1935, p.838.
66   Wolfe, *The Churches and the BBC*, p.19.
67   Machin, *Churches and Social Issues*, p.76.

of the Bishop of Birmingham. A subcommittee of psychologists produced a draft report which considered that cinematic role models encouraged: "fantasy day dreams and yearning to a degree ... that was unwholesome."[68] The church was not alone in it apprehension about cinema. Overy says: "The idea that films were likely to promote sexual licence remained a persistent concern of the respectable middle classes."[69] Machin described the reasons for the urgency shown by the church in attempting to come to terms with this new cultural development: "The churches were deeply interested in the cinema and its moral and cultural effects, for reasons which comprised the question of Sunday opening; the treatment of sacred subjects on film; the use of [the medium] for spreading a religious message; and the impact of film on the general moral health of society."[70]

Guy Rogers was able to say by 1930 that: "There is now little opposition to the theatre or cinema as such",[71] that it was the "tendencies in the modern use of leisure which the church must deplore." By this he was referring to the Sunday opening of cinemas, which had been spreading, albeit illegally, in the late 1920s. In July 1932 a bill was passed allowing for the opening of cinemas on Sundays, leaving local councils to decide whether they would allow films on Sunday or not, but as a result of this there were wide regional differences. London cinemas led the way, but there were fewer in Scotland and Wales.[72] In his chapter on Christian witness in *The Church and the People*, Rogers argued that the most difficult witness required of Christians was in relation to the use of leisure and the question of Sunday observance. He was anxious that people should not have to work on Sunday to provide leisure for others: "The labour involved in the further expansion of trading on Sunday, became important factors in deciding the social utility of the purpose."[73] He went on to explain that it was the commercial basis that he was particularly objecting to and advocated voluntary and free entertainment, with church halls and other public buildings being made available for young people to meet on Sunday evenings.

E. S. Woods, acting on his conviction that Sunday cinema should be managed and not banned, worked closely with other religious leaders and members of the local council to formulate the Croydon Scheme. This allowed for a committee to vet the films proposed for Sunday night viewing. It also ensured that the rights of the employees involved to a day off would be respected. It was agreed that a satisfactory arrangement would be made for a percentage of the profits to be given to charity. He justified this in a film shown in Croydon featuring himself arguing the case in a "talkie": "I am honestly convinced that such a use of a picture house on a Sunday is

---

68 Overy, *The Morbid Age*, p.152.
69 Ibid., p.152.
70 Machin, *Church and Social Issues*, p.76.
71 Rogers, *The Church and the People* p.193.
72 Machin, *Churches and Social Issues*, p.57.
73 Rogers, *Church and People*, p.197.

not at variance with the Christian view of the Christian use of Sunday."[74] Speaking at a lunch of the Sunday Films Association, of which he was chairman, he put forward his ideal for Sunday cinema: "Films shown should be of a classical character, dealing with historical romances, such as Disraeli, travel, science, sport and natural study." He assured his audience that there was "an ample supply of the better stuff and that there was a public for it".[75]

E. S. Woods saw that it was likely that Sunday opening of cinemas would continue and moved a resolution in the 1933 Convocation of Canterbury: "That this house is of the opinion that the church should approve the opening of cinemas on Sunday evenings provided … the pictures to be shown should be of a wholesome character." He went on to say that the church should admit that Sunday was "not an unsuitable day for some form of recreation", and that Sunday cinema went some way to solve the problem of catering for young people who had nowhere to go, with the proviso that it was "decent and wholesome". He realised that: "There are occasions when the church must set itself against the world but this is not one of them."[76] The Archbishop of Canterbury had taken a rather ambivalent line in supporting the original bill and his remarks had been taken in some quarters as support for Sunday cinema. He explained in Convocation that his principle had been as to ask: "whether it is in the ultimate interests of religion that they should attempt to say 'if you won't go to church on Sundays we will prevent you from going anywhere else'." The idea that this meant he was giving the lead to Sunday opening was wrong: "Nothing could be further from the truth."[77] R. G. Parsons proposed that: "the church should issue as soon as possible, with real authority, something quite plain, brief and unmistakeable which guided them on an effectual use of Sunday, which on the one hand would not be too sabbatarian, nor on the other, merely secular."[78] Guy Rogers had a slightly more pessimistic outlook on Sunday cinema after his struggles in court with the cinema proprietors over what was suitable for showing on a Sunday:

> The most flagrant breach of the agreement concerned the promise that was given by the trade in open court that they would exhibit only 'healthy and edifying films' on Sunday. It was my painful duty to appear before the magistrates to give an account of the films shown, which were regarded by the trade as such. Generally speaking, I am afraid promises given to secure an opening or a footing in the desired locality are apt to be forgotten when the purpose has been achieved.[79]

74   *The Times*, 14 November 1932, p.9.
75   *The Times*, 18 November 1932, p.12.
76   *The Times*, 25 January 1934, p.15.
77   Ibid.
78   Ibid.
79   Rogers, *A Rebel at Heart*, p.218.

In the late 1930s E. S. Woods expanded his idea that the cinema should not be fought but used by being an active tool in the work of the church. In July 1935 he became the chairman of an executive committee set up by the Church Assembly whose remit was "exploring the possibilities of utilising the cinematograph for purpose of religion", which, the report said, "has become a matter of some urgency." The Cinema Christian Council was formed, and in a report in *The Times* in March 1936 its aims were stated: "The council considered that the need for the production of films with a religious purpose is increasingly urgent and efforts must be made, if possible on a large scale to produce them."[80] In a letter to *The Times* in April 1937, Woods extolled the virtues of film and the importance of being involved in new technology: "Cinema is one of the most potent factors in influencing the lives of our people and especially the younger generation." He continued: "The writer of religious scenarios is free to write directly for the screen, he is unhampered by Hollywood traditions. The church and her worldwide organisation are established for distribution and it may be that a vast audience awaits the coming of such a moving religious picture gallery."[81] The pragmatic attitude of E. S. Woods echoed this and his efforts to embrace the cinema and use it to advantage seemed successful. Machin summed up the attitude of the churches to the cinema in the immediate pre-war era: "By the end of the 1930s the churches had little reason to think that the British cinema was a menace to morality and domestic stability."[82]

Conclusion

The subjects of marriage, divorce, sex and contraception were ones in which several former chaplains were in disagreement with mainstream opinion. The advocacy of divorce and remarriage in certain circumstances went directly against the teaching of the Anglican Church. This liberalism, however, was tempered by the strong emphasis of men like Pym, Barry and Rogers on marriage preparation and sex education. These are topics which at the beginning of the twenty-first century are still causing controversy and discussion. The contribution to the debate in the interwar years by former chaplains added significant arguments and also emphasised their willingness to hold and promulgate controversial views.

Despite an initially unsure attitude from the Anglican Churches former chaplains such as Pat McCormick and Dick Sheppard now took the lead, often facing opposition from the church establishment; and other chaplains were frequently to be found on the schedules of the *Radio Times* and *The Times*. This commitment stemmed from a desire to bring God to as many different people as possible, surely an attitude formed in the difficult conditions of the trenches. Radio seems to have been the perfect

---

80 *The Times*, 2 March 1936, p.17.
81 *The Times*, 28 April 1937, p.17.
82 Machin, *Churches and Social Issues* p.81.

opportunity for men who had complained about the limited nature of church services and the need to widen the appeal of the gospel.

The essentially pragmatic attitude of the Anglican Church to developments in the cinema was a result of the attitudes of former chaplains such as E. S. Woods and R. G. Parsons, who not only realised that outright opposition would be counter-productive, but also did much to ensure the church used the new technology to its advantage.

The changing nature of both church and society in the 1920s had necessitated the involvement of the church in controversies of a secular nature, which nevertheless had a bearing on the life of the church. Former chaplains, using their wartime experiences of the irrelevance of the church in everyday matters of concern to the average soldier, seemed to have sensed that entering the fray in such controversies would emphasise the relevance of the church in society. Their opinions and actions were such that they moved the Anglican Church forward throughout an era of rapid change.

7

Remembrance and Pacifism

A slogan of the British Legion, used in the post-war years, was "honour the living, serve the dead",[1] summed up the feeling that the commemoration of the fallen of the war should include measures to redeem the lives lost in battle with actions which would improve British society in the post-war world. Although the British Legion and the established church were to clash in the details of commemorative occasions,[2] the returning chaplains, in particular, were very aware of the need to reshape society radically if the sacrifices of the war were to have meaning. The idea that national life should be so ordered that war would never happen again was to inform the ideas of the pacifism, largely led by former chaplains, which was to emerge in the 1930s.

Bob Bushaway has described the themes of remembrance which were present in the interwar years as having a clear effect on the way that post-war society in Britain developed. He is of the opinion that the rituals developed: "resulted in a denial of any political critique of the Great War or of post-war society",[3] and that: "The rituals of remembrance in Britain, language, liturgy, hymnody, landscape...were created consciously for political reasons at a precise point in time."[4] Although the established church, including former chaplains, was to play a large part in this development of consolatory ritual, many chaplains regarded remembrance as a way to make sense of the deaths of so many by improving the social, economic and political conditions in post-war Britain.

Patrick Porter, in his essay "Beyond Comfort", has made a strong case that in the eyes of former chaplains the purpose of remembrance was to "Inculcate dissatisfaction,

---

1 Adrian Gregory, *The Last Great War: British Society and the First World War* (Cambridge, CUP, 2008), p.263.
2 Wilkinson, *The Church of England in the First World War*, pp.299-300.
3 Bushaway, 'Name upon Name' p.137.
4 B. Bushaway, 'The Obligation of Remembrance or the Remembrance of Obligation: Society and the Memory of World War', in *The Great World War 1914-1945: Lightning Strikes Twice, Vol 1*, Peter Liddle, John Bourne, Ian Whitehead (London, Harper Collins, 2001), p.490.

guilt and discomfort."[5] This was to encourage and mobilise efforts to transform society as a means of honouring the dead. He also made the point that "former chaplains played a significant role in defining the memory of the Great War."[6] This chapter will look at the ways in which the wartime experience of former chaplains had an effect on their ideas of remembrance, to what extent they were able to be a part of national commemoration and how during the course of the interwar years some became prominent in peace movements while others accepted the inevitability and the justice of another war.

The influence of the wartime experience of chaplains on the process of remembrance must be understood on several levels. The need to remember the dead resulted in their practical actions in keeping records of graves and writing letters to next of kin, but another longer-term response to the horrors of war was shown by their determination to honour the dead by continuing to work for a just and fair society.[7] Particularly in the earlier, more mobile stages of the war, before the Grave Registration Commission became active, chaplains were the people who marked graves and kept map references of where soldiers had been buried. Their lists and records were invaluable to the work of the Imperial, later, Commonwealth War Graves Commission when it was established in 1917. In a lull in battle on 10 September 1914, the Rev Douglas Winnifrith, attached to the 14th Field Ambulance went with his Methodist colleague, the Rev O. S. Watkins, to find bodies and bury them:

> We decided to go over the battlefield in different directions to bury any dead that we could find, irrespective of religious denomination. Whenever we found a fallen comrade we bore his body to the corner of a field to secure it ... and there dug a shallow grave.[8]

They marked the graves with a rough cross and kept a record of the names of the men they had buried. The war diary of the 14th Field Ambulance mentioned that on 10 September three officers and thirty-eight other ranks were found dead by the chaplains and buried.[9] Harry Blackburne also kept careful record of those he buried, with map references.[10] David Railton, who was to have the idea of the burial of the Unknown Warrior at Westminster Abbey, wrote after the war about the role of chaplains in identifying the graves of the dead, and of trying to be of comfort to the families at home:

5   P. Porter, 'Beyond Comfort: German and English Military Chaplains and that Memory of the Great War' in *The Journal of Religious History*, Vol. 29, no. 3, October 2005, p.258.
6   P. Porter, Beyond Comfort, p.260.
7   Ibid., p.258.
8   D. Winifrith, *The Church in the Fighting Line* (London, Hodder & Stoughton, 1915), p.70.
9   TNA, WO95/1540, 14th Field Ambulance War Diary.
10   Blackburne, *This Also Happened on the Western Front*, p.5.

Every padre serving with the infantry brigade was bombarded after each publication of casualties with the request, 'where-exactly where-did you lay to rest the body of my son? Can you give me any information?' To all these questions we were allowed to send map reference only. Oh, those letters of broken relatives and friends.[11]

Bob Bushaway described the growing importance of individual memorialisation, the detailed recording of names on rolls of service and then on rolls of honour.[12] This was important to the families of the citizen armies and to the towns and regions who had provided these armies. Lloyd George realised that: "The people of this country will take an intimate personal interest in its fate of a kind which they have never displayed before in our military expeditions."[13] The work of the chaplains in helping to realise this individual response to loss was a significant contribution to the consolatory nature of remembrance.

The experiences of other wartime chaplains also made them consider the meaning of war and how they could redeem the lives of those lost in practical ways. Tom Pym, writing in 1917, was thinking of the post-war situation and hoped that the idealism of the soldiers would not be wasted:

Many of those who gave their lives for England gave them not for the England of 1913 or 1914, but for England as she might be, as one day she shall – please God – become. For that ideal they have gladly died. In that hope and faith those of us who have survived must live and work. Their sacrifice must be made worthwhile.[14]

In a sermon preached at a memorial service for former Trinity College Cambridge men, in the college chapel on 2 November 1919, Pym related how his determination to honour the dead was engendered by his conversation with a dying soldier:

We cannot accept and try to profit by the sacrifice of the men who gave all for us and just go on living our lives simply for ourselves. We should be disloyal: I myself would be disloyal to a soldier who on a day near Christmas 1915 lay dying. He asked me if I thought his pain was doing any good, and if when he was gone ... there would ever come a time when men would not have to die as he was dying: I pledged him my own word and told him I was sure that those for whom he died would try and make the world a better place.[15]

11   D. Railton, *Our Empire*, Vol. 11, no 8, 1931, p.34.
12   Bushaway, 'Name upon Name', pp.139-140.
13   David Lloyd George, *The War Memoirs of David Lloyd George* (London, Oldhams, 1938), cited by Bushaway, ibid., p.140.
14   Pym and Gordon, *Papers from Picardy*, p.56.
15   Pym, *Tom Pym, A Portrait*, p.72.

A. E. Wilkinson, chaplain to the "Cast Iron Sixth" London Rifles, speaking to the Stock Exchange Battalion at an Armistice Day service in 1928, told the men to: "Recapture the spirit of service and self-sacrifice which was so manifest during the days of the war and to apply it to present-day problems by devoting our lives to service."[16] Former chaplains' attitudes to remembrance were therefore affected by their experiences. Many of them expressed the hope "that war would purge, renew and redeem society."[17]

During the war the belief had emerged that the sacrifices of the fallen could be compared with Christ's sacrifice on the cross. This belief was not an accepted part of Christian theology. Walter Carey, a former naval chaplain, explained that the sacrifice of soldiers was not comparable with the sacrifice of Christ on the Cross: "Let the church preach sacrifice at all sorts of services, but let her … keep the holy sacrifice as her central mystery and glory."[18] Adrian Gregory has coined the phrase "patripassionism"[19] to describe what he calls the ideas prevalent at that time of "the redemption of the world by the blood of soldiers."[20] The logical conclusion to this idea was that personal salvation could be acquired by death on the battlefield. Horatio Bottomley publicised the idea that soldiers were in no need of repentance.[21] Gregory implies that the idea of what he calls "secularised redemption" gained credence with Church of England priests.[22] The idea that personal salvation resulted from sacrificial death in battle did of course not fit with evangelical opinion, but was widely accepted as part of the consolatory ideas current in wartime. However, as Bushaway explains, it "Could not actually stand close theological scrutiny".[23]

Notwithstanding the reluctance of former chaplains to accept fully the role of remembrance as one of "collective healing", and the ceremonies of remembrance as commemorating sacrifice in a just cause, they were often involved in these ceremonies. At a local level they often took the lead in decisions and plans for local memorials and commemorations.[24] It is questionable whether this was because of the implicit acceptance of religious aspects of remembrance or the fact that they were leading members of the community in any case. What Mark Connelly described as the "language of consolation and hope" that the churches provided made it seem natural that they

---

16   Connelly, *The Great War, Memory and Ritual*, p.173.
17   P. Porter, 'New Jerusalems: Sacrifice and Redemption in the War Experiences of English and German Military Chaplains' in *Warfare and Belligerence, Perspectives in First World War Studies*, ed. Pierre Purseigle (Leiden, Brill, 2005) p.103.
18   Carey, *Sacrifice and Some of its Difficulties*, p.69.
19   Not to be confused with *Patripassianism*, a first century heresy which claimed God was passible and capable of suffering.
20   Gregory, *The Last Great War*, p.156.
21   Wilkinson, *The Church of England in the First World War*, p.184.
22   A. Gregory, *The Silence of Memory, Armistice Day 1919-1946* (Oxford, Berg, 1994), p.187.
23   Bushaway, 'Name Upon Name', p.159.
24   A. King, *Memorials of the Great War in Britain: The symbolism and Politics of Remembrance* (Oxford, Berg, 1998), p.30.

would have a role in the way communities remembered their dead. Connelly also contends that Anglican clergy in the East End allowed the sacrifice of the soldiers to be linked with that of Christ:

> Comfort came through an element that only the church could provide: namely that each dead man had achieved paradise: Anglican clergy tended to go one step further and openly associate their sacrifice with the sufferings of Christ, a trait very rarely seen in nonconformist churches.[25]

S. F. Leighton Green was the president of the local branch of the British Legion, at Mundesley, Norfolk, and on his death in 1929 members of the legion kept a watch over his coffin. He also kept close links with the Fourth London Regiment, whose chaplain he was in France.[26] Harry Blackburne was chairman of the British Legion at his parish at Ashford, and every year took the memorial service in the centre of town, in addition to having a service in the parish church, which was always full.[27] On Armistice Sunday 1919, The Comrades of the Great War[28] marched to the Cenotaph in the afternoon and were addressed by the Chaplain General, Bishop Taylor Smith. That evening Dick Sheppard had arranged a service of thanksgiving, at which he preached. The service was accompanied by the band of the Welsh Guards.[29]

On the wider front former chaplains, particularly those who were regular peacetime chaplains, were prominent in the unveiling of memorials and monuments in Britain and France. The diaries of senior army chaplains were kept full in the 1920s and early 1930s by taking part in ceremonies for the unveiling of memorials.[30] One of the last, at Thiepval on 1 August 1932, was attended by Bishop H. K. Southwell, former A. C. G. to the Fourth Army.

The most well-known example of how a former chaplain had an effect on the nation's rememberance of the war was the role played by David Railton, chaplain in France form 1916 to 1918, in the chain of events leading to the Unknown Warrior being brought in solemn ceremony to his resting-place in Westminster Abbey in November 1921. Railton, who won the Military Cross and was mentioned in despatches, was particularly moved by the grave of a soldier bearing the inscription "An Unknown Soldier" on the Somme in 1916. The idea that had then come to him: "Let this body

---

25 Connelly, *The Great War*, p.57.
26 S. J. Maclaren (ed.), *Somewhere in Flanders: Letters of a Norfolk Padre in the Great War* (Fakenham, Lark's Press, 2005), p.5 and p.40.
27 H. Blackburne, *Trooper to Dean: A Biography of Harry W. Blackburne, Dean of Bristol* (Bristol, J. Arrowsmith, 1955), p.67.
28 *Comrades of The Great War* was one of the original four ex-service associations that amalgamated on Sunday 15 May 1921 to form the British Legion.
29 *The Times*, 11 November 1919, p.14.
30 RAChD, Amport House, scrapbook of press clippings kept by Rev. Dr A. C. E. Jarvis during his time as Chaplain General c. 1930s,.

– this symbol of him – be carried reverently across the sea to his native land", had grown in his mind until August 1920, when he wrote to the Dean of Westminster, Hubert Ryle, explaining his idea of a burial of an unknown soldier in the Abbey, and offering his Union colour, used for services and burials in the war, for use in the service. Ryle was enthusiastic about the idea, and pressed for it as his own. Despite initial doubts from the King, Lloyd George, being aware of the overwhelming reaction to the temporary Cenotaph, at the Victory parade in August 1919 and on Armistice Day in November of the same year, saw the idea as a focus for public mourning and a possible distraction from post-war political agitation. The tomb had a great resonance with the British public, and thousands filed past to pay their respects in the seven days that the grave was left open. On the first day alone, 40,000 mourners passed the tomb.[31] Every bereaved person and family now had a grave to represent their missing son, husband or father. Railton was not present at the abbey on 11 November 1920, but in 1921 took part in a service on Armistice Day in which he presented his Union colour which had been used to cover the coffin on its journey, to the Abbey to be hung above the tomb. *The Times* then acknowledged Railton as "the author of the idea of the burial of the Unknown Warrior in Westminster Abbey".[32] Railton's experiences in the war had brought home to him the needs of the families of the missing and those buried abroad to a have a national symbol of remembrance, grief and mourning, but in the midst of war he had been thinking that remembrance involved practical action in peacetime. On 9 January 1917 he wrote: "If God spares me I shall spend half my life in getting their rights for the men who fought out here."[33]

In his work on the various ways in which the East End communities of London set about memorialisation, Mark Connelly has described the clear role that the Anglican clergy performed in the 1920s and 1930s in Armistice Day celebrations and in organising the building of memorials, both in public places and in churches. Among these were several former chaplains. Guy Rogers was reported in the *Stratford Express* when he took Armistice Day services in the parish of West Ham. He was also invited to share in services of dedication in Nonconformist churches. When attending a service at Stratford Presbyterian church he stressed their "Common churchmanship", explaining that: "they did not talk of Church of England dead or Presbyterian dead, but Christian dead".[34] In Poplar and Stepney the Old Comrades Association of the 17th London Regiment had their annual services conducted by their chaplain G. H. Lancaster, and he was joined in 1924 by C. C. T. Wood, also a former chaplain of the 47th London Division. Connelly considers that: "The sermons were tailored to

31   N. Hanson, *The Unknown Soldier* (London, Doubleday, 2005), pps. 472-474.
32   *The Times*, 13 Nov 1920, p.9.
33   IWM, 80/22/1, the Papers of David Railton, p.24.
34   Connelly, *The Great War*, p.67.

suit the audience and both men drew together a number of themes inspired by their own joint war experiences."[35]

Former chaplains were understandably a popular choice to take part in Armistice Day services, as they could use their wartime experiences to make links with their congregation, both ex-servicemen and the bereaved, but they also used their sermons at Armisticetide to question the post-war status quo. Rogers reminded his congregation:

> They remembered that day many were living in affluence and wealth while numbers of those who had guarded the wealth of the country during the war were still living in poverty. … They remembered that day the failure to seize the opportunity that was given to the men who died, of remaking the world.[36]

Former chaplain Mervyn Evers, also in 1923, addressed the Territorial Army. He spoke of his experience on the Western Front but also criticised the current situation: "Who, in 1918, when the war was over, would have thought that five years later they would have the problem of unemployment on a gigantic scale?"[37]

Reading accounts of the ceremonies at the Cenotaph in the early 1920s, it is difficult to escape the conclusion that the role of the church representatives, and the religious content of the proceedings, played a minor part in comparison to the civic and military roles. In some ways the state had hijacked some of the rituals of religion to create rituals of remembrance, and the resulting ceremonies were "religious occasions in form only."[38] Lloyd George had experienced some opposition from Archbishop Randall Davidson when he had suggested that the service be secular, but in the end the Lord's Prayer and a hymn were included. However *The Times*, in an in editorial on 23 October 1923, urged that the government reconsider its decision not to have a service at the Cenotaph because Armistice Day fell on a Sunday, and considered that:

> It has become part of the expected order of things, and as long as there is an established church which represents, however imperfectly the whole people, it will be prudent of authority to follow the precedent … laid down for maintaining intact year by year a religious ceremony which more comprehensively than any other consecrates for thousands a national day of the most solemn remembrance.[39]

According to Lutyens, the architect of the Cenotaph, there was some consternation in the church establishment at its design: "There was some horror in church circles.

---

35   Ibid., p.153.
36   Ibid., p.171.
37   Ibid., p.171, and *Stratford Express*.
38   Bushaway, ' Name upon Name', p.159.
39   *The Times*, 23 October 1923, p.13.

What! A pagan monument in the midst of Whitehall?"[40] It is Gavin Stamp's opinion that it was the architecture of the Cenotaph which influenced the largely secular commemorative symbolism of the Imperial War Graves Commission.[41] The decision not to allow a cross as a headstone was bitterly opposed by some of the bereaved. Florence Cecil, wife of the Bishop of Exeter, wrote: "It is only in the hope of the cross that most of us are able to carry on – to deny us the emblem of that strength and hope adds heavily to the burden of our sorrows."[42] Neville Talbot, on a Toc H pilgrimage to Poperinghe and Ypres in May 1930, saw the Menin Gate for the first time and was disappointed: "There was no touch of Christian symbolism on it."[43]

It can be seen that the views of former chaplains and to some extent the church establishment clashed with some contemporary ideas of the role of remembrance as a comforting and unifying set of actions, which honoured the sacrifice of the dead and justified their death in terms of national and religious significance, as Porter contends: "implicit in the message of healing is the assurance that the ordeal is over and the price worth paying."[44] It was the aim of the chaplains to continue the redemptive sacrifices of the war by ensuring that the fight for a fair and just society continued.

Christopher Chavasse, in his parish of St George's, Barrow-in–Furness, often returned to the linked themes of remembrance and building for the future in his letters to his parishioners in the parish magazine. Writing in November 1920, he commented on the irony of Armisticetide services taking place under the shadow of the miners' strike:

> Where is the brotherhood of the six years of agony? Where is the patience that endured and so finally triumphed? … the world can quite easily recuperate after the war, if we all work in our brotherhood. Instead the grim spectre of unemployment will stalk our towns. Meanwhile it is for us to refrain from all recrimination and bitterness … for such cause wounds that are long in healing."[45]

In 1920, Chavasse inaugurated a war memorial fund that had two aims, one a practical one, to refurbish the Parish Hall to be a centre for a men's institute and the other to build a memorial chapel in St George's Church. By December the Men's Institute was up and running in the "Memorial Hall". Chavasse declared that: "All youths and men of 16 years and over are eligible for membership … and we are confident that

---

40   Gavin Stamp, *The Memorial to the Missing of the Somme* (London, Profile Books, 2006) p.43.
41   Ibid., p.71.
42   Ibid., p.87.
43   Nottinghamshire Record Office DD 1332 /198, Neville Talbot's account of the pilgrimage of padres to Talbot House, 27 April –1 May 1930. p.10.
44   Porter, 'Beyond Comfort', p.289.
45   Barrow-In-Furness Record Office, BPR11/PM/2, *St George's Parish Magazine*, February 1921.

they will roll up in great numbers."[46] Chavasse was concerned with industrial justice and the social gospel and often, in his vicar's letter, linked hopes for the future with the suffering of the war. It was his experience of war at a personal level as chaplain which gave meaning and gravitas to the ideas he encouraged his parishioners to adopt.

The Rev A. R. Browne-Wilkinson, MC, a former chaplain, was appointed to Daybrook parish Nottingham in 1919, and in the interwar years often spoke about the effects of the war and the need for positive modes of remembrance. In August 1919 he wrote about the signing of the Treaty of Versailles:

> Now that we have peace, what are we going to do? Perhaps we can best sum up what we *ought* to do in one word – 'remember'. Remember that the war will have been lost if after all the evil spirit of selfishness and self-seeking triumphs over the spirit of duty and service.[47]

In the same article he encouraged his parishioners to: "Remember the hundreds and thousands of our gallant dead, and that we cannot discharge our duty to them by erecting memorials of brick and stone, the only memorial worthy of them is the building up of that new order in the world for which they died".[48]

Chapter 3 described how a creative tension developed between the desire of Toc H to honour the elder brethren, recapturing what was splendid about Talbot House, and to move forward as an active force for good which would suit the needs of the post-war world. The comment made in 1923 in an article, "Our room on earth", shows how intermingled the remembrance of the lost and the hope for the future were in Tubby Clayton's mind:

> To the survivors, half ashamed, the deepest of all war debts is from the living to the dead. We can only pay by being and doing what they would wish. With this aim in view we, of Toc H, began to build a new society of serving brethren.[49]

The work of Toc H in the interwar years was led and supported by many former chaplains among the padres who served Toc H. In 1930 there were twenty association padres with seventy-one honorary padres and sixteen overseas padres who served as branch and area chaplains, keeping up the "ceremony of light" which perpetuated the memory of those who had fallen. John Leonard, in his online edition of Pat Leonard's memoirs, sums up the ethos of Toc H towards remembrance: "There was a very strong feeling that such sacrifice and suffering in the war must be met

---

46 Barrow-In-Furness Record Office, BPR11/PM/2, *St George's Parish Magazine,* December, 1920.
47 Nottinghamshire Record Office PR 19, 762/5, *Daybrook Parish Magazine,* August 1919.
48 Ibid.
49 *The Times,* 15 December 1923, p.13.

with grateful determination. It must be justified by those to whom the future was entrusted."[50]

Tubby Clayton instituted "memorial rooms" in each Toc H mark as a means of keeping the younger generation in touch with the example of the fallen "elder brethren". He explained in a letter to a Toc H Mark in Liverpool how these worked: "Families dear to Talbot House for their son's sake desired … to equip their rooms, either by sending in the actual furniture of the boy's room which he had left for Flanders, or by a gift equivalent in value, coupled with photographs and books and trophies from school or college days."[51] He believed that the "Silent Witness" of these men in the memorial rooms could inspire the post-war generation. He hoped they would conclude that: "man can be irrationally noble, and die with that degree of cheerfulness and vision which well becomes a man in a great cause."[52]

The example of Toc H supports Porter's theory that the attitude of former chaplains to remembrance was one of reformation rather than remembrance and comfort, and aimed to "mobilise rather than console".[53] It is also, perhaps, an example of Jay Winter's "fictive kin", groups of men and women responsible for individual memorials or acts of remembrance whose bonds continued their association long after the unveiling of the memorial or the setting up of the act of remembrance.[54] The concept of pilgrimages to the Great War battlefields began soon after the war, and has been closely linked by historians such as Alex King to a kind of "battlefield tourism" that developed as sites became more accessible and visitors were catered for. David Lloyd has described the pilgrimages undertaken by Toc H as being indicative of "the close link between religious belief and the organisation of battlefield pilgrimages".[55] Toc H was involved with the league of St Barnabas, an organisation set up to help relatives of the fallen to visit the battlefields. In 1923 the Rev R. H. Royle, representing Toc H, took part in a ceremony at Lijssenthoek Military Cemetery, which was accompanied by the choir of All Hallows.[56] In 1920 Tubby Clayton took a small party of friends to visit the battlegrounds of Ypres, at a time when the countryside had not been restored to any great extent and battlefield debris was still to be seen in the fields. As a result

50   Philip Leonard-Johnson, *Pat Leonard DSO – A Memoir* (2010) http://www.toch-uk.org.uk/documents/Pat%20Leonard%20Memoir%20%28Final%29.pdf.
51   LMA, CLC/347/ M/S 30385, an open letter from Tubby Clayton to a leader at Gladstone House of Toc H, dated 1932.
52   Ibid.
53   P. Porter, 'Beyond Comfort', p.258.
54   Jay Winter, *Remembering War: The Great War between Memory and History in the Twentieth Century* (London, Yale University Press, 2006).
55   D. Lloyd, *Battlefield Tourism, Pilgrimage and the Commemoration of the Great War in Britain, Australia and Canada* (Oxford. Berg, 1998), p.146.
56   University of Birmingham Special Collections, Toc H Archives, Order of Service, Palm Sunday, 1923.

of this visit Toc H published *The Pilgrim's Guide to the Ypres Salient*.[57] It considered that such a guide would be needed by pilgrims "revisiting the scene of *Tales of Talbot House*."[58] A review of the book in *The Times* described it as: "An accurate and comprehensive practical handbook for visitors to the graves and battlefields, ... with several useful maps."[59] In 1921 at Whitsun a larger group of 400 pilgrims set out: they had been given "routine orders" about what to bring. Among the acceptable or *"très trop"* items were old clothes, shorts, trench maps and a pipe. Among the definitely unacceptable *"non bon"* items were summer suitings, spats, Michelin guides and mirrors.[60]

Before Toc H acquired Talbot House again in 1929, the owner of the house did not allow groups to visit until 1926, when small groups were permitted to see the upper room, now partly returned to its role as a hop loft. Jock Gilllespie, one of the pilgrims, described the experience:

> Finally it was our turn to go upstairs. As we mounted the narrow stairway we met the first party coming down and we saw by their faces that they had not only seen, but also understood their vision. We all instinctively knelt as we entered for we knew the ground whereon we stood was holy.[61]

In 1929 Lord Wakefield bought Talbot House for Toc H, and it has remained a place of pilgrimage and refreshment for all those who want to remember the men who died on the Ypres Salient and to recapture the spirit of the wartime Talbot House. It was not meant only as a shrine of remembrance but also as a place where new generations of pilgrims and Toc H members could learn about the war and in learning, remember. Alec Paterson stated in 1933:

> We have to go back to our beginnings to understand our growth and see our objective. The lad who was a baby in the war gains more by going to the old house and imagining the refreshment of the tired soldier than by listening to many poor reminiscences of mine or any other. The old house is more than a place of sentiment – it is a fact of history.[62]

Neville Talbot wrote a long and moving account of the pilgrimages of wartime padres to Poperinghe and Ypres in 1930. He recounted how the padres present were:

57   *The Pilgrim's Guide to the Ypres Salient*, (London, Herbert Reiach for Toc H, 1920), now unavailable.
58   B. Baron, *The Birth of a Movement: 1919–1922* (London, Toc H, 1946), p.41.
59   *The Times* 29 June 1920, p.19.
60   Baron, *Birth of a Movement*, p.42.
61   Lever, *Clayton of Toc H*, p.147.
62   Ibid., p.151.

Full of the sense that they could not either take in or begin to express more than a fragment of the meaning which brought them together – to stand in the Upper Room or at the vast cemetery of Tyne Cot was to feel afresh how things are too deep for expression."[63]

Talbot described, how, after initial consternation and resentment that the house had changed, the party went up to the partially restored Upper Room and knelt in prayer, each chaplain in turn being inspired to pray spontaneously. Talbot remembered: "all this was truly and very tremendous."[64]

Another aspect of Tubby Clayton's role in remembrance was his attitude on the crop of war books that has been described as "the war books boom" of 1929 into the early 1930s. Authors such as Ford Maddox Ford, Erich Maria Remarque, Siegfried Sasson, Robert Graves, Vera Brittain: all shared elements of what Samuel Haynes has called "a common language", which included:

The idealism betrayed, the early high mindedness turned … to bitterness and cynicism; the growing feeling among soldiers of alienation from the people at home for whom they were fighting … a bitter conviction that that the men in the trenches fought for no cause, in a war that could not be stopped.[65]

In 1929 Tubby Clayton published *Plain Tales from Flanders*. A review in *The Times* considered that the book was an antidote to those war books "in which all the horrors and brutalities are treated with a sort of gruesome pleasure." The reviewer realised that not all men were of the calibre of some of the characters described by Tubby, but also that it was not true to say that: "The mud of warfare could not be washed away from the souls of those who were slimed with it."[66] He quotes a passage to show Tubby's opinion of the men: "It was not in hate but in love, that your son, your brother, your father went about his duty in Flanders. It was love with him all the way: love that led him there for your sake." In a speech to the schools section of Toc H in 1930,[67] Tubby was pressing for a schools pilgrimage to the Salient in order to counteract, in the minds of young people, the impression of war given by recent war books. He said that the deliberate and dignified reticence with which men fought and suffered and died in the Great War had been betrayed by practically every publisher in the land. He was concerned that young people would become influenced by "this curiously perverted form of peace propaganda". He thought that the pilgrimage was necessary in that "the stains had got to be taken off the war memorial". In a sermon preached at

63   Nottinghamshire Records, DD1332/198, Talbot, p.1.
64   Ibid., p.6.
65   S. Hynes, *A war imagined, The First World War and English Culture* (London, The Bodley Head 1990), p.439.
66   *The Times*, 8 October 1929, p.22
67   *The Times*, 7 January 1930 p.7.

St Mary's University Church on Armistice Day 1928 he had warned against taking the "blotterature" of the war period too seriously. "We who know these men also know that that blotterature is not true."[68] Having given several examples of the spirit of unselfish sacrifice from his wartime experiences, Tubby returned to his familiar theme of the burden being passed on to the youth of a new generation. He imagined the advice of the dead:

> Do not imagine that an age of supreme sacrifice can well be followed by an age of supreme self-indulgence. Your age, which has entered into an inheritance which we purchased, will not lack its sufficiency of ambitious and successful men. Let some of you be ambitious and successful in a deeper direction. Be ambitious to serve the cause of Christ with every silent power in you. Be ambitious to devote your lives to the spreading of a new spirit between man and man.[69]

Many chaplains maintained close links with their ex-comrades and some were involved in commemorating the fallen by writing regimental histories. E. C. Crosse wrote a history of the Seventh Division, *The Defeat of Austria as seen by the Seventh Division*. Canon Coop,[70] who served as the senior chaplain to the 55th Division in France from 1915-1918 wrote the official history of the division, *The Story of the 55th (West Lancashire) Division* in 1919. He also was very involved in the attempts to place a cockade with the divisional arms, the Lancashire rose, on the grave of every fallen soldier belonging to the division. In a letter to General Jeudwine in October 1919 he recounted his efforts on a recent trip to the battlefields of France to place new cockades on recently made graves and to replace some that had been stolen on others. "I have just got back home after our tour to mark the remainder of our graves. ... We did not find as many of our graves as we had hoped. The number of 'Unknown British Soldiers' was appalling." Coop was upset because many of the graves had been concentrated in large cemeteries and "Our dead were not where we had expected to find them". However he was glad to report that "The cockades put up in February show no signs at all of deterioration."[71] In Coop's church of St Margaret's Anfield, where he was incumbent when he died in 1926, he had placed underneath the Roll of Honour a small altar which he had used in the war, covered by an altar cloth with the red rose embroidered on it. Coop's attitude to the dead was that of remembering the role played by individuals in the war. He did this in a non-sectarian manner which helped the cohesive remembrance of the war in Liverpool. This echoes the concern felt by many former chaplains about the importance of this aspect of remembrance.

---

68   P. B. Clayton, *Plain Tales From Flanders* (London, Longmans, Green & Co., 1930), p.155.
69   Ibid., p.156.
70   General H. S. Jeudwine commanded the 55th Division from January 1916 to the end of the war.
71   IWM 72/82/1, the Jeudwine Papers.

The role of former army chaplains in remembrance seems to have been ambivalent and multi-faceted. On one hand they stood apart from aiding and abetting the constructed view of remembrance as being one of social cohesion and collective recognition of sacrifice, but they were also prominent in services and rituals designed to promote an acceptance of the post-war status quo. Their focus was on the building of a new society, but they also saw a role in involving the church in acts of collective remembrance and pilgrimage. It is clear that many of them felt a deep sense of loyalty to old comrades and former regiments and felt keenly the loss of the "elder bretheren". Their experiences, as outlined in previous chapters, inclined them to look for reform in church and state and it was in this way that the idea of the redemptive nature of the sacrifices of war was worked out.

Former Chaplains and Pacifism

The role that former chaplains played in the pacifist movement in the interwar years differed as circumstances changed from the emphasis on the League of Nations and collective security of the 1920s, through the anti-war period of the late 1920s and early 1930s to the international crises of the later 1930s. Michael Snape has argued that: "The radicalising effect of the First World War ... propelled a vocal element of former chaplains into the interwar peace movement",[72] whereas Martin Ceadel, though admitting that the war did have an effect on the development of pacifism says that "seeds sown in the war in Dick Sheppard, Charles Raven and Vera Brittain were slow to develop".[73]

Their view of the war as sacrificial had prevented most of the chaplains from joining in the widespread denigration of war in the late 1920s and early 1930s, as exemplified by the war book boom. To have seen the war as something failed and to be regretted would have lessened the impetus of creating a new world as a redemption of the sacrifices made by the combatants. In speeches of ex-chaplains the emphasis was on the future. More typical was the association of former chaplains with the idea of the continued remembrance of the sacrifices made in war, and the need to keep them in mind whilst focusing on the maintenance of peace and social developments as exemplified by Tubby Clayton's "Living Memorial" of Toc H. Faith in the Treaty of Versailles and the League of Nations focused on the expectation that there would be no more war, and in the real possibilities of international arbitration and multi-lateral disarmament, whereas the pacifism to emerge in the 1930s was to challenge the concept of collective security and be of a pacifist rather than a pacificistic

---

72   Snape, *Clergy under Fire*, p.274.
73   M. Ceadel, *Pacifism in Britain, 1914-1945. The Defining of a Faith* (Oxford, The Clarendon Press, 1980), p.59.

nature.[74] Martin Ceadel, in his study of interwar pacifism, has said of the late 1920s anti-war-feeling, "the brand of pacifism which emerged from this anti-war feeling was internationalism".[75]

However, some of the chaplains were expressing anti-war, if not pacifist sentiments quite soon after the war. Neville Talbot presided over a meeting at the Corn Exchange in 1919.The resolution passed was that the peace treaty terms offered "No guarantee of a lasting peace". He asked: "were they not tired to death of the barrenness and feebleness of hatred, fear and stupidity?"[76] Geoffrey Studdert Kennedy, quite early on after the war started to repudiate some of his more bellicose war writings. He was a speaker in the "No More War" demonstration in Hyde Park in July 1923. A resolution was carried at this meeting declaring that: "the time had come for the peoples to insist upon universal disarmament and a whole-hearted and organised cooperation of the peoples working with and through a perfected and all-inclusive League of Nations."[77] In Lies, published in 1919, he admitted that: "If war is good then I am morally mad and I know of no difference between good and evil",[78] and: "if war is to go on forever, then I am in the dark, and I can find no meaning and no God in history, at least no God that I can love or respect."[79] Gerald Studdert Kennedy said of Studdert Kennedy:

> His anti-war speeches seem to have been unforgettable, but their emotional violence must be seen in relation, not only to his experience of the horrors of war, but also in revulsion against his own involvement in the military process. During the war he had been a highly effective preacher who had gone further than some in translating Haig's expressed wishes into combative incitement.[80]

F. R. Barry, writing in 1931 also expressed regrets about the role of the church in the war. "The Christian church has not yet recovered from its humiliating surrender in blessing the arms of all the late belligerents."[81]

A resolution of C.O.P.E.C. in 1923 had resolved that: "All war is contrary to the spirit and teaching of Jesus Christ". This robust approach caused some consternation shown by letters in the press, with Raven and Temple having to write to The Times to explain the stance of C.O.P.E.C. William Temple explained: "The important part,

74 'Pacifism – War is always wrong and should never be resorted to. Pacificisim – War is wrong but is sometimes necessary; its prevention should be an overriding political priority'. Ibid., p.3 Also A. J .P. Taylor, The Trouble Makers: Dissent Over Foreign Policy, 1792-1939, (London,Hamish Hamilton, 1957), p.51 .

75 Ibid., p.62

76 Wilkinson, The Church of England and the First World War, p.265.

77 The Times, 30 July 1923, p.12.

78 Studdert Kennedy, Lies!, p.162.

79 Ibid., p.159.

80 Studdert Kennedy, Dog Collar Democracy, p.58.

81 Barry, The Relevance of Christianity, p.275.

however, is that the conference made it quite clear that in adopting this resolution it was not committing itself to pacifism."[82] Later Raven believed that C.O.P.E.C. had been equivocal about pacifism, because the time was not ripe for its discussion so soon after war.[83]

In August 1928 Pat McCormick preached in St Martin-in-the-Fields, where he was then incumbent, on the General Treaty for the Renunciation of War, or The Kellogg-Briand Pact, which had been signed on 27 August. The pact, between the United States, the United Kingdom, Italy, Japan and Germany prohibited war as "An instrument of national policy", except in matters of self-defence. McCormick said: "For ten years we had been making efforts – to win the peace which we talked about at the armistice. At last we see the dawning of a new day, to some extent worthy … of those millions of lives laid down in the war." He continued by stating that the signing of the pact was only a beginning, but now it was an international crime to resort to war to settle a dispute. He looked to a "spiritual community of nations", and ended by saying, "with God all things are possible".[84] Raven also considered that the pact had changed the situation:

> Until 1928 it needed some courage to denounce war from a public platform, and with the exception of the Society of Friends no Christian church had expressed any strong sense of its devotion. The Autumn saw a definite change.[85]

A resolution of the Council of Christian Churches on social Issues, meeting in January 1930, welcomed the Kellogg-Briand Pact and in Point Four of their resolution called on the:

> Respective authorities of all Christian communities to declare in unmistakeable terms that they will not countenance any war, or encourage their countrymen to serve in any war, with regard to which the government of the country had refused an offer to submit to pacific methods of settlement.[86]

This was signed by former chaplains Raven, Pym, Rogers and Southwell among others, and it showed that mainstream Christian opinion was still pacificist rather than pacifist. It also shows a continued faith in collective security and international arbitration. It was this faith in collective action and the policing potential of the League of Nations that was the default opinion of the Church of England. Martin

---

82   *The Times*, 16 April 1924, p.10.
83   Charles Raven, *War and the Christian* (London, SCM Press, 1938), p.18.
84   *The Times*, 28 August 1928, p.14.
85   Charles Raven, *Is War Obsolete?* (London, Allen and Unwin, 1935), pp.22-23.
86   *The Times*, 1 January 1930, p.9.

in his 1965 study of pacifism stressed that that mainstream position of the Church of England was to support the League of Nations.[87]

In 1931, F. R. Barry wrote at some length in *The Relevance of Christianity* on the Christian attitude to war and disarmament :

> Deeper than all temporary experiments for assisting economic recovery is emancipation of nation states from the ruinous wastage of competing armaments. Education, housing public health and all that most vital concerns of Christian citizenship are sacrificed to the blood lust of Moloch. … So urgent and so imperious is this burning question of disarmament that it ought now in the mind of Christian citizens to take priority over all other issues. … The states signatory to the Kellogg pact have renounced war as an instrument of policy. Armaments belong to a world order which is legally as well as morally obsolete.[88]

He then went on to predict that: "The time may come when Christian citizens must choose between their Christianity and their political allegiance. In any future war it will be the duty of Christians to refuse to support or cooperate with their government."[89] When Hitler occupied the Rhineland in 1936, Barry said to Viscount Davidson, a member of Baldwin's government: "If you allow our people to be involved be involved once again in the Franco-German quarrel, you cannot justify it to God or man."[90] Although Barry recanted his pacifism, his attitude in 1936 exemplified the thoughts of those clergy whom he later described as "living in a fool's paradise". He considered that in the years leading up to Munich most of the former chaplains were pacifists.[91]

Tubby Clayton was as anxious as any former chaplain there should be no more war. His aim was always to hold the memory of the Great War as sacrosanct; writing energetically against the denigration of the war that was prevalent in the early 1930s. As the events of 1938 unfolded he was asked to write a piece for the Toc H Journal, which was later published as a leaflet, *In My View*. It was a careful, nuanced piece in which he supported the terms of the Munich agreement on the grounds that Germany was actually much larger and stronger than Britain, which had been somewhat complacent during the interwar years : "We have evolved a singular capacity for stifling and arresting progress likely to change our comfortable outlook." He also believed that the Treaty of Versailles was "formed in anger" and had caused distress to the German people. Although admiring the "discipline" of Germany, he is very critical of the treatment of Jews. "To my mind, with my lifelong Jewish Friends, I hate the treatment

---

87   Ceadel, *Pacifism in Britain*, p.182.
88   Barry, *The Relevance of Christianity*, pp.271-272.
89   Ibid., p.276.
90   Barry, *Period of my Life*, p.127.
91   Ibid., p.128.

this immortal race is receiving in the length and breadth of Germany". He asked Toc H groups to learn some German so that they would be equipped to "send two or three members [to Germany] on their Summer leave, and Germans should be asked to visit here."[92] In a letter to William Lambert In September 1938, he is more trenchant and open in his views, criticising the "fatal error of those who would not let this country arm" and admitted, "I regard pacifism as a dangerous delusion too loudly trumpeted in recent years."[93]

Neville Talbot, in an article in the *Natal Mercury* at Christmas 1931, was pessimistic about the way in which the new decade had opened:

> The peace of the world is war-haunted; and fear is widespread … for the things that are coming on the earth. The cynic may well ask whether any of the visions seen in the lurid glare of the World War have been translated into reality: whether any of the lessons taught by Armageddon have been taken to heart.

He criticised spending on arms by all the great powers, while the world was slipping into "An unparalleled world crisis". His solution was an increase in cooperation between peoples. "Let us leap over the parapets of hate and get through separating entanglements, and then we can meet our fellow world citizens and shake them by the hand. That is the way to keep Christmas in this epoch-making year." He was critical of the effects of the Treaty of Versailles: "What a different peace it would have been could the peacemakers could have joined in the Lord's Prayer and acted upon it."[94] He placed some faith in the forthcoming Disarmament Conference, due to take place in February 1932.

The international events of the early 1930s, Japan's action in Manchuria 1931, Mussolini's invasion of Abyssinia in 1935, Hitler's move into the Rhineland 1936, and the Spanish Civil War in 1936 saw the growth of both secular and Christian pacifist movements. Although many chaplains changed their views on pacifism, two former Anglican army chaplains were to be prominent in these pacifist developments.

Charles Raven and Dick Sheppard

During the Great War Charles Raven served with the 1st Berkshire Regiment and saw action which, according to his biographer Dillistone, had a profound effect on him. Dillistone described an experience that Raven had of a God's presence on one occasion in the trenches when he was very afraid: "For the next nine months He was never

92   LMA, CLC/347/MS2996/01, pamphlet *In My view*, published by All Hallows Church in *The Vicar's Maxims* series, December 1938.
93   Letter from Tubby Clayton to William Lambert, leprosy worker in West Africa, cited in Lever, *Clayton of Toc H*, p.213.
94   Nottinghamshire County Record Office, DD 1332/76, *Natal Mercury*, Christmas 1931, press cuttings in the papers of Neville Talbot.

absent, ... It was He that was with me when I was blown up by a shell, and gassed and sniped at, with me in hours of bombardment and the daily walk with death."[95] While at the front Raven wrote, "Pacifists and C.O.s may talk about the sanctity of human brotherhood, we out here have discovered something of its reality."[96] The discussions on war and pacifism at C.O.P.E.C.had caused him to consider pacifism seriously, and after having become a pacifist in 1930, he felt that the topic was an ideal follow-up to C. O. P. E. C: "If a single issue was to be chosen, only the cause of peace was large enough and exciting enough to be a worthy expression of our studies."[97] Significantly, almost 100 members of the Fellowship of Reconciliation had attended C.O.P.E.C. in some capacity.[98] However, the public reaction to the C.O.P.E.C. resolution on war had caused both Temple and Raven to write to the press denying that absolute pacifist connotations be given to the resolution.[99]

Charles Raven was convinced by pacifism after the "Christ for Peace campaign" in 1929. Raven committed himself to pacifism in 1930 and "never wavered".[100] He joined the Fellowship of Reconciliation in 1931, and in 1932 became its president. "To the fellowship, Raven brought prestige, a reputation for strong, even arrogant leadership and above all else, an outstanding intellect. A brilliant academic, he nevertheless had the gift of making theology acceptable to the man in the street."[101] On 10 May 1932 Raven signed a letter as part of protest against the progress of the Disaffection Bill. The 1934 Incitement to Disaffection Act made it an offence to seduce a servicemen from his "duty or his allegiance", thus expanding the ambit of the law.[102] The act was widely criticised as being an unnecessary restriction on freedom of speech.[103] Lord Ponsonby attacked it in the House of Lords: "We foresee that in times of panic, or should the cloud of war appear on the horizon, this measure will be used for the suppression of what has been hitherto considered perfectly legitimate opinion."[104] Two years after accepting the post of chairman of the Fellowship of Reconciliation, Raven was admit-

95   Dillistone, *Charles Raven*, p.81.
96   Ibid., p.86.
97   Raven, *Is War Obsolete?* pp.22-23.
98   Jill Wallis, *Valiant for Peace: History of the Fellowship of Reconciliation, 1914-89* (London, The Fellowship of Reconciliation, 1991), p.54
99   *The Times*, 16 April 1924, p.10. Letters from Charles Raven and William Temple to the editor.
100 Dillistone, *Charles Raven*, p.211
101 Wallis, *Valiant for peace*, p.77
102 Select Committee on Religious Offences in England and Wales, First Report, 2003, www.parliament.uk.
103 The 1934 Act eventually produced the only occasion on which the higher courts have had to pronounce on this form of legislation, (*R v Arrowsmith* [1975] QB 678), Select Committee on Religious Offences in England and Wales, First Report, 2003, www.parliament.uk.
104 House of Lords Debate, 13 November 1934, vol. 94 cc. 379-91 (Lord Ponsonby of Shulbrede speaking).

ting that "all was far from well."[105] This must be seen in the context of disillusion about the Lambeth resolution,[106] the failure of the Simon Commission on India,[107] and the breakup of the disarmament conference of 1933.[108] Raven became involved in preparing for the Universal Christian Council for life and work, which was a follow-up to the conference called for by Nathan Söderblom in Sweden in 1923.[109] Bell gave a taste of its remit in a letter to *The Times* on 25 August 1932: "We are studying what church life in the modern world ought to mean ... we are cooperating with other international organisations in insisting that it will be a scandal to the conscience of mankind if the disarmament conference was without effective results."[110]

Raven was initially influenced by pacificist ideas. In an article in *Reconciliation* January 1934, he shocked other pacifists by saying "mere abstention will not suffice to make war impossible."[111] He thus supported the League of Nations Union and said: "While refusing to submit our own consciences to the dictates of political common sense or to make the church an appendage of the League of Nations, it ought to be possible for Christians to acquiesce in the internationalism of armed force while advocating and developing another way of reconciliation."[112] Raven's ideas on pacifism were those of a liberal theologian and he seemed to have based his attitude to pacifism on his ideas of the natural sciences and his concept of a "new reformation". In line with his naturalist interests Raven worked out: "that pacifism was thus a natural adaptation to ensure human survival in an era of total war, as well as a step nearer the Christian religious ideal."[113] In 1935 Raven gave The Halley Stewart lectures on the topic of *Is*

---

105 Letter from Raven to F. O. R. executive, 23 September 1924, cited in Wallis, *Valiant for Peace*, p.77.
106 Although the Lambeth Conference resolutions on 'The Life and Witness of the Christian Community – Peace and War' affirmed 'That war as a method of settling international disputes is incompatible with the teaching and example of our Lord Jesus Christ' (Resolution 25), it was ambivalent about pacifism. 'The Conference holds that the Christian Church in every nation should refuse to countenance any war in regard to which the government of its own country has not declared its willingness to submit the matter in dispute to arbitration or conciliation' (Resolution 27). http://www.lambethconference.org/resolutions/1930/1930-27.cfm.
107 The Simon Commission went to India in 1928 to review the Government of India Act 1919. Its report in 1930 was widely criticised. http://www8.open.ac.uk/researchprojects/makingbritain/content/simon-report.
108 The progress of the Geneva Peace Conference was halted by the withdrawal of Japan from the League of Nations in March 1933 and the withdrawal of Germany in October 1933. http://www.globalsecurity.org/military/world/naval-arms-control-1932.htm.
109 Nathan Söderblom, Archbishop of Uppsala from 1914. He was a strong advocate of intercommunion between the Swedish Church and the Church of England. He was awarded the Nobel Peace Prize in 1930 for his work for church unity and world peace. http://www.nobelprize.org/nobel_prizes/peace/laureates/1930/soderblom-bio.html.
110 *The Times*, 25 August 1932, p.6.
111 Ceadel, *Pacifism in Britain*, p.159.
112 Dillistone, *Charles Raven*, p.219.
113 Ibid., p.165.

War Obsolete? Dillistone argued that, "Through these lectures Raven had cleared his mind, worked out an impressive apologia on behalf of pacifism and at least indirectly issued a challenge to his fellow Christians to enlist in the same crusade."[114] It was at this stage that he embraced a purely pacifist attitude towards war.

He described in *War and Christianity* the issues he saw as important in debate about Christian pacifism:

1. The character of authority.
2. The origin of evil in God's world.
3. An examination of the cross in the way of redemption.
4. How do I reconcile my obligation to the state and my comrades with the demands of Christian conscience?[115]

Raven considered that it "was not until Armisticetide 1928 that a change of attitude towards the discussion of war became obvious", and that in the next few years "a deeply felt wave of pacifism spread over the country."[116] Talking about the events of 1933-38 he acknowledged that: "only those who had serious grounds for their faith and had learnt to see the issues plainly and take the long view were likely to stand firm."[117] He continued, "The problem of war is the dominant moral and religious issue of the day. Both its character and its urgency make it essential for the churches to face it."[118] He concluded, "War is evil and for the Christian a flat denial of his faith."[119]

Raven's pacifism seemed to grow originally from his experience of war, but was informed by C.O.P.E.C. and his ideas on a "New Reformation". It was theologically based but also owed much to his ideas on evolution. Edward Madigan is of the opinion that Raven joined the F.O.R. "Perhaps because it was the most overtly Christian and the one most interested in discovering a theological basis for defending the absolute rejection of war."[120] Raven felt that in the later 1930s the threat of war gave the church a definite cause: "A concrete situation",[121] on which "Christians would be constrained to stand and deliver an unequivocal reply".[122] He was possibly glad to find a cause which might prove more durable than that of C.O.P.E.C.

Although Dick Sheppard was an undoubtedly major influence on the development of pacifism through his leadership of the Peace Pledge Union in the interwar years, the extent to which his pacifism was influenced by his short time as chaplain to an

114 Dillistone *Charles Raven*, p.219.
115 Raven, *Is War Obsolete?*, p.43.
116 Ibid., p.19.
117 Ibid., p.23.
118 Ibid., p.43.
119 Ibid., p.51.
120 Madigan, *Faith Under Fire*, p.236.
121 Raven, *War and the Christian*, p.13.
122 Ibid., p.43.

Australian hospital on the Western Front is open to question. Although his experience was brief, and was never meant to be protracted, as he had just been appointed vicar of St Martin-in-the-Fields, he seem to have exhausted himself by working long hours and becoming very emotionally involved with his pastoral duties.[123] He returned in a state of collapse and concentrated on his work at St Martin's, where his open-house policy in his use of the church and crypt in wartime London contained a strong element of identification with the troops as he provided a place for rest and comfort as troops moved to and from the front.

In *We Say "No", A Plain Man's Guide to Pacifism,* written in 1935, he recounted the experience of talking to a dying man in the trenches, and the effect this had on him:

> In September 1914 I knelt by a dying soldier. I had just arrived in France. He was the first soldier I saw die. As I bent to catch his painfully spoken words, I discovered he had little need of my ministry, he was thinking of a life that was still unborn. His wife was expecting a baby about Christmas. He died thanking God, that if the child was a boy, he would never have to go through the hell of war. That man believed that what he had been told, that he was fighting in the war to end war ... those sons are of military age now.[124]

However, according to Maude Royden, close friend and fellow peace campaigner, during the war he had no doubts as to its legitimacy:

> I asked him whether he had ever felt any questions about the righteousness of the war at that time, and he told me he had not. Many army chaplains had, and many soldiers who were not chaplains. Dick assured me, that astonishingly as it may seem he had no doubts at all: War seemed to him to be then absolutely necessary and therefore right, even though he, as a Christian priest, must not take a sword in his hand.[125]

The first manifestation of ideas, which were perhaps part of his move towards pacifism, came at Armistice Day, 1925. Sheppard had, with many others, become appalled with the elements of celebration on Armistice Sunday, and particularly objected to an Armistice Day ball at the Albert Hall. At short notice, he managed to get the ball cancelled and took a short service in the Albert Hall himself. William Paxton, National President of the Brotherhood Movement remembered, "He organised a

123 Ellis Roberts, *H. R. L. Sheppard,* p.84
124 H. R. L. Sheppard, *We Say "No", A Plain Man's Guide To Pacifism* (London, John Murray, 1935), p.1
125 Maude Royden, 'Dick Sheppard, Peace Maker' in *Dick Sheppard, An Apostle of Brotherhood* ed. William Paxton (London, Chapman & Hall, 1938), p.75.

religious service in the Albert Hall and in the presence of thousands of people, he pleaded for a fresh dedication to the cause of peace."[126]

In the 1920s and early 1930s, Sheppard had obtained a reputation as an anti-church establishment figure who often clashed with the church authorities on issues such as unity and intercommunion. In 1927 he published *The Impatience of a Parson*, which contained criticism of the established church, but also more than a hint of his growing commitment to pacifism:

> We cannot any more think of war as anything but a damnable arrest of develop-
> ment and decency: it is not only the willingness to suffer agony; it is the willing-
> ness to inflict it. War cannot be reconciled with Christianity: there is no such
> thing as a Christian war.[127]

In a letter to Laurence Houseman on 31 January 1927 he said: "I shall be obliged to identify myself with your pacifism." On 4 February he continued, "I am a pacifist now – I cannot but identify myself with pacifism, for I am a pacifist and not prepared to pretend I am anything else", but it is clear that he still had to work his ideas out. "Of course I am still in a haze about what is right and wrong, as far as the state goes. Surely the state must protect its citizens?"[128]

In 1932 he became involved in a scheme with Maude Royden to create a "Peace Army", which would travel to Manchuria and physically interpose itself between the Japanese army and the Chinese people. A letter to the press in February 1932 elicited 800 volunteers, but the scheme never happened, partly because of Foreign Office disapproval and partly because the situation in Manchuria improved. Sheppard tried to get Lloyd George interested in the ideas and, in the opinion of Martin Ceadel, this attempt gave an insight into the way he perceived the idea of pacifism: "An attempt which demonstrated how far Sheppard saw the peace question in terms of mobilizing men of good will behind an inspiring leader, rather than in terms of defining a specific pacifist policy which could be applied to the international situation."[129]

Sheppard continued to work out his pacifist beliefs culminating in the publication of *We Say "No"* in 1935. On 16 October 1934 he wrote an open letter to the press in which in 500 words he justified his reasons for writing, which Ceadel summarised as: "The urgency of the international situation, the increasing tendency to violence exemplified by the fascist and communist movements and his belief that the average man was seeking an alternative policy."[130] Sheppard stated that many people were convinced

---

126 William Paxton, 'Dick Sheppard, National President of the Brotherhood Movement', in Paxton, *An Apostle of Brotherhood*, p.12
127 H. R. L. Sheppard, *The Impatience of a Parson* (London, 1927), p.57.
128 Laurence Housman (ed.), *What can we believe? : Letters Exchanged Between Dick Sheppard and L. H.* (London, Cape, 1939), pp.81-82.
129 Ceadel, *Pacifism in Britain*, p.96.
130 Ibid., p.177.

that war was: "Not only a denial of Christianity, but a crime against humanity."[131] He offered the opportunity for men in agreement with him to write a postcard using the words of what became the famous "peace pledge". "We renounce war and never again, directly or indirectly will we support or sanction another."[132] The response was enormous, with a total of 50,000 postcards received in response to his appeal.

Sheppard did not follow up this initiative until 4 July 1935, probably as a response to the growing Abyssinian crisis. He held a meeting of all the signatories of the Peace Pledge at the Albert Hall, who were addressed by Sheppard, Edmund Blunden, Siegfried Sassoon, General Crozier and Maude Royden. After this meeting the Sheppard Peace Movement was launched, soon to be renamed the Peace Pledge Union. Its launch attracted some influential sponsors from a variety of Christian, secular, cultural and political circles. Events of 1935 and 1936 increased public sympathy for the pacifist cause at the same time as the League of Nations looked ever less credible as a means of avoiding war. In October 1937 Sheppard's policy of creating the Peace Pledge Union as a heterogeneous organisation containing all strands of pacifism was vindicated by his victory in Glasgow University's Rectorial election as a purely pacifist candidate. The leading article in the *Student Pacifist* (the paper for his campaign), speaking of the Peace Pledge said:

> This was no crank idea foisted on an unthinking public by wealth and privilege. It was a logical sequel to the fact that over all the land thinking men and women were despairing of the prevailing panaceas for the prevention of war and were turning to pacifism with as a personal philosophy and national policy.[133]

A few days after this victory he was dead, his compulsive overworking and his asthma contributing to a fatal heart attack.

There is no doubt about the contribution of Dick Sheppard to the peace movement between the wars, and his undoubted skilled leadership of the Peace Pledge Union. Although the growth of the movement owed much to his leadership, the headline in the *Peace News* on his death was, "The movement will stand without me",[134] and it is perhaps a tribute to his leadership that it did. The statement from P. P. U. asserted that: "While the Peace Pledge Union throughout its membership is overwhelmed by grief at the news of its founder's death, the work which Dr Sheppard began and which he died for, will go forward with redoubled vigour and fulfilment."[135]

Notwithstanding his stature and reputation as a pacifist leader in this era, there are still some questions to be asked about Sheppard in terms of his motivation and his use

131 *Manchester Guardian*, 16 October 1934, p.20.
132 Ibid.
133 LPL, MS 3744 *Student Pacifist*, 12 October 1937.
134 LP L, MS 3744 *Peace News*, 7 November 1937.
135 Ibid., 6 November 1937.

of his wartime experiences as credentials in the peace movement. Ceadel is sceptical of Sheppard's motivation. Commenting on Sheppard's acceptance of a canonry at St Paul's in September 1934 :

> For a person who had vaunted his "impatience" with the stuffiness of established religion, this long pondered and soon regretted decision was a surprising one. It is tempting, therefore to see his simultaneous decision to renew his pacifist stand as in some way a compensation for accepting a conventional preferment.[136]

A more charitable interpretation could be that his health had improved due to his new breathing machine, obtained in late 1933, and he was therefore able to give more attention to his new post and peace campaigning. Also, fast-moving international events had caused him to firm up the ideas he had expressed since 1927 into full-blown absolutist pacifism, which demanded action.

Sheppard had been moved by his experiences in the war, and it is possible that his short time there had indeed influenced him as much as longer spells experienced by less intense and healthier chaplains. There exists, however a distinct impression that he, or others, exaggerated his war service in order to give his pacifism more credibility. Entries in *Crockford's Clerical Directory* have him described as a Temporary Chaplain to the Forces, whereas he was never in fact attached to the Chaplains' Department.[137] His close friend Maude Royden had an impression that his war record was more wide-ranging than it actually was. In her tribute to him in 1938 she said of him:

> Ultimately at one with the men of his regiment, he went over the top with them again and again, but always weaponless, unarmed: It was prophetic of the position he was to take up later but now no longer an individual who, because he happened to be a ordained priest must not fight. He was to convince us ordinary men and women who were not priests, but Christian all the same, that war was not possible for us either.[138]

This shows not only a lack of understanding of the role of a chaplain but a determination to link his pacifism with his war experiences. Michael Snape has cited evidence to show that some of his followers were convinced that he had been awarded a Military Cross.[139] It must be remembered that Sheppard was a major and well-loved celebrity

---

136 Ceadel, *Pacifism in Britain*, p.176.
137 *Crockford's Clerical Directory* (1937), p.1202, cited by M. F. Snape, 'Church of England Army Chaplains in the First World War: Goodbye to "Goodbye to All That"' in *Journal of Ecclesiastical History*, Vol. 62, no. 2, April 2011, p.338.
138 Roydon, 'Dick Sheppard, Peacemaker', p.76.
139 L. Smith, *Pacifists in action: The experience of the Friends Ambulance Unit in the Second World War*, (York, William Sessions Ltd., 1998) p.15, cited by Snape, 'Church of England Army Chaplains in the First World War: Goodbye to "Goodbye to All That"', p.338.

in his life and that a certain amount of hyperbole and rumour would have surrounded his life and actions. However, there seems to be little evidence that he corrected these exaggerated accounts of his war service. He was held in very high esteem by a number of high profile former chaplains, including Harry Blackburne, Pat McCormick and Tom Pym, Blackburne addressing him in letters as "Beloved Dick".[140] It is unlikely that this should have been so if it was felt that he was capitalizing on his war experience. It is significant in examining the role of chaplains in post-war society that it was felt to be so important that a priest with a high public profile in the pacifism movement could be shown to have been at the front and endured it rigours with the men he was now asking to renounce war.

Sheppard's pacifism was always of a more emotional type than that of an academic like Raven. He was sometimes equivocal about whether absolute pacifism would be sustainable in war. A letter from him to the *Manchester Guardian* protesting about taking part in ARP arrangements nevertheless continued, "I would do my best to be of assistance in the unthinkable event of another war."[141] Adrian Hastings has described him as: "a man of the most intense emotional susceptibility but almost no capacity for cool sustained analytical thinking or carefully planned action."[142] Ceadel thinks that a number of P. P. U. members came to believe that Sheppard would have abandoned or modified his pacifism in 1939 or 1940, basing their ideas on his ambivalence on a number of issues expressed in *We Say "No"*, and "his belief about the Great War that the self-sacrifice of the soldiery was greater than that of the conscientious objector."[143] William Paxton remembered, "On one occasion I heard someone condemning a friend of ours who had 'ratted' on the pacifist question. 'Go easy, old man', said Dick. 'When the guns begin to fire who can say how many of us will fail?'"[144] His death removed the future dilemma but it is possible that as his pacifism was an emotional pacifism, at war it could have been an emotional patriotism.

Sheppard's role in Christian pacifism was considered by Charles Raven to have been important to the church as a whole. Writing to Archbishop Lang after Sheppard's death he emphasised the importance of appointing a Christian leader for the P. P. U.:

> Dick Sheppard held together a very influential group of people and many of them formerly critical of and even hostile to Christianity. His influence changed their attitude …but many of them are still only sympathetic and will easily slip back into estrangement.

---

140 LP L, MS 3744, letter from H. Blackburne to Dick Sheppard, p.11.
141 *Manchester Guardian* 11 May 1935.
142 A. Hastings, *A History of English Christianity* 1920–1990,(London, SCM Press, 1991), p.332.
143 Ceadel, *Pacifism in Britain*, p.247.
144 Paxton, 'Dick Sheppard, National President of the Brotherhood Movement', p.12.

The letter goes on, "This would not matter so much for the peace movement. There are other specifically Christian peace societies, but it would matter for the church, for the P. P.U. is proving a very effective evangelistic agency."[145]

It is clear then that Sheppard played an important role in the development of the pacifist movement and was an undoubted motivator of the P. P. U. during the interwar years. It is less clear to what extent this pacifism was informed by his war service and to what extent this was exaggerated to enhance his standing in the movement. Martin Ceadel and Edward Madigan have both quoted Baldwin's famous dictum that "the bomber will always get through"to suggest that it was in fact the fear of a new war rather than memories of an old one which motivated the peace movement and its famous figures such as Raven and Sheppard. However, the ideas of war and remembrance, with regret leading to pacifism, played a large part in the psyches of former chaplains and it is not too much to assume that Sheppard's undeniable heavy workload in the cause of pacifism owed much to his brief experience as a chaplain in the Great War.

Conclusion

Chaplains returning from the Great War were determined that part of the redemption of sacrifice was to be that there would be no more war. In this their ideology was part of the general feeling that the war had been "The war to end all wars". They played their part in the national rituals of remembrance, which have been considered by some historians to have been mechanisms to promote social cohesion and acceptance of the existing social order. However, their combination of remembrance of the dead with change for the future, as epitomised by Toc H as a "living memorial", prevented them from being merely the official functionaries of a state-inspired semi-religious commemoration. The fact that it was important for leaders of the peace movements to emphasise strongly their credentials as former chaplains to enhance their influence shows how much effect the Great War had on the thinking of many sections of society. It was more credible to decry a future war if one had been shown to have fully appreciated the horrors of the last one.

The majority of views held concerning war and peace in the Anglican Church in the 1930s were to support the efforts of the League of Nations and the national government to keep peace, but there was a growing awareness, especially after the Munich Crisis, that this support did not preclude the idea that Britain, as part of the League of Nations and as a major European power, should play a part in defeating the expansion of fascism. Former chaplains like Barry, although joining in the general relief at Munich, soon changed from a pacifist position to that of support for war, even castigating themselves for having supported pacifism:

---

145 LPL. Lang Papers 393, letter from Charles Raven to Archbishop Lang, 17 November 1937.

I must admit with shame that after Munich I shared in the popular hysteria. Only slowly and painfully did I realise the wickedness of Nazism and fascism and the moral duty of saving the Western World from being enslaved to their obscene domination.[146]

The different attitudes taken by former chaplains in the face of another war show the different ways in which their experiences in the Great War had effected their thinking during the brief period of the interwar years. Men who had worked out a definite theological and intellectual rationale for their absolute pacifism, such as Charles Raven, remained convinced of the need to avoid war, but for many former chaplains, their horror of war, and consequent pacificistic thinking, was replaced by the need to support another, very different war against fascism.

146 Barry, *Period of my Life*, p.128.

Conclusion

The interwar years were a time of change and adjustment for Britain, in which the nation grappled with the effects of a world war while at the same time experiencing continuities from the pre-war economy and Victorian and Edwardian social attitudes. The immediate and longer term effects of total war, in which civilians as well as the armed forces had played a vital part, dominated politics, industry and society, while the rituals of remembrance were a reminder of the enormous personal and corporate cost of war, which encouraged a new sense of engagement in the post-war world.

Against this background, the Anglican Church, particularly the chaplains returning from war, struggled to emerge from the disappointment of finding that the conditions of total war had failed to produce a religious revival, and the realisation that the Christianity of the troops was, when it existed, of a far more diffusive nature than had been thought. It was certainly not strong enough to bring the men who had served in the army to regular attendance at church on their return. Revisionist historians have questioned the concept of the First World War as a distinct watershed in British society, so pre-war influences on chaplains, in terms of their backgrounds and previous careers, have been assessed, together with an overview of the strength of the Anglican Church at the beginning of the war. In 1914 the church was overcoming some of the problems of the late nineteenth century and was optimistic about further progress. The pre-war experiences of the men who came forward as chaplains were diverse, and as a group they were not inexperienced. However, to a great extent their lives and opinions were altered by the experience of war. The chaplains' experiences and the issues they brought up affected their ideas of their role in the post-war world. They had experienced the opportunity to work in cooperation with chaplains of other denominations and they had ministered to men of every background. They had occasion to grapple with difficulties in their own faith and to question preconceived theological tenets and church party affiliations. Their awareness of the diffusive Christianity prevalent in the trenches had given them fresh ideas for harnessing the increased religious awareness of men who were returning, by fresh approaches to the liturgy of the church and the role of the church in social and industrial issues. Most importantly, they had experienced freedom from restraints imposed by the structure and discipline of the Anglican Church at home. This allowed them to develop a flexible attitude which was to be reflected in their post-war ministries.

The chaplains were very conscious about the way in which their work in the war would have an effect on their post-war ministries and produced collectively a large body of work in which they articulated this awareness. Although as individuals they wrote about inspiring occasions and services at the front, and their post-war accounts of their time at war are in the main positive, collectively they were very conscious of the failure of the Anglican Church to have an obvious effect on the majority of the troops. This realisation informed their views and actions in their post-war careers in a number of ways. One of the early indicators that they were to have a significant effect on the organisation and administration of the post-war Anglican Church was shown while the war was still continuing in the rebellious attitude of some chaplains, towards the institutions, procedures and services of the church. A symptom of this attitude was seen in the "Plus and Minus" scheme discussed by some senior chaplains in the spring of 1918. This and other expressions of discontent with the government of the church led serving chaplains to be prominent in the Life and Liberty Movement which was to be instrumental in the genesis of the Enabling Bill, passed in 1919.

The economic effect of the war, linked to the continued decline of Britain's staple industries, coal, steel and textiles, resulted in economic hardship, unemployment and consequent industrial strife throughout the interwar years. The slump which followed the brief post-war boom brought into focus the economic difficulties which were to continue in some parts of Britain throughout the interwar years. Many of the former chaplains worked towards both amelioration of the conditions caused by unemployment and solutions to its root causes. The work of C. O. P. E. C .has been seen as being too idealistic and not producing enough practical applications, but there is no doubt that the principles of the main reports of C.O.P.E.C. were ones which were to reappear in the foundations of social reform in the years leading up to the Beveridge Report and the formation of a National Health Service. C.O.P.E.C. was the idea of William Temple, ably assisted by former chaplains. Temple had been close to several prominent chaplains such as Pym, Raven, Blackburne and Talbot during the war and immediately after it. Some of his initiatives, such as the Life and Liberty Movement, were inspired or certainly encouraged by the opinions of serving chaplains.

Individual former Anglican chaplains such as Bishop Timothy Rees, John Groser and Tom Pym became prominent in working for a just industrial society. A great deal was achieved by the work of the Industrial Christian Fellowship (ICF), which, although not overtly political, was involved in many of the issues involved in industrial relations during the 1920s and 1930s. As well as organising crusades in many deprived areas which concerned themselves with the material as well as the spiritual plight of the local population, they campaigned for changes in government policy which would be to the benefit of the poorly paid and unemployed. Their chief missioner, Geoffrey Studdert Kennedy, as well as participating in crusades, spoke on all kinds of public platforms expounding the Christian response to the problems of industry and society. P. T. R. Kirk, the ICF leader, became involved in an interdenominational group attempting to mediate in the General Strike. Gerald Studdert Kennedy explained how the ICF received much support from parishes where the priest was a former chaplain. A significant number of former chaplains were also on its committee. Through its contacts with both influential figures in industry and with unions through the Brotherhood, the ICF was able to play a significant role in the industrial and economic affairs in the interwar period. The ICF has continued to flourish into the twenty-first century, providing funds for research on industrial relations and giving advice through its publications on modern industrial dilemmas. Although the ICF is not an Anglican institution, many of its main supporters were influential figures in the Anglican Church. These included former chaplains who had a high profile in Anglican Church government and were instrumental in encouraging debate in Convocation and Church Assembly on social and industrial issues. They were instrumental in creating a climate of opinion within the Anglican Church more in tune with the social and Industrial issues of the interwar years.

The work of the Toc H movement can be seen as complementary to the work of the ICF. It was founded by P. B. 'Tubby' Clayton, and aimed at a better and more equal society by encouraging men of all classes to be united in the service of their fellow men as a memorial to the men who had fallen in the war. The difference in Toc H's attitude was that its emphasis was on fellowship in service, its members drawn from all walks of life, being organised by the "jobmaster" to provide service according to their talents. The organisation, although Anglican in origin, was interdenominational and spread to become a worldwide movement which has provided service and fellowship to generations. It was active during the Second World War, and like the ICF, still exists today.

The record of former chaplains in their efforts to engage with social and industrial problems during the interwar years is impressive. Behind the larger-than-life figures of Geoffrey Studdert Kennedy and "Tubby" Clayton were the priests who took part in committees and debates at parochial, diocesan and national level, who arranged crusades, spoke out in the local and national press on industrial matters and preached in market places alongside communists. The Anglican Church had a history of social action stretching back into the nineteenth century, but the circumstances of the interwar years demanded an immediate and articulate response from it which was present in no small measure due to the efforts of former chaplains.

Former chaplains also had a role in training the clergy, in developments in academic theology and in the support of Christian-based educational institutions. Some of the senior and more perceptive and experienced chaplains, such as Neville Talbot, were aware of a distance between some chaplains and the ordinary soldier. This prompted them to question the way in which ordinands had been prepared for their ministry before the war in universities and theological colleges. The reactions of some ill-prepared and inexperienced Anglican chaplains to conditions at the front prompted some criticism. To combat this criticism the necessary training in pastoral work was considerably developed, together with an awareness of the new discipline of psychology. This caused a sea change in post-war ordination training. The Test School at Knutsford contributed to the widening class composition of the Anglican clergy by ensuring that ordinary, perhaps hitherto poorly educated, ex-servicemen had the chance to catch up on their educational qualifications in an atmosphere far removed from the traditional theological college. It was the vision of chaplains such as P. B. Clayton and F. R. Barry, who had been debating the nature of the Anglican ministry as part of their response to war, that ensured the success of this venture, which laid the ground for a much broader selection of candidates for ordination as the twentieth century progressed. The development of the concept of a more professional priesthood for the Church of England is one of the results of the insights of some Anglican chaplains as a result of their wartime experiences. Former chaplains contributed extensively to the development of continued theological debate within the church and grappled with new disciplines such as moral theology and psychology, and they explored the way in which new ideas and research into the functioning of the human mind had relevance for the way in which to live a Christian life.

The interwar years saw challenges and changes to the institutional structure of the Anglican Church, for example, the Enabling Act, which resulted in parochial changes such as Parochial Church Councils as well as wider changes such as the creation of new dioceses. There was controversy over proposed changes to the Prayer Book and widely differing opinions on moves toward unity with other churches. Some former chaplains, who had already been instrumental in the Life and Liberty Movement, were involved from early war days in moves toward unity. Neville Talbot wrote about unity in several books and was present at the Lambeth Conference discussions in 1920, which resulted in the important Lambeth resolution on unity, "An Appeal to all Christian People". Nine former chaplains took part in the Mansfield Conference in 1920, which produced a resolution advocating exchange of pulpits with other Christian denominations and also promoted joint communion services. Other chaplains were prominent in the wider orbit of international unity between churches, in the Lausanne Conference on Faith and Order in 1927, and in discussion on unity with the Church of Scotland in 1932 and 1933. Chaplains such as Guy Rogers, who was a leading advocate and indeed practitioner of intercommunion, explained that the motivation for many chaplains in their support for church unity was a desire to recapture the spirit of unity and interdenominationalism that had prevailed in the trenches. The cause of church unity did not develop much further in the interwar years than the Lambeth resolution of 1920: one of the main problems being the validity of non-Episcopal orders. However, throughout this period, former chaplains and those who had experienced ministering at war, such as Dick Sheppard, kept the topic alive and went much further than some of their colleagues in acting against church policy on unity and intercommunion.

Chaplains ministering to congregations at the front had often been highly critical of the services of the church, seeing them as arcane and irrelevant to the spiritual needs of the ordinary soldier. In several wartime reports they were vociferous in their comments that services should be revised if the church was to attract worshippers in the post-war world. A major controversy which engulfed the Anglican Church in the 1920s was that of the proposals to revise the Book of Common Prayer. After several years of heated discussion at the Church Assembly, a proposal was put forward to Parliament in December 1927 and was rejected. A revised proposal was rejected in

February 1928. Many former chaplains had been active in proposals for Prayer Book revision, mainly cooperating on a proposal called the "Grey Book'" which incorporated their ideas of lectionary revision and changes to the communion service. Although the Grey Book proposals did not have a large effect on the eventual revised proposal which went to Parliament in 1928, most of the former chaplains involved supported the revision and were consciously aware that their opinions had been formed to a large extent by their wartime experiences. Their emphasis on the importance of Holy Communion was to be instrumental in encouraging developments leading to the Parish Communion movement later in the century.

In addition to being involved in controversies concerning the life of the church, former chaplains were also involved in some more wide-ranging controversies of the interwar years. The mainstream of Anglican opinion was firmly against the remarriage of divorced people and of admitting them to Holy Communion. By 1936, however, Convocation at Canterbury acknowledged that the attitude of the church was out of line with changing social mores, and there was a role for the church in supporting limited demands for reform in the divorce laws. Former chaplains were prominent in pressing for a more compassionate attitude from the church on remarriage and consequent admission to Holy Communion. Rogers freely admitted to performing marriages where one of the partners had been divorced. Rogers, Pym and Linton Smith were firmly in favour of adequate marriage preparation, thus dealing with the causes rather than the consequences of marriage breakdown. Among former chaplains, Kenneth Kirk was a dissenting voice, arguing for the sanctity of marriage and the safeguarding of moral standards. Another controversy in which some former chaplains were to be involved, that of the use of contraception, also showed the necessity to think beyond narrow theological or doctrinal restraints. Again, former chaplains were arguing against the mainstream of Anglican opinion, refuting the idea that contraception was wrong in all cases. In their advocacy of the use of contraception in certain circumstances, Barry and Rogers went far beyond the exceptions allowed by the Lambeth Conference in 1930. The question of remarriage in church after divorce still causes controversy in today's church, the use of contraception less so, but former chaplains were in the vanguard of change in these matters. Their arguments, based on the compassion of God rather than on theological arguments, could have been influenced by their experiences in the war, when often the necessity to show the love of God was more important than points of church doctrine or morality.

The development of radio broadcasting and the cinema into mass media in the interwar years posed further challenges to the church. There was concern that listening to the radio on Sunday would detract from church attendance and that the content of films shown in the cinemas would undermine the moral standards of the nation. Former chaplains proved adept at seizing the opportunities posed by the new media by encouraging the development of broadcast church services against some stiff opposition from laymen and clergy, and the efforts of Dick Sheppard and Pat McCormick made St Martin-in-the-Fields synonymous with the success of early broadcasting on the B. B. C. Less successfully, attempts were made to harness the power of the cinema to promote Christianity. The pragmatic attitude of E. S. Woods and others to cinema-going encouraged local councils to cooperate with the local churches in discussions about timing and content of cinema showings. Former chaplains were involved in many of the controversies of the Anglican Church in the interwar years. Although they did not always speak with one voice they were active in words and deeds in pursing their objectives. Their concern with issues of unity with other churches and the liturgy of the church was clearly linked to their war service. They were evidently prepared to challenge mainstream opinion in the established church. Their speeches, books and actions can be said to have led the way in dealing with some of the more controversial issues both internally and in wider society that the church had to tackle in this era and to have established a groundwork which the church would find helpful in the rest of the twentieth century.

The attitude of the former chaplains to remembrance led some to adopt a pacifist position. They were much in demand to help form and consolidate rituals of remembrance in the post-war years. However, their emphasis was mostly on the concept of redemptive sacrifice and the necessity to reshape society in the name of those who had died. A clear example of this was the 'Living Memorial' of Toc H. They also had to combat attempts to make remembrance a secular function as epitomised by the non-religious symbolism of the Cenotaph and the refusal of the Imperial War Graves Commission[1] to allow crosses as headstones. A former chaplain, David Railton was, however, instrumental in the burial of the Unknown Warrior at Westminster Abbey, which gave families of the soldiers without a known grave a place to mourn. This grave remains a major focus for remembrance. An important legacy of the participation of former chaplains in rituals of remembrance is the continuation of the Anglican Church's involvement today. Even in a secular society the example of the chaplains' participation in remembrance after the Great War remains. While representatives of all major religions are invited to participate in national and local ceremonies, it is mainly in the buildings and under the auspices of the Anglican Church that such ceremonies take place.

The role that former chaplains played in the pacifist movement in the interwar years differed as circumstances changed during the interwar years, from the emphasis on the League of Nations and collective security of the 1920s, through the anti-war period of the late 1920s and early 1930s to the international crises of the later 1930s. Many former chaplains such as Neville Talbot and Geoffrey Studdert Kennedy spoke with an anti-war voice in the years immediately after the war but generally the pacifism shown by former chaplains was linked to support of collective security and the League of Nations union. Charles Raven and Dick Sheppard made an undeniable and major contribution to the organisation of the pacifist cause with their work with the Fellowship of Reconciliation and the Peace Pledge Union respectively. These organisations are flourishing today and are further instances of institutions formed by or supported by former Anglican chaplains which continue to have an effect on

---

1   The name was changed to The Commonwealth War Graves Commission in 1960.

twenty-first century society in that they provide a structure for pacifist action and forums for pacifist debate.

The ideas of chaplains returning from the Great War emphasised reformation rather than remembrance, although they did play their part in the rituals of remembrance and pilgrimage that took place in the interwar years. The focus of their views and actions in these years was on renewal of the Anglican Church and its place and purpose in the post-war world. They contributed to this renewal directly by their involvement in changes to the institutional organisation of the church, their advancement of the cause of church unity and intercommunion, their contribution to new training methods for ordinands and their advocacy of a revised liturgy for the church. Indirectly they placed the Anglican Church at the centre of important institutions such as Toc H and the Industrial Christian Fellowship. Their work attempting to improve social and industrial conditions, to achieve developments in education, in responding to moral and technical developments in the 1920s and 1930s and in rationalising the implications of further war, were all informed by their wartime experiences, whether implicitly or explicitly. Their common experiences of war had given them a characteristic pragmatism and made them adaptive to change. Post-war these aspects of their characters informed their actions to a significant extent. The causes they espoused were ones which echoed down the twentieth century and are still relevant today.

The work and influence of the former Anglican chaplains has to be considered as part of the wider development of the Anglican Church in the interwar years. Current scholarship on the development of the church in the era has considered some former chaplains as prominent individuals in the church and has pointed to the significance of their war service, but has not considered them as a group who together greatly enhanced the internal development of the church as well as encouraging its engagement with problems in society. Although they were not the only Anglican voices to be concerned with these reforms, in proportion to their numbers they achieved prominence in many institutions of the church and society, from Bishop's Palace and Convocation to crusade meetings and picket lines. Much of the evidence for this has been taken from the careers of former chaplains who expressed their ideas in books, articles, and debates, and whose contributions to the post-war church can be clearly analysed. Future research on the subject will need to concentrate on examining more deeply the contribution of individual ex-chaplains at parochial, diocesan and national level. However, in the absence of detailed research from local archives on more obscure chaplains returning to their parishes, it is possible to assert that much of what we know about specific chaplains was echoed in the lives and work of many of the priests whose ministries had been changed by their experiences in war.

The interwar years have been described as "the long peace". As the former chaplains were coming to terms with the way in which the Great War had affected their lives and ministries the threat of the next war loomed. In the twenty years after their wartime chaplaincies, these men had gone some way to fulfilling the hopes and aspirations articulated on their return from the front and could claim to have contributed greatly to both developments in the Anglican Church and in wider society.

Appendix

Chaplains mentioned in text

F. R. Barry, TCF 1915-1919 (DSO 1916). Deputy Assistant Chaplain General, Head of Knutsford Ordination Test School 1919-1923. King's College London 1923-1927. Vicar of St Mary's University Church Oxford 1927-1933. Canon of Westminster 1933-1941. Bishop of Southwell from 1941.

Julian Bickersteth, TCF 915-1919 (mentioned in despatches 1917, MC 1918). Head teacher, St Peter's Adelaide 1920-1933. Headmaster Felsted School from 1933. Archdeacon of Maidstone and Canterbury from 1943.

H. W. Blackburne, CF 1903-1924 (MC 1914, DSO 1917). Vicar of Ashford 1924-1931. Canon of St George's Windsor 1931-1934. Dean of Bristol from 1934.

R. V. H. Burne, TCF 1917-1918. Tutor at Knutsford Ordination Test School 1919-23. Principal 1923-1937. Canon of Chester Cathedral from 1933.

Walter Carey, TCRN 1914-1919. Bishop of Bloemfontein from 1921.

C. M. Chavasse, TCF 1914-1918 (MC 1917, Croix de Guerre, 1918). Vicar of St George's Barrow-in-Furness 1919-1922. Rector of St Aldate's Church Oxford 1922-1928. Master of St Peter's Hall Oxford 1929-1939. Bishop of Rochester from 1939.

J. F. Clayton, TCF 1916-1919 (MC 1918). Tutor at Knutsford Ordination School 1919-1920. Domestic Chaplain to the Bishop of Durham 1921-1926. Lecturer at Sarum Theological College 1926-1929. Warden of St Nicholas's Hall, Bristol 1929-1933. Ripon Hall 1935-1939. Prebendary of Hereford Cathedral from 1937.

P. B. Clayton. TCF 1915-1919 (MC 1917). Founder of Toc H Movement, Vicar of All Hallows, London, from 1922.

E. C. Crosse, TCF 1915-1918 (MC and DSO 1917). Headmaster, Christ's College New Zealand 1921-1930. Headmaster, Ardingly College from 1933.

Herbert Fleming, TCF 1914-19. First Hon. Administrative Padre to Toc H.

A. R. Goodwin, TCF 1918-1919. Part-time chaplain to Toc H in the interwar years. Vicar of Pleasly Hill 1921-1923.Rector of Bamford 1923-1925. Curate of St John the Baptist, Kidderminster 1925-1927. Rector of Blakedown, 1927-1931. Rector of Himley 19311-1936. Vicar if Welshhampton from 1926.

John Groser, TCF 1916-1919 (mentioned in despatches 1917). Curate, Lostwithiel 1920-1922. Curate, St Michael's Bromley by Bow 1922-1928. Vicar of Christ Church Watney St, from 1929.

Bishop L. H. Gwynne, Bishop of Diocese of Khartoum (Sudan) 1908. TCF 1914-1919. Deputy Chaplain General in France 1915-1919. Returned to Sudan to resume his post in 1919. Lord Bishop in Egypt and the Sudan, 1920-1945

Mervyn Haigh, TCF 1916-1919 (mentioned in despatches 1918). Tutor at Knutsford Ordination Test School 1919-1924. Principal Secretary to Archbishop of Canterbury 1924-1931. Bishop of Coventry from 1931. Bishop of Winchester from 1942.

W. T. Havard, TCF 19115-1919 (mentioned in despatches 1916, DSO 1917). Chaplain Jesus College, Oxford 1919-1921. Vicar of St Paul-at-Hook 1922-1924. Vicar of Swansea 1928-1934.Bishop of St Asaph from 1934

A. C. E. Jarvis, Assistant chaplain EEF 15-1916. Principal Chaplain, Mesopotamia, 1916-1919. Serbian Order of the White Eagle, 1917. Chaplain General to the Forces 1925-1931. Hon Canon in Sheffield Cathedral 1931-36. Vicar and provost of Cathedral Church, Moorfields from 1938.

Robert Keable, Chaplain to the South African Labour Corps, serving mainly at Le Havre. Resigned and left the Anglican Ministry 1919.

Bernard Keymer, TCF 1916-1918, chaplain in RAF 1918.

Kenneth Escott Kirk, TCF 1914-1919. Regius Professor of Moral Theology, University of Oxford 1933. Bishop of Oxford from 1937.

P. T. R. Kirk, TCF 1915-1918. General Director of the Industrial Christian Fellowship from 1919. Vicar of Christ Church, Westminster 1922.

M. P. G. Leonard, TCF 1914-1919, (DSO 1916). Chaplain Cheltenham College 1919-1922. Chaplain to Toc H Manchester 1922-1929. Toc H Admin HQ 1929-1931. Curate of All Hallows, London 1931-1936. Rector of Bishop's Hatsfield from 1936. Provost and Rector of St Mary's Cathedral city and diocese of Glasgow from 1944. Bishop of Thetford from 1953.

M. Linton Smith, TCF 1915-1917 (DSO 1917). Suffragan Bishop of Warrington 1918, Translated to Hereford 1920, Translated to Rochester 1930-1939.

Geoffrey Lunt TCF 1917-1919. Vicar of All Souls' Northampton 1919-1926. Archdeacon in Egypt and sub-dean of All Saints Cathedral, Cairo 1926-1928. Vicar of St Mary's Portsea 1928-1934. Bishop of Ripon from 1934.

W. P. G. McCormick, TCF 1914-1919 (DSO 1917). Vicar and Rural Dean of Croydon 1919-1927. Vicar of St Martin-in–the-fields from 1927.

J. V. Macmillan, TCF 1915-16, 1917-19. Vicar of Kew 1916-1921. Archdeacon of Maidstone and Canon of Canterbury Cathedral 1921-1934. Suffragan Bishop of Dover from 1927. Bishop of Guildford from 1943.

F. B. Macnutt, Canon of Southwark Cathedral, TCF 1915-1918, becoming senior chaplain. Vicar of St Martin's Leicester 1918-1938. Canon of Canterbury Cathedral from 1938.

E. Milner-White TCF 1914-1918, (DSO 1918). Dean and Fellow, King's College, Cambridge 1918-1941. Dean of York from 1941.

R. H. Moberly, TCF 1917-1919. Curate of Benoni, Transvaal 1914-1925. Principal of Bishop's College, Chesunt 1925-1936. Bishop of Stepney from 1936.

R. G. Parsons, TCF 1916-1917. Vicar of Poyton 1916-1919. Rector of Birch in Rushholme 1919-1932. Suffragan Bishop of Middleton 1927. Bishop of Southwark from 1932.

Tom Pym TCF 1914-1919 (DSO 1917). Assistant Chaplain General 1918. Warden of Camberwell House Settlement 1919. Canon Missioner to the Diocese of Southwark 1925-1929. Canon of Bristol Cathedral 1929-1932. Fellow and Chaplain of Balliol College Oxford 1932-1938.

Oliver Quick, TCF 1917-1918. Canon of Carlisle Cathedral and examining chaplain to the Bishop of Newcastle 1923-1930. Canon of St Paul's Cathedral 1930-1934. Professor of Divinity, Durham Cathedral 1934-1939. Regius Professor of Divinity University of Oxford from 1939.

David Railton, TCF 1911-1919. Vicar of St John the Baptist, Margate 1920-1925. Curate of Christ Church Westminster 1925-1927.Vicar of St James, Bolton 1927-1931. Vicar of Shalford 1931-1935. Rector of St Nicholas Liverpool 1935-42, Archbishop's Visitor to the R.A.F. 1943-45.

Charles Raven, TCF 1917-1918. Dean and fellow of Emmanuel College Cambridge 1909-1920. Rector of Blechingley 1920-1924. Canon of Liverpool Cathedral 1924-1932. Regius professor of Divinity, University of Cambridge from 1932. Master of Christ's College Cambridge from 1939.

Timothy Rees, TCF 1916-1919. Community of the Resurrection, Bishop of Llandaff 1931-1939.

T. Guy Rogers, TCF 1915-1916, MC 1916. Vicar of West Ham 1917-1925. Rector of St Martin's Birmingham from 1925.

A. C. Rose, TCRN 1914-1919. Warden of Bishop's Hostel Lincoln 1921-1927. Vicar of Brighton with West Bletchington 1927-1934. Suffragan Bishop of Dover from 1935.

H. F. Sawbridge, TCF 1915-1919 (MC 1916). Lecturer Knutsford Ordination Test School 1919-1922. Chaplain to Toc H 1922-1931.

E. G. Selwyn, TCF 1918-1919, Rector of Red Hill 1919-1931. Dean of Winchester from 1931.

H. R. L. Sheppard, Chaplain to an Australian field hospital 1914. Founder of the Peace Pledge Union 1927. Vicar of St Martin-in-the-fields 1914-1926. Dean of Canterbury Cathedral 1929-1931. Dean of St Pauls 1934-1937.

B. F. Simpson, TCF 1916-1918 (MC 1918). Rector and Rural Dean of Stepney 1920-1926. Vicar of St Peter, Cranley Gardens 1926-1932. Suffragan Bishop of Kensington from 1932.

H. K. Southwell, TCF 1915-1919. Mentioned in despatches 1915and 1916 Assistant Chaplin General 1916-1919 Provost of Lancing 1902-1937,Bishop of Lewes 1920-1926.

G. A. Studdert Kennedy, TCF 1914-1918 (MC 1916). Vicar of St Paul's Worcester 1914-1921. Vicar of St Edmund's Lombard Street London from 1921. Chief Missioner for the Industrial Christian Fellowship from 1921.

Edward Keble Talbot, TCF 1914-1920. Superior of the Community of the Resurrection from 1922.

Neville Talbot TCF 1914-1919 (MC 1915). Senior chaplain Sixth Division 1915. Senior Anglican chaplain of XIV corps 1916 and Assistant Chaplain General to Fifth Army 1916. Bishop of Pretoria 1920-1934. Vicar of St Mary's Nottingham and assistant bishop of Southwell from 1934.

A. R. Browne Wilkinson TCF 1918-1919. Priest in Charge of St Paul's Daybrook, 1919-1924. Diocesan missioner Southwark diocese 1920-1926. Principal St Christopher's College, Blackheath 1926-1931. Vicar of Bedale 1931-1938. Canon of Chichester Cathedral from 1938.

A. E. Wilkinson, CF (TA) 1913-1918 (mentioned in despatches 1918). Vicar of St James, Croydon, 1919-1931. Vicar of Merstham from 1931.

E. S. Woods, TCF 1914-1919. Vicar of Holy Trinity, Cambridge 1918-1927. Vicar of Croydon 1927-1937. Bishop of Croydon 1930-1937. Bishop of Lichfield from 1937.

C. S. Woodward, TCF 1916-1917(MC 1916). Vicar of St Peter's Cranley Gardens 1918-1926. Canon of Westminster 1926-1933. Bishop of Bristol from 1933.

H. E . Wynn, TCF 1914-1919. Dean of Pembroke College Cambridge 1920-1936, Tutor from 1936.

Bibliography

Archival Material

Cheshire County Record Office
Ducdame, the Magazine of the Ordination Test School at Knutsford (D 3917/32).
Le Touqet Times, R. V. H. Burne Collection.

C M S Archives, University of Birmingham
XACC/18/Z/1 Army Book of L. H. Gwynne.
XACC/18/F/1 Diaries of Bishop L. H .Gwynne.

Toc H Archives, University of Birmingham
Section 6 G1 Annual Reports, 1921-1941.

Cumbria County Record Office
(BPR 11/PM/2) St George's Parish Magazines 1919-1922.

Imperial War Museum
IWM (80/22/1) E. C. Crosse papers.
IWM (90/7/1) C. I. S. Hood papers.
IWM (72/82/1) H.S. Jeudwine papers.
IWM (7/107/1) T. G. Rogers papers.
IWM (1/51/94) H. Spooner papers.

Lambeth Palace Library
The papers of Bishop Bell, Vols. 193, 206, 367.
The papers of Archbishop Randall Davidson, Vols. 201, 216, 217.
The papers of Archbishop C.G. Lang, Vols. 106, 114, 117, 118, 150 and 393.
The papers of Archbishop William Temple, Vols. 46 and 42 and 148.
(MS 4042): The minute book of the ICF Council for 1920-1926.
(MS 2077): The papers of B. K. Cunningham.
(MS 3428): The papers of John Groser.
(MS 3744): The letters and papers of H. R. L. Sheppard.

London Metropolitan Archives
P. B. Clayton Collection CLC 437
Papers relating to the Tower Hill Trust LMA/4544

The National Archives
TNA, WO/95/2023: the war diary of the senior chaplain to the 8th Division, the Rev. G. A. Weston.
TNA, WO 95/1540: the war diary of the 14th Field Ambulance.

Nottinghamshire County Record Office
DD 1332/112/4: Pamphlet, Conference on the Preparation of the Ministry, p. 2.
DD 1332 /198: Neville Talbot's account of the pilgrimage of padres to Talbot House April 27–May 1 1930, p. 10.
PR 19, 762/5: *Daybrook Parish Magazine*, August 1919.
DD 1332/76: *The Natal Mercury*, Christmas 1931, press cuttings in the papers of Neville Talbot.

Royal Army Chaplains' Department Archives
The papers of the Very Rev. H.W. Blackburne, DSO MC.
Scrapbook of press clippings kept by Rev. Dr A. C. E. Jarvis during his time as Chaplain General c. 1930s

Private Papers
The diaries of the Rev. B. O'Rorke.

Newspapers, Journals and Magazines

The Times, 1916-1985.
The *Church Times*, 1916-1939.
The *Challenge*.
The *Guardian*.
The *Manchester Guardian*.
The *Observer*.
Toc H Journal.

Published Primary Sources

Anonymous, *Can England's Church Win England's manhood?* By an Army Chaplain (Macmillan, 1917).
(The) Archbishops' Fifth Committee of Enquiry, *Christianity and Industrial Problems* (SPCK, 1918).
(The) Archbishops' Second Committee of Enquiry, *The Worship of the Church* (SPCK, 1918).

(The) Archbishops' Third Committee of Enquiry, *The Evangelistic work of the Church* (SPCK, 1918).

Baron, B., *The Birth of a Movement 1919-1922 – The Story of Toc H* (Westminster, 1952).

Barry, F. R., *Religion and the War* (Methuen, 1915).

Barry, F. R., *Christianity and Psychology* (SCM Press, 1923).

Barry, F. R., *St Paul and Social Psychology. An Introduction to the Epistle to the Ephesians* (Humphrey Milford, 1923)

Barry, F. R., *One Clear Call – An Appeal to the Church of England* (W. Heffer & Sons, 1922).

Barry, F. R., *The Relevance of Christianity* (Nisbet & Co., 1932).

Barry, F. R., *Period of My Life* (Hodder and Stoughton, 1974).

Barry, F. R., *Christianity and Psychology* (SCM Press, 1923).

Bickersteth, J. (ed.), *The Bickersteth Diaries* (Leo Cooper, 1996).

(The) Bishop of Kensington's Report, *The evidence received from chaplains in the Navy and Army in responses they have given to the following letter* (Church Army Press, 1916).

Blackburne, H., *This Also Happened on the Western Front. The Padre's Story* (Hodder & Stoughton, 1932).

Burne, R. V. H. *Knutsford: The study of the Ordination Test School, 1914-40* (SPCK, 1959).

Carey, W., *Sacrifice and Some of its Difficulties* (Mowbray, 1918).

Cairns, D. (ed.), *The Army and Religion* (YMCA, 1919).

Clayton, P. B., *Tales of Talbot House, Everyman's Club in Poperinghe and Ypres, 1915-1918* (Chatto and Windus, 1919).

Clayton, P. B., *The Smoking Furnace and the Burning Lamp: Talks on Toc H* (Longmans Green, 1927).

Clayton, P. B., *To conquer hate* (Epworth Press, 1963).

Clayton P. B., *Plain Tales from Flanders* (Longmans, Green & Co., 1930).

Clayton, P.B. (ed.), *A Birthday Book, Published for the Coming of Age Festival of Toc H* (Toc H Incorporated, 1936).

Coop, J. O., *The Story of the 55th (West Lancashire) Division* (*Liverpool Daily Post*, 1919).

C.O.P.E.C., *The C.O.P.E.C. Commission Reports* (C.O.P.E.C. Commission, 1924).

C.O.PE.C., *The Purpose, Scope and Nature of the Conference* (C.O.P.E.C. Commission, 1923).

C.O.P.E.C. Commission Report: *The Nature of God and his Purpose for the World* (C.O.P.E.C. Commission, 1924).

Creighton, Louise (ed.), *Letters of Oswin Creighton, C.F.: 1883-1918* (Longmans Green & Co., 1920).

Crosse, E. C., *The Defeat of Austria as Seen by the Seventh Division* (Dean and Sons, 1919).

Dearmer, Percy, *Christianity and the Crisis* (Gollancz, 1933).

Drury, William, *Camp Follower* (Privately published, 1968).

Furse, M., *Stand Therefore!* : *A Bishop's Testimony of Faith in the Church of England* (SPCK, 1953).

Garbett, C.F., The *Work of a Great Parish* (Longmans, Green & Co, 1915).

Garbett, C. F., *In the Heart of South London* (Longmans, Green & Co., 1931).

Garbett, C.F., *The Challenge of the Slums* (Longmans, Green & Co., 1933).

The General Report of the Pan Anglican Congress (Church of England, 1908).

Gore, Charles, (ed.), *Lux Mundi: A series of Studies in the Religion of the Incarnation* (John Murray, 1889).

Gordon G. and Pym, T., *Papers from Picardy* (Constable, 1917).

Hankey, D., *A Student in Arms* (Andrew Melrose, 1917).

Housman, L. (ed.), *What can we believe?* : *Letters Exchanged Between Dick Sheppard and L. H. Housman* (Cape, 1939).

Joynson-Hicks, W., *The Prayer Book Crisis* (G. P. Putman, 1928).

Keable, R., *Standing By: Wartime reflections in France and Flanders* (Nisbet & Co., 1919).

Kirk, Kenneth, *A Study in Silent Minds, War Studies in Education* (SCM, 1918).

Kirk, Keneneth, *Some Principles of Moral Theology and their Application* (Longmans, Green & Co., 1920).

Kirk, Kenneth, *Ignorance, Faith & Conformity* (Longmans, Green & Co., 1925).

Kirk, Kenneth, *Conscience and its Problems* (Longmans, Green & Co., 1927).

Kirk, Kenneth, *The story of the Woodard schools* (Hodder & Stoughton, 1937)

Kirk, P. T. R. 'The Industrial Christian Fellowship' in D. P. Thompson (ed.), *Modern Evangelistic Movements* (Thomson & Cowan, 1924).

Kirk, P. T. R., *The Movement Christwards* (A. R. Mowbery, 1931).

Kirk, P. T. R. 'Studdert Kennedy, ICF Crusader', in J.K. Mozley (ed.), *G. A. Studdert Kennedy, By His Friends* (Hodder and Stoughton, 1929).

(The) Lambeth Conferences (1867-1948): The reports of the 1920, 1930 and 1948 conferences, with selected resolutions from the conferences of 1867, 1878, 1888, 1897 and 1908 (SPCK, 1948).

Lloyd George, David, *The War Memoirs of David Lloyd George* (Odhams, 1938).

Macnutt, F. B. (ed.), *The Church in the Furnace, Essays By Seventeen Temporary Church of England Chaplains on Active Service in France and Flanders* (Macmillan, 1918).

McCormick, Pat, *Be of Good Cheer* (Longmans, Green & Co., 1934).

Middleton, R. D. *The Church among Men – A Study in Pastoral Theology* (SPCK, 1923).

Paxton, W., 'Dick Sheppard, National President of the Brotherhood Movement' in Paxton (ed.), *Dick Sheppard. An Apostle of Brotherhood* (Chapman and Hall, 1938).

Pym, Tom, *Psychology and the Christian life* (SCM Press, 1921).

Quick, Oliver, *The Christian Sacraments* (Nisbet, 1927).

Quick, Oliver, *Doctrines of the Creed* (Nisbet, 1938).

Selwyn, E.G., *Essays Catholic and Critical, by Members of the Anglican Communion* (SPCK, 1926).

Sheppard, H. R. L., *We Say "No", A Plain man's Guide to Pacifism* (John Murray, 1936).

Sheppard, H. R. L., *The Impatience of a Parson: a plea for the recovery of vital Christianity* (Hodder and Stoughton, 1927).

Railton, D., *Our Empire*, Vol. 11, no 8 (1931).

Raven, C., *War and the Christian* (SCM Press, 1938).

Raven, C., *Is War Obsolete? A Study of the Conflicting Claims of Religion and Citizenship* (Allen and Unwin, 1935).

Raven, C., *Creator Spirit: A Survey of Christian Doctrine in the Light of Biology, Psychology and Mysticism* (Martin Hopkinson, 1927).

Rees, T., *Sermons and Hymns Collected and Prepared for Publication by John Lambert Rees* (A.R. Mowbray & Co., 1946)

Rogers, T. G., *A Rebel at Heart: The Autobiography of a Nonconforming Churchman.* (Longmans Green & Co., 1956).

Rogers, T. G. (ed.), "The Inner Life" In *Essays in Liberal Evangelicism* (London, Hodder & Stoughton, 1925).

Rogers, T. G. (ed.) "Religious Authority" In *Essays in Liberal Evangelicism* (Hodder & Stoughton, 1925).

Rogers, T. G., *The Church and the People: Problems of Reunion, Sex and Marriage, Women's Ministry, Etc.* (Sampson Low, Marston & Co., 1931).

Rogers, T. G., (ed.), *Christ in the Changing World* (Hodder and Stoughton, 1932).

Rogers, T. G., "The new Catholicism, Intercommunion" in G. L. H. Harvey (ed.), *The Church in the Twentieth Century* (Ayer, 1936).

Royden, Maude, "Dick Sheppard, Peace Maker" in William Paxton (ed.), *Dick Sheppard, An Apostle of Brotherhood* (Chapman and Hall, 1938).

Studdert Kennedy, G. A., *Rough Talks by a Padre, delivered to officers and men of the B.E.F.* (Hodder and Stoughton, 1916).

Studdert Kennedy, G. A., *The Hardest Part* (Hodder and Stoughton, 1918).

Studdert Kennedy, G.A., *Rough Rhymes of a Padre* (Hodder & Stoughton, 1918).

Studdert Kennedy, G. A., *Lies!* (Hodder & Stoughton, 1919).

Studdert Kennedy, G. A., *More Rough Rhymes of a Padre* (Hodder & Stoughton, 1920).

Studdert Kennedy, G. A., *Peace Rhymes of a Padre* (Hodder & Stoughton, 1920).

Studdert Kennedy, G. A., *The Sorrows of God and Other Poems* (Hodder & Stoughton, 1921).

Studdert Kennedy, G. A., *Democracy and the Dog Collar* (Hodder and Stoughton, 1921).

Studdert Kennedy, G. A., *The Word and the Work* (Longmans & Co., 1925).

Talbot, N., *Thoughts on Religion at the Front* (Macmillan & Co., 1917).

Talbot, N., *Religion Behind the Front and After the War* (Macmillan, 1918).

Talbot, N., *Before we meet at the Lambeth Conference* (Longmans Green, 1930).

Talbot, N., *Thoughts on Unity* (SCM Press, 1920).

Talbot, N., *The Returning Tide of Faith* (Nisbet & Co., 1923).

Wand, W., *The Changeful Page, The autobiography of William Wand* (Hodder and Stoughton, 1965).

Winifrith, D., *The Church in the Fighting Line* (Hodder and Stoughton, 1915).

Woods, E. S., *Getting Ready for Reunion* (W. Heffer & Sons, 1926).

Woods, E. S., *Every-day Religion* (SCM, 1921).

Secondary Sources, Incorporating Journal Articles

Barber, M., Taylor, S. and Sewell, G. (eds.), *From the Reformation to the Permissive Society: A miscellany in celebration of the 400th anniversary of Lambeth Palace Library* (Boydell Press, 2010).

Baron, B., *The Doctor, The Story of John Stansfeld of Oxford and Bermondsey* (Edward Arnold, 1952).

Baron, B., *The Birth of a Movement: 1919–1922* (Toc H, 1946).

Barron, Hester, "'Tis very embarrassing, say what you like, to be a good vicar in a valley on strike': The Church of England and its relationship with the Durham miners at the time of the 1926 lockout". *Twentieth Century British History, Vol. 17.*, 2006.

Barnes, J., *Ahead of his Age – Bishop Barnes of Birmingham* (Collins, 1979).

Barry, F. R., *Mervyn Haigh* (SPCK, 1964).

Bell, G. K. A., *Randall Davidson, Archbishop of Canterbury* (Oxford University Press, 1935).

Benstead, Charles R., *Retreat: A Story of 1918* (Methuen, 1930).

Boggis, Jack, "John Groser, Some Memories". *The Christian Socialist*, May 1966.

Bickersteth, J., (ed.), *The Bickersteth Diaries 1914-1918* (Pen and Sword, 1995).

Blackburne, H., *Trooper to Dean, A biography of Harry W. Blackburne, Dean of Bristol* (J. W. Arrowsmith, 1955).

Brabant, F.H., *Neville Stuart Talbot 1879-1943 A Memoir* (SCM Press, 1949).

Briggs, A., *The History of Broadcasting in the United Kingdom, Vol 1.* (Oxford University Press, 1961).

Brown, Callum, *Religion and Society in Twentieth-century Britain* (Pearson Longmans, 2006).

Brown, Callum, *The Death of Christian Britain: Understanding Secularisation 1800-2000* (Routledge, 2009).

Brown, Malcolm, *The Imperial War Book Museum book of 1918: Year of Victory* (Pan, 1998).

Brill, Kenneth, *John Groser, East End Priest* (Mowbray, 1971).

Bullock, F. W., *A History of training for the ministry in the Church of England in England and Wales 1875-1974* (Home Words Publishing, 1976).

Burne, R. U. H., *Knutsford. The Story of the Ordination Test School 1914-1940* (SPCK, 1959).

Bushaway, B., "The Obligation of Remembrance or the Remembrance of Obligation: Society and the Memory of World War" in John Bourne, Ian Whitehead and Peter Liddle, *The Great World War 1914-1945: Lightning Strikes Twice Vol. 1* (Harper Collins, 2001).

Bushaway, B., "Name upon Name, The Great War and Remembrance" in P. Porter (ed.), *Myths of the English* (Polity Press, 1993).

Ceadel, Martin, *Pacifism in Britain, 1914-1945. The Defining of a Faith* (Clarendon Press, 1980).

Chapman, Paul, *A Haven in Hell: Talbot House, Poperinghe (Cameos of the Western Front)* (Pen and Sword, 2000).

Connelly, M., *The Great War, Memory and Ritual: Commemoration in the City and East London, 1916-1939* (Royal Historical Society, 2001).

Cox, J., *The English Churches in a Secular Society – Lambeth 1870-1930* (Oxford University Press, 1982).

Crockford's Clerical Directory, 1940 (Oxford University Press, 1940).

Davies, Horton, *Worship and Theology in England, Vol. 5, The Ecumenical Century, 1900-1965* (Oxford University Press, 1996).

Dillistone, F. W., *Charles Raven: Naturalist, Historian, Theologian* (Hodder and Stoughton, 1975).

Dowland, David, *Nineteenth Anglican Theological Training, The Red Brick Challenge* (Oxford University Press, 1997).

Drury, William, *Camp Follower* (Privately published, 1968).

Durham, John, *Talbot House to Tower Hill, A 'Tubby' Clayton Anthology* (Toc H Incorporated, 1960).

Durham, John, *Tubby on Toc H* (Toc H incorporated, 1962).

Ellis Roberts, R., *H. R. L. Sheppard, Life and Letters* (John Murray, 1942).

Garbett, C. F., The *Work of A Great Parish* (Hodder and Stoughton, 1915).

Gardiner, Juliet, *The Thirties, An Intimate History of Britain* (Harper Collins, 2010).

Gibraltar, W. E., "The Pan Anglican Congress" in *The Irish Church Quarterly*. Vol.1., No 4 Oct., 1908.

Gray, Donald, *Earth and Altar. The evolution of the Parish Communion in the Church of England to 1945* (Canterbury Press, 1986).

Gray, Donald, *Percy Dearmer, A Parson's Pilgrimage* (Canterbury Press, 2000).

Graves, Robert, *Goodbye to All That: An Autobiography* (Penguin, 1929).

Grey, A. H., Iremonger, F. A., et al., *St Martin-in-the-Fields Calling, Broadcast Addresses* (Atheneum Press, 1932).

Gregory, Adrian, *The Last Great War: British Society and the First World War* (Cambridge University Press, 2008).

Gregory, Adrian, *The Silence of Memory, Armistice Day 1919-1946* (Berg, 1994).

Groser, John, *Politics and Persons* (SCM Press, 1949).

Gummer, Selwyn, *The Chavasse Twins* (Hodder and Stoughton, 1963).

Haig, Alan, *The Victorian Clergy* (Croom Helm, 1984).

Hanson, N., *The Unknown Soldier* (Doubleday, 2005).

Harcourt, M., *Tubby Clayton. A personal saga* (Hodder and Stoughton, 1956).

Harvey, G. L. H. (ed.), *The Church in the Twentieth Century* (Macmillan, 1936).

Hattersley, Roy, *Borrowed Time: The story of Britain Between the Wars* (Little, Brown, 2007).

Hastings, Adrian, *A History of English Christianity 1920-2000* (SCM Press, 2001).

Holmes, R., *Tommy, the British Soldier on the Western Front 1914-1918* (Harper Collins, 2004).

Howson, P. *Muddling Through: The Organisation of British Army Chaplaincy in World War One* (Helion, 2013).

Hylson Smith, K., *Evangelicals and the Church of England 1734-1984* (Continuum Publishing, 1992).

Hynes, S., *A War Imagined, The First World War and English Culture* (Bodley Head, 1990).

Iremonger, F., *William Temple, Archbishop of Canterbury: His Life and Letters* (Oxford University Press, 1948).

Iremonger, F., *Men and Movements in the Church* (Longmans, 1928).

Jackson, H.C., *Pastor on the Nile: Being some account of the life and letters of Llewellyn H. Gwynne* (SPCK, 1960).

Kemp, E. Waldram, *The Life and Letters of Kenneth Escott Kirk* (Hodder & Stoughton, 1959).

Kent, John, *William Temple: Church State and Society in Britain 1880-1950* (Cambridge University Press, 1992).

King, A., *Memorials of the Great War in Britain: The Symbolism and Politics of Remembrance (Legacy of the Great War)* (Berg, 1998).

Knight, Frances, "Internal Church Reform 1850-1920. An Age of Innovation in Ecclesiastical Reform" in Paula Yates and Joris van Eijnatten (eds.)*The Churches: The Dynamics of Religious Reform in Church, State and Society in Northern Europe, 1780-1920* (Leuven, 2010).

Lambert Rees, J., *Timothy Rees of Mirfield and Llandaff* (Mowbray, 1945).

Lawson, J., Silver, H., *A Social History of Education in England* (Methuen, 2007).

Leonard, John, Leonard-Johnson, Philip, *The Fighting Padre: Letters from the Trenches 1915-1918 of Pat Leonard DSO* (Pen and Sword, 2010).

Lever, T., *Clayton of Toc H* (John Murray, 1972).

Lloyd, D., *Battlefield Tourism, Pilgrimage and the Commemoration of the Great War in Britain, Australia and Canada 1919-1931* (Berg, 1998).

Lloyd, Roger, *The Church of England in the Twentieth Century 1900-1965* (SCM Press, 1968).

Lockhart, G. J., *Cosmo Gordon Lang* (Hodder and Stoughton, 1949).

Louden, S., *Chaplains in Conflict, The Role of Army Chaplains since 1914* (Avon Books, 1996),

Machin, G. I. T., *Churches and Social issues in Twentieth-Century Britain* (Clarendon Press, 1998).

Machin, G. I. T., "Marriage and the Churches in the 1930s: Royal Abdication and Divorce Reform 1936-37", *Journal of Ecclesiastical History*, Vol. 42 (1991).

Maclaren, S. J. (ed.), *Somewhere in Flanders: Letters of a Norfolk Padre in the Great War* (Lark's Press, 2005).

Madigan, E., "The Life Lived Versus Balaam's Ass's Ears: Neville Stuart Talbot's Chaplaincy on the Western Front", *Royal Army Chaplains Department*, Vol. 47 (2008).

Madigan, E, *Faith under Fire, Anglican Chaplains and the Great War* (Palgrave Macmillan, 2011).

Madigan, E. and M. Snape(eds.), *The Clergy in Khaki: New Perspectives on British Army Chaplaincy in the First World War* (Ashgate, 2013).

Maiden, J. *National Religion and the Prayer Book Controversy, 1927-1928* (Boydell Press, 2009).

Marrin, A., *The Last Crusade – The Church of England in the First World War* (Duke University, 1974).

Machin, G., *Churches and Social Issues in Twentieth-Century Britain* (Oxford University Press, 1998).

McKibbin, R., *Classes and Cultures England 1918-1951* (Oxford University Press, 2000).

Mcleod, Hugh, *Religion and Society in England 1850-1914* (Palgrave Macmillan, 1996).

Methuen, C., in "Lambeth 1920: The Appeal to all Christian People: An account by G. K. A. Bell and the redactions of the appeal", in M. Barber, S. Taylor and G. Sewell (eds.), *From The Reformation to the Permissive Society* (Church of England Record Society, 2010).

Mews, S., "The Churches", in M. Morris (ed.), *The General Strike* (Historical Association, 1976).

Moorman, J. R. H., *B. K. Cunningham, A Memoir* (SCM Press, 1947).

Moorman, J. R. H., *A History of the Church in England* (A and C Black, 1973).

Morgan, D. Densil, *The Span of the Cross: Christian Religion and Society in Wales 1914-2000* (University of Wales Press, 2011).

Mozley, J. K. (ed.), *G. A. Studdert Kennedy, By His Friends* (Hodder and Stoughton, 1929).

Mowat, C., *Britain Between the Wars 1918-1940* (Methuen & Co, 1955).

Mozley J. K (ed.), *G A Studdert Kennedy, By His Friends* (Hodder and Stoughton, 1929).

Nicolson, J., *The Great Silence: 1918-1920, Living in the Shadow of the Great War* (John Murray, 2009).

Norman, E. H., *Church and Society in England 1770-1970: A Historical Study* (Oxford University Press, 1976).

Northcott, R. J., *Dick Sheppard and St Martin's* (Longmans Green & Co., 1937).

Northcott, R.J. *Pat McCormick* (Longmans Green & Co., 1941).

Oliver, John, *Church and Social Order: Social Thought in the Church of England, 1918-39* (Mowbray, 1968).

Overy, R., *The Morbid Age, Britain between the wars* (Allen Lane, 2009).

Parker, L., *The Whole Armour of God: Anglican Army Chaplains in the Great War* (Helion, 2009).

Paxton, William (ed.*), Dick Sheppard, An Apostle of Brotherhood* (Chapman and Hall, 1938).

Perry, R., *Ardingly 1848-1946, A History of the School* (The Ardinians Society, 1951).

Pickard, Tom, *Jarrow March* (Allison and Busby, 1981).

Porter, P., "New Jerusalems: Sacrifice and Redemption in the War Experiences of English and German Military Chaplains", in Pierre Purseigle (ed.), *Warfare and Belligerence, Perspectives in First World War Studies* (Brill, 2005).

Porter, P., "Beyond Comfort: German and English Military Chaplains and the Memory of the Great War" in *Journal of Religious History*, Vol. 29, no. 3 (October 2005).

Pugh, M., *We Danced All Night: A Social History of Britain Between the Wars* (Bodley Head, 2008).

Purcell, William, *Woodbine Willie: An Anglican incident, being some account of the life and times of Geoffrey Anketell Studdert Kennedy, poet, prophet, seeker after truth, 1883-1929* (Hodder and Stoughton, 1962).

Pym, D., *Tom Pym. A Portrait.* (W. Heffer & Co., 1952).

Quick, Oliver Chase, *The Christian Sacraments* (Nisbet, 1927).

Quick, Oliver Chase, *Doctrines of the Creed* (Nisbet, 1937).

Ramsey, A. M., *From Gore to Temple: The development of Anglican theology between Lux mundi and the Second World War, 1889-1939* (Longmans Green, 1960).

Reckitt, M. B., *Maurice to Temple: A century of the Social Movement in the Church of England. (Scott Holland lectures 1946* (Faber and Faber, 1946).

Robertson, D.H., "A Narrative of the General Strike of 1926" *The Economic Journal* Vol. 36, no. 143 (Sept., 1926) p.376

Robbins, Keith, *England, Ireland, Scotland, Wales: The Christian Church 1900-2000* Oxford History of the English Church (Oxford University Press, 2008).

Royden, Maude, "Dick Sheppard, Peace Maker" in *Dick Sheppard, An Apostle of Brotherhood* ed. William Paxton, Philip Inman and others (Chapman & Hall, 1938).

Schweitzer, A., *The Quest of the Historical Jesus* (Adam and Charles Black, 1910).

Schweizter, R., *The Cross and the Trenches: Religious Faith and Doubt Among British and American Great War Soldiers* (Praeger, 2003).

Scott, C., *Dick Sheppard, A Biography* (Hodder and Stoughton, 1979).

Studdert Kennedy, Gerald, *Dog Collar Democracy, The Industrial Christian Fellowship 1919-1929* (Macmillan Press, 1982).

Studdert Kennedy, Gerald, "Woodbine Willie: Religion and Politics after the Great War". *History Today* December (1986), p. 42.

Smith, E. H. F., *St Peter's, The Founding of a College* (Colin Smythe, 1978).

Smith, L., *Pacifists in action: The experience of the Friends Ambulance Unit in the Second World War* (William Sessions Ltd., 1998).

Smyth C., *Cyril Foster Garbett, Archbishop of York* (Hodder and Stoughton, 1959).

Snape, M.F., *God and the British Soldier, Christianity and Society in the Modern World* (Routledge, 2005).

Snape, M. F., "Archbishop Davidson's Visit to the Western Front May 1916", in *From the Reformation To The Permissive Society*, M. Barber, S. Taylor and G. Sewell, (eds.) (Boydell Press 2010).

Snape, M. F., *The Royal Army Chaplains' Department, 1796-1953: Clergy under Fire* (Boydell Press, 2007).

Snape, M. F. *The Back Parts of War: The YMCA Memoirs and Letters of Barclay Baron 1915-1919* (Boydell and Brewer, 2009).

Snape, M.F., "Church of England Army Chaplains in the First World War: Goodbye to' Goodbye to All That'", *Journal of Ecclesiastical History*, Vol. 62, No. 2, April 2011.

Stamp, Gavin. *The Memorial to the Missing of the Somme* (Profile Books, 2006).

Taylor, A. J .P., *The Trouble Makers Dissent Over Foreign Policy, 1792-1939* (Hamish Hamilton, 1957).

Thompson, D. M. "War, the Nation, and the Kingdom of God: The origins of the National Mission of Repentance and Hope 1915-1916" *Studies in Church History*, vol. 20, 1983.

Thompson, Kenneth, *Bureaucracy and Church Reform: The Organizational Response of the Church of England to Social Change, 1800-1965* (Clarendon Press, 1970).

Todman, Dan, *The Great War, Myth and Memory* (Hambledon and London, 2005).

Tomkins, O., *Edward Woods* (SCM Press, 1957).

Walker, J., *The Blood Tub: General Gough and the Battle of Bullecourt 1917* (Spellmount, 1998).

Wallis, J., *Valiant for Peace: History of the Fellowship of Reconciliation, 1914–89* (Fellowship of Reconciliation, 1991).

West, F., *F. R. B., Portrait of Bishop Russell Barry* (Grove Books, 1980).

Williams, Sarah, *Religious Belief and Popular Culture: A Study of the South London Borough of Southwark 1880-1930* (Oxford Historical Monographs, 1999).

Wilkinson, A., *The Church of England and the First World War* (SCM Press, 1978).

Wilkinson, A., *Dissent or Conform? – War, Peace and the English Churches 1900-1945* (SCM, London, 1986).

Wilkinson, A., *Christian Socialism: from Scott Holland to Tony Blair* (Presbyterian Pub Corp, 1998).

Wilkinson, A., *The Community of the Resurrection: A Centenary History* (SCM Press 1992).

Wilkinson, A., "The Paradox of the Military Chaplain", *Theology* (1984).

Winter, Jay, *Remembering War: The Great War between Memory and History in the Twentieth Century* (Yale University Press, 2006).

Winter, Jay, *War and Remembrance in the Twentieth Century (Studies in the Social and Cultural History of Modern Warfare* (Cambridge University Press, 2000).

Wolfe, K.M., *The Churches and the British Broadcasting Corporation 1922-1956: the Politics of Broadcast Religion* (SCM, 1984).

PhD Theses

Stuart P. Mews, "Religion and English Society in the First World War", Cambridge PhD thesis, 1974.
Catriona Noonan, "The Production of Religious Broadcasting: The Case of the B.B.C.", Glasgow PhD thesis, 2008.

Websites

http://justus.anglican.org/resources/bio/199.html (accessed 18 September 2012)
http://www.bbc.co.uk/radio4/features/daily-service/history/ (accessed 2 February 2011) Daily Service website.
http://www.churchhouse.org.uk/ (accessed 19 September 2012)
http://www.globalsecurity.org/military/world/naval-arms-control-1932.htm (accessed 4 October 2012)
http://www.lambethconference.org/resolutions/1930/1930-27.cfm (accessed 4 October 2012)
http://www.nobelprize.org/nobel_prizes/peace/laureates/1930/soderblom-bio.htm (accessed 4 October 2012)
http://www.oikoumene.org/en/who.../faith-and-order/history (accessed 12 May 2012)
http://www.parliament.uk (accessed 29 August 2010)
http://www.royall.co.uk/royall/St-Michael-All-Angels.php (accessed 18 September 2012) The articles of Prebendary A. Royall.
http://www.toch-uk.org.uk/documents/Pat%20Leonard%20Memoir%20%28Final%29.pdf (accessed February 2011) Philip Leonard-Johnson, *Pat Leonard D S O – A Memoir* (2010).
http://www8.open.ac.uk/researchprojects/makingbritain/content/simon-report (accessed September 24 2012)

Index